The Hare Krishnas
IN INDIA

The Hare Krishnas
IN INDIA

Charles R. Brooks

PRINCETON UNIVERSITY PRESS

PRINCETON, NEW JERSEY

Library of Congress Cataloging-in-Publication Data
Brooks, Charles R., 1946–
    The Hare Krishnas in India / Charles R. Brooks.
    p.   cm.
    Bibliography: p.
    Includes index.
    ISBN 0–691–03135–5 (lib. bdg. : alk. paper) ISBN 0–691–00031–X (pbk.)
    1. International Society for Krishna Consciousness—India—Vrindávan.
2. Vrindávan (India)—Religion. I. Title.
BL1285.832.V75B76 1989
294.5′512—dc19   88-22655
                                                              CIP

CONTENTS

TABLES AND FIGURES

INDIAN words in this book have been anglicized. The closest English equivalent is given upon a word's first occurrence. Full transliterations with diacritical marks are listed in the glossary. Sanskrit and Hindi vowels are pronounced as follows:

a (as the *u* in *but*: *paṇḍita*)   *ā* (as the *a* in *father*: *ghāṭa*)
i (as the *i* in *bit*: *Viṣṇu*)   *ī* (as the *ee* in *meet*: *śrī*)
u (as the *u* in *put*: *guru*)   *ū* (as the *oo* in boot: *mūrti*)

The diphthongs are *e* (as the *ai* in *bait*: *Rādhe*); *ai* (as the *i* in *bite*: *Vaiṣṇava*); *o* (as the *o* in *blow*: *mokṣa*); and *au* (as the *ow* in *cow*: *Gauḍīya*). The underdotted *ṛ* is also a vowel in Hindi and Sanskrit and is pronounced *ri* (as in *Vṛndāvana*).

As for consonants, both the retroflex sibilant *ṣ* and the palatal sibilant *ś* are pronounced as *sh* (*Kṛṣṇa* = *Krishna*; *Śiva* = *Shiva*). *C* sounds like the *ch* in *church*, but with less aspiration (*Caitanya* = *Chaitanya*). There are two *t*s and two *d*s, one dental and the other retroflex. Both are anglicized as simply *t* or *d* (*ghāṭ* = *ghat*; *Gauḍīya* = *Gaudiya*). There are four *n*s—one guttural, one palatal, one lingual, and one dental. The dental *n* carries no diacritical markings and is pronounced like the English consonant. The retroflex *ṇ* is a rather distinct sound produced by curling the tongue backward. This *n* occurs in both *Kṛṣṇa* and *Viṣṇu*. The other *n*s, the palatal *ñ*, and the guttural *ṅ*, are less common. The aspirated consonants are *bh*, *dh*, and *th*. *Bh* is pronounced as in *clubhouse* (*Bhāgavad-gītā*); *dh* as in *roundhouse* (*dhāma*); and *th* as in *hothouse* (*tīrtha*).

The most noticeable difference between Sanskrit and Hindi pronunciations is that Hindi tends to drop the final *a*. For example, *dhāma* in Sanskrit is pronounced *dhām* in Hindi. In most cases, I have dropped the final *a* to more closely approximate the pronunciation of words in Vrindaban usage.

Compound words that are written without a break in the Devanagari script have been transliterated with a hyphen between the individual components (*Radhakrishna* = *Radha-Krishna*). For ease in reading, I have pluralized Sanskrit and Hindi words by adding an *s* as in the anglicized form. Proper nouns have been handled in the same manner as other words except in cases where another anglicized version is more familiar or more commonly used in the vernacular (*Vṛndāvana* = *Vrindaban*; *Haridvāra* = *Hardwar*).

The Hare Krishnas

IN INDIA

CHAPTER 1

Introduction

EVERY morning at 7:00 the Taj Express pulls out of the New Delhi railway station, its air-conditioned class compartments full of Indian and foreign tourists headed for Agra and a day of marveling at the Mughal splendor of the Taj Mahal. About forty-five minutes before arriving at the Agra Cant station, the Taj halts briefly at Mathura, and from the second-class cars disembarks a varied swarm of passengers: urban civil servants dressed in polyester shirts and pants; Punjabi men sporting colorful turbans and stately beards, their wives in traditional pants and long blouses; Rajasthani farmers with gold rings in each ear, accompanied by wives in saris of brilliant colors. Still others are sparsely clothed in coarse cotton and barefoot, having renounced all worldly possessions to become *sadhus* (religious ascetics), or to take up the life of mendicant widow after a husband's death. Here and there in the crowd can also be seen individuals slightly taller than the rest, with lighter skin—American or European—dressed in the saffron *dhoti* of a *sannyasi* (renunciate) or the dingy loincloth of a sadhu, hair closely cropped except for a lock in the back, a style ubiquitous among the Indian men that crowd the station platform.

This mass of humanity, however diverse, shares one motive as it pushes its way toward the station exit, and many shout out "*Jai ho*" ("Victory"), "*Giri Raj ki jai*" ("Glory to Krishna"), or "*Hare Krishna*" ("Oh Krishna"),[1] raising hands above heads in exaltation as

---

[1] These phrases are used as salutations and exclamations. *Jai ho* is often shouted at the first glance of a rising sun or moon, or upon sighting a sacred person or object. *Giri Raj* is one of Krishna's many names, referring to the Govardhan mountain about twenty miles from Vrindaban, a place of mythological significance, often considered to be identical to Krishna himself. *Hare Krishna* is an invocation to Krishna excerpted from the *mahamantra*, the chant which forms the center of ISKCON doctrine and well-known throughout India. It has, since the arrival of Western devotees in Vrindaban, been used as a salutation between members. Before their presence there, the most common greetings among residents of the town were "*Jai Radhe*" ("Victory to Radha"), and "*Radhe Shyam*" ("Radha-Krishna"). *Hare Krishna* has now also become a frequent salutation among Indians as well, especially when foreigners are present or at times the Indian actors wish to identify with them. Conversely, if a person wishes to symbolically distance himself from ISKCON, one of the other salutations will be used. In this instance, the *Hare Krishna* exclamation was invoked by both Indian and foreign pilgrims.

they spot the sign on platform number one that announces "Alight Here for Vrindaban Pilgrimage." Further on a more recent billboard extends a "Welcome to the Land of Sri Krishna Consciousness." They have all come to *Braj* (the linguistic and cultural area in the southwestern corner of present-day Uttar Pradesh) on pilgrimage—to walk in the same soft and clinging dust in which their god Krishna walked and to bathe at the same *ghats* (river landings) where he teased the *gopis* (village milk-maids) by stealing their saris while they swam.[2] They will, during their pilgrimage, relive in ritual and imagination many of the scenes from Krishna's life which occurred, according to popular consensus, about five thousand years ago.

Leaving the dim station interior for the bright hot morning light, the pilgrims are confronted by a hoard of rickshaw and horse-cart drivers, all intent upon securing their business, each insisting that his vehicle is superior to the competition. Few in the crowd, however, will linger long in Mathura, for their destination is Vrindaban. Located some six miles to the north, Vrindaban is considered the "center of the lotus of Braj,"[3] and is renowned as the idyllic setting of Krishna's childhood

---

[2] During the month of Karttik, according to the residents of Vrindaban, the gopis went to this spot on the river (today known as *Chir ghat*) to bathe and offer prayers to the goddess Katyayani, beseeching her to give them Krishna as their husband. On the cold morning of the month's full moon, the object of their prayers happened by and playfully took their saris from the river bank and hung them in a nearby *kadamb* tree (which still stands). From a vantage point in the same tree, Krishna called for the girls to come out of the water and retrieve their clothes. At first refusing, they finally emerged, covering themselves modestly with their hands, but Krishna was not fully satisfied with this display; he wanted a full view. Demanding that they make obeisances to him with folded hands raised overhead, he again denied them their garments. Finally relenting, the gopis bared themselves before Krishna, who then kept his end of the bargain and returned their saris. (The story appears in *Bhagavata Purana* 10:22, 7–27. The textual account, however, says these events occurred in the month of Margashirsha instead of Karttik.) Brahman pilgrim guides who take pilgrims to this site today usually make two points concerning this story. First, Krishna is a playful god, and while religion should be taken seriously, it must also be joyous. Second, in order to approach God, one must bare his soul before coming into his intimate presence.

[3] Sripad Baba, a Vrindaban sadhu who has established Vraja Academy, explains that "Vraja is like an ocean where Mathura rests as a lotus floating upon it, and Vrindaban is the lotus's heart filled with nectar." According to a pamphlet written by Padmalocanadas, an English devotee who has lived in Vrindaban 11 years, *Braj-mandal* (*mandal* means circle, and is often used in a symbolic manner to refer to the universe, or as a circular pattern used as a meditation aid) measures 168 miles in circumference. "It is stated in the *Adi-varaha-purana* that if one takes the city of Mathura as the center, and measures out 42 miles in each of the four directions, then this is how *Braj-mandal* can be calculated. . . . On the modern day map this will include places such as Agra, Kosi, Bharatpur, Aligarh, etc. Within this circle is an inner section which is in the shape of a lotus. This has a perimeter of 96 miles. Within this area Krishna performs most of his pastimes, very rarely going to other areas" (Padmalocanadas n.d.: 2–3).

and adolescence—the period in which his activities are the most esoteric and religiously significant for the *bhakta* (devotee). It is the events
of Krishna's Vrindaban *lila* (sports, play) which symbolize for the pilgrims the highest ideal: an intimate personal relationship between deity
and devotee. And it is in Vrindaban where this divine relationship can
be most easily realized.

Today, however, is not an ordinary day, for it is the eve of the festival of Holi,[4] and at every village along the tracks from Delhi, the train
has been pelted with cow dung and colored water by jubilant children.
Now as the pilgrims disembark at Mathura, the very town of Krishna's
birth, everyone is drenched by the spray from large syringes filled with
colored water, and the mood is one of intoxicated celebration. Many in
the crowd wear clothing still colored from past Holis and put aside to
be worn only at the next Holi. Others began the day clad in fresh white
handwoven cotton clothing purchased just for the occasion, knowing
that by day's end it would be colorfully dyed. There are no protests
against this constant bombardment of colored water and powder which
continues unabated from the first steps onto the railway platform,
through the station, and into the yard, for as one elderly pilgrim
shouted to half-frightened foreign tourists still on the train, ''This is the
joy of our civilization!''

Those who arrived on the Taj Express now find themselves on the
road with many others of like mind who have come from all parts of
India by bus, car, scooter, oxcart, horse cart, camel, or on foot. They
share a mood which is simultaneously solemn and joyfully playful, for
their Lord Krishna is a fun-loving trickster who is worshiped as much
for his pranks as for his miracles. In spite of this playfulness, Krishna
is still the full incarnation of Vishnu, highest of gods,[5] and each person
anticipates an awesome experience of direct contact with him—an experience possible not only because he resided in the earthly Vrindaban

---

[4] For a first-person account of the festival of Holi, see Marriott 1966.

[5] Even for Hindus who are not Krishna-bhaktas, he is still a significant figure in their pantheon,
an *avatar* (incarnation) of Vishnu. In modern Hinduism, Vishnu is one of the chief gods, sharing
equally the business of the cosmos with Brahma (the creator), and Shiva (the destroyer); Vishnu
himself is the preserver. This conceptualization is perhaps more popular among foreign scholars
than with Indians, however, since most elevate their own *ishta devata* (personal deity) to the
position of Supreme Lord, and for the Vaishnava, Vishnu holds this status. But for Krishna-
bhaktas, especially the *Gaudiya sampradaya* (the Bengal Vaishnava sect founded by Shri Chaitanya), Krishna is no longer a derivation or manifestation of Vishnu, but God himself in an almost
monotheistic sense. For them, Krishna is not just an incarnation of Vishnu; rather, all other avatars
are incarnations of Krishna. Therefore, Krishna descended onto the earthly plane at Vrindaban as
himself, and there can be no higher form.

five thousand years ago, but also because (it is firmly believed) he is eternally present there.

The ride to Vrindaban normally takes about forty-five minutes by horse cart, but this day more than an hour is required, as at every turn in the road all are stopped and persuaded to step down so that they may receive the hospitality of Holi. These roadblocks are composed largely of young men who, filled with *bhang* (a drink made with *Cannabis*), embrace each person they encounter, spreading bright red or green powder across his or her forehead. It is Vrindaban and the surrounding Braj which are famous for having the best Holi in India, and the local residents are not about to jeopardize this reputation. After all, was not Holi Krishna's favorite celebration?

Finally, the families, groups of old friends, and solitary pilgrims reach the outskirts of Vrindaban where many prostrate themselves in the dust, rub it over their head and eyes, and perhaps even taste some of the Vrindaban soil, treating it as the most sacred *prasad* (literally, "grace," spiritualized food). Tears form in many eyes as emotions of a destination reached and expectations of extraordinary experiences to come overwhelm them. Now, before they disperse into various *dharm-shalas* (pilgrim lodges) around town to avoid the midday heat, they are eager to visit some of the most important sites of the town.

Ram Gopal is a *rickshaw-wala* who travels between Mathura Cant station and Vrindaban several times on a good day, and today his business is very good. He explains to his clients that for over a week now, no accommodations have been available in either Mathura or Vrindaban. He is therefore "prayerful" that everyone has written ahead for lodging well in advance. But for most pilgrims, physical comfort is their last concern, and they are prepared to sleep by the river or on the steps of a temple; for it is simply being in the land of Krishna at this auspicious time that is the fulfillment of their most ardent desires. The reality that they are now in Vrindaban *dham* (holy land) floods their consciousness and overshadows any worry about food or shelter.

Volunteering to assist his riders on their initial tour of the sacred town, Ram explains, "There are four temples that you must visit immediately! It is now time for *darshan* (viewing of the sacred images), so it is a must that we hurry. Otherwise you will wait until evening for your first darshan." So it is agreed: hurriedly the rounds should be made.

Immediately past the toll gate on the Mathura-Vrindaban road, Ram makes a left and heads to the area of town called Raman-Reti. As he turns onto the old Chhatikara road (now officially Bhaktivedanta Marg), the flood of people slows traffic practically to a halt. This steady stream of humanity circulates from dharmshalas to shops to temples to tea stalls, with everyone heading generally in the same direction—two kilometers from the main intersection of Bhaktivedanta Marg and Mahatma Gandhi Marg, to the Krishna-Balaram temple. Over the noise of the crowd Ram explains that Krishna-Balaram is the first temple that should be seen (see appendix 1).

As slow progress is made toward the *mandir* (temple), Ram Gopal points to the spire of Madan-Mohan, the first in a series of temples whose construction began in the late 1400s when Vrindaban was changing from a wilderness retreat to a pilgrimage town. Built by the medieval saint Sanatan Goswami, and patronized by the tolerant Mughal emperor Akbar, this temple once housed the image of Krishna called Madan-Mohan which supposedly was commissioned by Krishna's own earthly great grandson, and rediscovered by Sanatan. Over the years many miracles were attributed to this deity, but the original image no longer resides beneath the tower which dominates Vrindaban's riverfront skyline. Today the image called Madan-Mohan is worshiped at Karauli in the state of Rajasthan, taken there in order to avoid the destructive wrath of Akbar's notorious grandson, Aurangzeb.

Further on is Fogal Ashram, a large dharmshala where many pilgrims stay and where a large entourage of sadhus and *vairagis* (Vaishnava sadhus) obtain free food and shelter throughout the year. Ram laughs that Vrindaban is "75 percent sadhu, 25 percent people." His comments, which are accurate and detailed, are given freely, he says, and he is quick to point out that there is no competition between himself and the hereditary Brahman pilgrim guides or *pandas*. These pandas claim a monopoly on this activity at most *tirthas* (pilgrimage site; literally, a ford, or place to "cross over" to the spiritual world), and often possess records indicating a client relationship with some families for generations.[6] "However," Ram continues with a smile, "if you are happy with my services today, I can return this evening and tomorrow to be your escort without charge. Or you may also find your own panda and pay his fee."

Vrindaban town of ten years ago ended just past Fogal Ashram for

---

[6] The term *panda* is used to designate the Brahman pilgrim guide and is derived from the Sanskrit *pana*, meaning "to deal with." The pandas in many large tirthas, such as Varanasi, are highly organized with well-preserved, meticulous records. In Vrindaban, though the claim is often made for records dating back some ten generations, this is difficult to substantiate.

all but the most stalwart pilgrims, the area still being forested—a retreat
for sadhus who wished to conduct their spiritual practices in solitude.
Since the opening of the Krishna-Balaram temple in 1975, however,
Raman-Reti has become an integral part of the town. Now there are
temples, ashrams, and dharmshalas extending to Bhaktivedanta Gate
which marks the southwestern extremity of Vrindaban. "Today," Ram
comments, "*Brajbasis* (residents of Braj) complain that you must go
all the way to Krishna-Balaram to hire a rickshaw. If you need a ride
to Mathura, you can always find one there."

As the temple is approached, pilgrims congest the dusty street. There
is a gentle but steady pushing that begins a hundred meters from the
temple itself, extends into the narrow alleyway leading up to its entrance gate, and into the courtyard. Once inside, all strain on tiptoes to
catch their first glimpse, over the heads of the crowd, of the sacred
images whose darshan they seek.

Everyone knows the proper ritual etiquette to receive the full effect
of darshan. Having repeated the process before in many other temples,
they are prepared to repeat it many times more during their Vrindaban
yatra (pilgrimage journey). As each individual crosses the temple
threshold, he rubs his hands or fingertips across the entrance floor,
transferring the dust of all devotees who have gone before to his own
forehead. This ritual both establishes his humility and transfers the
shakti (energy) and blessing of all the great souls, or *mahatmas*, who
have passed there before.

Once inside the temple courtyard, the pilgrims are swept into a
clockwise movement, inching slowly toward the holy images in a flow
which will allow them each a few seconds before the three altars. Toward the temple front, steps are confronted, taking the worshiper to an
elevated stage area upon which he can meet the deities eye-to-eye. During this time, priests of the temple circulate as best they can, making
their way through the crowd with good-natured shoves and spraying
gallons of saffron-colored, rose-scented water over the hot congrega-
tion which receives it with enthusiastic cheers. Center front is located
the *samaj* (a group of singers and musicians), singing rhythmic songs
to the accompaniment of *pakhawaj* (a two-headed drum, same as *mridanga*), *kartals* (hand cymbals), *tamboura* (a droning stringed instrument), and harmonium, and many sing along, keeping time with their
clapping hands. Throughout the dense crowd small groups of enthusiastic devotees also burst into spontaneous dancing to the encouraging
shouts of the throng.

As the people climb the stairs to the elevated stage, they are faced with an image of the temple's founder, stage left and situated at a right angle to the altars. This lifelike figure is sitting on a marble throne and is covered with garlands of jasmine and rose blossoms. If living, he would have a commanding view of the crowd and an unobstructed view of all the *murtis* (images). Pilgrims gaze at the guru's form, some stopping to fully prostrate themselves before it, risking being trampled in the process. Money and flowers are tossed upon his throne, private mantras are muttered, and exclamations of "mahatma" and "sadhu" are heard.

In each of the three main shrines, marble statues about four feet tall stand, clothed in silks and jewels, with offerings of rich, expensive food placed before them. Priests attend each image as if it were living royalty and every pilgrim gazes intently into the deities' eyes to receive the transmission of sacred blessings. Upon the third altar stand Radha and Krishna, lavishly decorated for Holi. It is this divine couple that the pilgrims have especially come to see, and lovingly gaze upon the statues as if they were dear friends meeting after a long separation. The priests accept more offerings of sweets and flowers extended by the crowd, wave these items around the images, and return the now-consecrated objects back to eager hands. Some of the *pujaris* (priests) spray scented streams of colored water from hidden recesses behind the inner sanctum, to the crowd's surprise and delight.

Having received the darshan, some slowly merge with the crowd in the central courtyard for an extended view of the entire chaotic scene. Many join in the chanting which now and then erupts into more dancing. But most, now fully satisfied, hurry back outside to waiting *tangas* (horse carts) and rickshaws and on to other temples and sacred sites.

Similar scenes are enacted in most of Vrindaban's temples daily, but the events at Krishna-Balaram are unique in ways not revealed by a description of ritual and devotee enthusiasm. The distinction, however, is strikingly apparent to anyone present there, for the priests are unmistakably non-Indian. To be precise, the head pujari is French, the temple manager is American, the Brahman cook responsible for preparing the deities' food offerings is English, and the samaj is composed of all these nationalities plus German, Australian, Puerto Rican, and Japanese, along with a few Indians.

THE PROBLEM

Members of the International Society for Krishna Consciousness (ISK-CON), foreigners to India, yet Hindus by a complex process of conversion and culture change,[7] have successfully established a temple in the traditional pilgrimage town of Vrindaban, and it has become a popular part of that town's sacred complex. This much was apparent from the scene witnessed my first day there, the day before Holi, 1982. Being previously aware of the ISKCON temple's existence, I had come to Vrindaban to discover whether or not significant interactions were occurring between these non-Indian devotees of Krishna and the Indians of the town.

Furthermore, since in the traditional view, it is an impossibility for foreigners to become Hindu, much less Brahman, as these Western devotees claim to be, a paradox is created by their very presence. Pragmatically, then, I wished to know how this conflict was being resolved in the situations of everyday life in Vrindaban, and what consequences were resulting from that resolution.

At every phase in the process leading up to my being in Vrindaban, I was cautioned not to expect any significant degree of social intercourse between foreign and native groups. This doubt was expressed by Indologists and other scholars, as well as by traditional Indians, reflecting long-accepted notions that severe constraints embedded in the Indian sociocultural system would stifle all but the most superficial encounters. My expectations were different, however, resting upon the fundamental assumption that people who occupy the same habitat sooner or later become involved in a common web of life.

I was similarly encouraged by the empirically based knowledge that ideational notions do not always coincide with practical actions. Even in the face of admitted constraints, these underlying suppositions suggested to me that a good probability for interaction existed, especially if the foreign actors employed an active strategy to win acceptance, as was implied by their human and financial investment in the town.

Apparently, highly staged symbolic interactions were taking place at the Krishna-Balaram temple. On my first day there, I witnessed thousands of Indian pilgrims worshiping in a temple built and staffed by foreigners, and the pilgrims participated enthusiastically. They seemed to accept the mediation of non-Indian priests between themselves and

---

[7] I have earlier suggested (Brooks 1979) that ISKCON, as it emerged in the United States during the 1960s and 1970s, was an example of a revitalization movement, defined by Wallace as any "deliberate, organized, conscious effort by members of a society to construct a more satisfying culture by rapid acceptance of a pattern of multiple innovations" (Wallace 1966: 143–44). See also Judah (1974) and Daner (1976) for intepretations focusing upon the processes of change and socialization of individuals who joined ISKCON during its formative years.

their gods, and showed respect and deference to the Westerners by ritual gestures.[8] This suggested to me that the broader arena of Vrindaban town would be a productive setting for research; that other types of significant encounters were occurring. I therefore determined to investigate the nature and extent of interactions between the foreign bhaktas and the Indian population, both resident and pilgrim.

Documenting interactive episodes constituted the project's basic strategy. The study was further framed by the following related questions:

1. What specific types of interaction are occurring between the foreign devotees of ISKCON and Indian pilgrims? Between foreigners and Vrindaban residents?

2. What objects and symbols are designated as important by the actors in these situations? Is there agreement on these objects and symbols? On their meaning? If not, how is disagreement resolved?

3. What physical, sociocultural, and individual consequences result from the interactions? Are the results interpreted as ''change'' by the actors?

4. What are the historical and contemporary contexts which provide resources for interpretation and explanation of situations by the actors?

These questions reflect a specific problem focus, coupled, however, with a commitment to open-ended research. While their exact content developed during the course of the study, they were informed and guided by a particular sociological perspective.

THE THEORETICAL PERSPECTIVE OF SYMBOLIC INTERACTIONISM

In all phases, from conceptualization to the final interpretations, this study has been guided by the perspective of symbolic interactionism. ''Symbolic interactionism'' labels a distinctive approach to the study of human social life, yet is difficult to define succinctly. This is not surprising since the perspective attempts to reflect what is, in itself, seen as an uncertain, emergent, and ever-changing domain. Epitomizing the attitude that society ultimately consists of individuals engaged in an open, sometimes frankly unknowable process, the perspective consequently cannot be strictly formulated or highly structured. A

---

[8] Two gestures were prevalent: the traditional salutation of respect (consisting of bringing the hands, palms together, to the forehead); and a demonstration of one's inferiority (performed by touching the feet of the other person).

study guided by the principles and logic of interactionism,[9] will, rather, convey something of the flow and order of the living experience, constructing for the reader an authentic image of the situated reality under scrutiny.

Symbolic interactionism is a perspective which presents a processual view of the social world, focusing upon the importance of situated activity and offering a unified methodological and interpretive strategy for its study. The principles and premises of interactionism have been explicated by Herbert Blumer in his *Symbolic Interactionism: Perspective and Method* (1969); in 1937, Blumer himself coined the words which have come to label the approach.[10] A student and interpreter of George Herbert Mead, Blumer presents a theoretical and methodological perspective that is particularly suited to the empirical study of everyday life.

Symbolic interactionism is an approach, I think, employed by most ethnographic anthropologists; it is consistent and continuous with the traditions of Boas and Malinowski, and informs what Pelto has called "a very generalized 'meta-theory' of anthropology" (1970: 18). While many anthropologists implicitly accept the major tenets of symbolic interactionism for their interpretation of day-to-day human behavior, the assumptions are rarely explicitly stated. Yet, symbolic interactionism itself can be termed a social "theory," one that is especially suited to guide research and interpretation of social and cultural change. If the word *theory* is to be used to refer to symbolic interactionism, however, it must be defined within the context that Blumer intended.

The use of theory in the social sciences can never attain the ideal that has been established by theoretical inquiry in the physical or "natural" sciences. In the physical sciences, theory is composed of "definitive concepts" which "provide prescriptions of what to see" (Blumer 1969: 148). In other words, the scientist assumes, if his theoretical concepts are correct, that they will function to categorize and explain his data time after time, experiment after experiment. Theory directs his research expectations and perceptions so that each experiment acts as a confirmation of it, or else the theory must be revised or changed. Rep-

---

[9] In this book I use the terms *interactionism* and *symbolic interactionism* interchangeably.

[10] Blumer (1969: 1) states that "the term 'symbolic interactionism' is a somewhat barbaric neologism that I coined in an offhand way in an article written in *Man and Society* (Emerson P. Schmidt, ed. New York: Prentice-Hall, 1937.) The term somehow caught on and is now in general use."

licability is the hallmark of scientific truth in the physical sciences, and an elegant theory, a priori, will suggest what the results should be.

Social life, however, is not so replicable, and definitive concepts—concepts that have precise, unchanging referents—cannot handle the variability and diversity of social reality. Rather, social theory must by composed of "sensitizing concepts," concepts that suggest directions along which to look, and as such allow the social scientist to discover and attempt to understand the empirical distinctiveness of different social phenomena.

Geertz has offered basically the same argument by explaining that in the natural sciences theory ideally functions to simplify that which at first seems too complex to understand. But in the study of man, he suggests "that explanation often consists of substituting complex pictures for simple ones while striving to retain the persuasive clarity that went with the simple ones" (1973: 34). In the social sciences, what is needed is not a theory that prescribes what should occur, but one that guides the observer in discovering the unique complexity of the social world he is studying. Moreover, a social theory should also provide guidelines for making some sense of that complexity—a direction for interpretation of the data.

The perspective of symbolic interactionism provides such a theoretical orientation. It does not claim to provide definitive concepts and categories capable of predicting social reality, but it does provide a set of generalized assumptions which can assist in discovering and understanding the dynamics of a particular social reality.

Change with Continuity

Society does not exist apart from activity. Instead of people fitting into already existing, freestanding structures of stable categories and fixed statuses with unchanging roles, the interactionist views society as an ongoing process. Roles and their content, along with any other observable patterns of interaction, develop during the course of activity and can never be fully anticipated or predicted. Structure, if we are to use that term, exists in situations of interaction insofar as actors attempt to maintain a single definition of the situation which is expressed and sustained in the face of a multitude of potential disruptions. This does not imply that there will be only one definition of a situation, but that the various actors in the situation will attempt to present and maintain their own definition, often in the face of challenges.

Process implies change. Even within the most traditional societies that seem to have centuries of apparent structural continuity, the demands and uncertainties of everyday life dictate an element of unpredictableness. In such environments, as in all others, expected lines of action based upon historical and cultural precedents can still become unexpectedly blocked, compelling the actors to redefine the situation. This becomes all the more certain when impressions of stability are overtly, deliberately challenged by external forces, as they currently are in Vrindaban by the foreign devotees of ISKCON. When such obvious challenges to established values and meanings occur, symbolic interactionism provides an especially useful perspective for the investigation, description, and interpretation of the social world in process.

If an individual is confronted with disruptions or ambiguities in cultural norms and expectations, there is a tendency for explanation and resolution. Goffman (1971: 183) points out that actors engage in "remedial interchanges," where they attempt to reinforce definitions of themselves and the situation that ultimately are seen as acceptable and satisfactory for all parties to the interaction; this is especially the case during encounters in "public."[11] The situations of interaction in Vrindaban reflect this human tendency in that both foreign and Indian actors are attempting to present themselves as competent in a common cultural system, a system that the Indians have inherited and the foreigners have chosen to learn. Although actors from both sides appropriate the system in varying degrees, sometimes define common symbols differently, and often view the others with some degree of suspicion, they still share the primary resources of cultural knowledge. Empirically, then, we must observe the dynamics of significant situations, note differences in the actors' interpretations, and watch for the negotiations and compromises which occur. If there is conflict, is it maintained or resolved? Does resolution result in changes in attitude, belief, and meaning, or is there agreement to maintain tension created by the differences? In Vrindaban, how do residents deal with the phenomenon of foreign Hindus who claim to be Brahman, and how do the devotees of ISKCON deal with local people? Is there convergence, coexistence, or hostility? These questions must be considered for each situation and in the general context of ISKCON's position in Vrindaban's sociocultural system.

---

[11] Goffman uses the term *public life* to include face-to-face interactions in the "front regions," which, he points out, may include "private domestic establishments" (Goffman 1971: ix n.). It should also be pointed out that actors attempt to reinforce definitions in other types of interchanges as well.

Many Indians culturally have difficulty accepting foreigners as valid members of their native system, but at the same time search for clues that the outsiders who do attempt integration have acquired, or are achieving competence. On the other hand, the ISKCON devotees conceive that their understanding of the Indian system actually approaches the cultural ideal more closely than that of the native members. Since the system itself has some degree of inherent flexibility, there is room for resolutional dynamics to occur. If in this process there is a broadening of norms and meanings to encompass the Western devotees, however, some alteration to the system as understood and practiced by the Indians prior to encounters with the foreigners may also result. These changes, however, since they occur within the symbolic framework of Vrindaban culture, may not be perceived as change to the local people. In fact, they often say that Vrindaban never changes; it changes the people who come there. Analytically, however, changes will likely occur on both sides whenever people deal with a new situation, and the observer must be sensitive to these changes and their consequences.

The present situation in Vrindaban is especially revealing because there foreign devotees are interacting with Indians on Indian terms; they are using Indian categories of persons and things. But as Sahlins has shown, if these common categories are differently valued, in the process of interaction they may be functionally redefined. He states that "the specificity of practical circumstances, people's differential relations to them, and the set of particular arrangements that ensue . . . sediment new functional values on old categories" (Sahlins 1982: 67–68). Indeed, it is the use of traditional Indian categories by the foreign devotees in Vrindaban that predisposes the traditional system toward changes—sometimes obvious, sometimes subtle. In the attempt by Indians to maintain and reproduce their system in these cross-cultural interactions, it is being transformed. As Sahlins has pointed out, we should question "whether the continuity of a system ever occurs without its alteration" (67).

Yet in the face of change, the human compulsion is to continue everyday life, attempting to make sense out of it in terms of past experiences, and Sahlins recognizes this by adding that not only does he question continuity without change, but also "alteration without continuity" (ibid.). This impulse to interpret new situations as logically continuous from previous ones, though in fact considerable redefinition is required, is seen by the symbolic interactionists as an underlying fact of social life. Change will inevitably occur, and inevitably it will be explained in terms of tradition.

That human social interaction leads to change, with that change being explained by invoking historical or cultural precedent, is a recurrent interactionist theme. Ambiguity and conflict in a situation thwart routine behavior and understanding. At the same time, it gives rise to the opportunity for a reassessment of assumptions that appear empirically invalidated. This provides a chance for realignment between symbols and referents, for reformulations of meaning. Concurrently, situationally determined new forms will be interpreted as logically consistent with familiar, preexisting ones, if at all possible.

The Vrindaban context provides many situations of ambiguity and conflict which challenge traditional assumptions. But the Indian mind is not the rigid ''traditional Indian mind'' of the media, novels, and textbooks. Factually, for Vrindaban, conflicts, contradictions, ambiguities, surprises, and other blockages to expected behavior activate cultural and historical resources that are in reserve for such situations. This allows individuals to successfully cope with meaning challenges, resulting not so much in a disruption of everyday life as an opportunity to invoke and employ the resources. Ultimately, the new meanings will be logically explained and incorporated into a now broader system, still interpreted as traditional.

These are all, of course, micro-level concerns, and are consistent with the idea that symbolic interaction attempts only to make understandable the social dynamics operating between real people in a specific environment. But as Srinivas (1966: 2) has pointed out, ultimately there should be ''movement'' between the insights of micro-studies and the broader macro-perspective. Inasmuch as this book describes Indian situations, therefore, it is appropriate to consider what questions it raises and what insights it may offer for a more complete understanding of the complexities of Indian culture and social organization.

PROBLEMS WITH THE INDIAN MACRO-PERSPECTIVE

Standard analysis of Indian society attempts to deal with the staggering variation that empirically exists by insisting upon the application of a reified, philologically, and textually derived ''caste'' concept. Although problems long noted with this approach have led to numerous modifications and reconstructions of the old concept—some showing an inherent possibility for mobility within the ''caste system''—these solutions still suggest that the overwhelming concern of the Indian people and the primary determinant of interaction between them is caste. Situations that do not fit into this pattern are either considered modifications of the standard model or examples that are only superficially atypical (Leach 1962: 3).[12]

Since the processes occurring in Vrindaban that are described in this book gain little or no intelligibility by imposing the standard caste template, it would be tempting to conclude that this is simply an aberrant situation where the true Indian paradigm is somehow nullified because of outside contamination. I suggest that this is not the case. The dynamics of Vrindaban's present sociocultural reality are distinctly Indian, and they point to the general untenability of the position that claims human behavior in India is solely determined by the structural force of the caste system. Such a position ignores the general interactionist view of social reality "as consisting of the collective or concerted actions of individuals seeking to meet their life situations" (Blumer 1969: 84). What is needed is a more responsive Indological perspective that, while not ignoring the cultural aspects of hierarchy that do exist broadly across the subcontinent, goes beyond the mere application of caste as a priori social fact, and is capable of better understanding the complex and varied particulars of social and cultural phenomena in modern India.

This does not entail a high level of abstraction, nor does it necessarily ignore the wealth of ethnographic data compiled over the past decades in support of the caste model. Rather, it only forces us to admit to what Rudolph and Rudolph (1967: 10) have labelled "recessive themes" that are just as important and just as available as sociocultural resources to the Indian population as the "dominant" ones. This also implies that a "historical particularist" approach is needed for the interpretation of Indian situations rather than, or in complement to a

[12] While the word *caste* is used today as if it were an inherently Indian concept, it is important to note that there is no such Indian word, and that no Indian term fully equates with it. Dumont points out that the word is of Portuguese and Spanish origin, meaning "something not mixed" and derived from the Latin *castus*, "chaste." In English, *cast* was used in the sense of "race" from about 1555 and identified with its Indian meaning at the beginning of the seventeenth century. It has been used in a "technical" sense from around 1700 (Dumont 1970: 21). This information indicates, I think, that the caste concept represents an abstraction formulated by observers in their own particular Western context to distinguish the Indian social system from their own. Considering the obviously *etic* nature of the term, it is logical to question its usefulness in particular contexts. Even when caste apparently exists, it is wise to consider that it may only be "an 'idiom,' a language borrowed from elsewhere to talk about social relationships" in Indian contexts (Stirrat 1982: 30).

structural-functional one. We should admit that, taken as whole, India is far from being completely understood, that our approach should be admitedly open-ended, and that we should realize, as Kolenda (1981: 89) has said, that "essential pieces undoubtedly have not even been discovered."

In order to place these assertions in a broader context, I will briefly review some of the persistent concerns of Indian sociologists and anthropologists as they have been variously handled, highlighting those that seem to offer direction for the problem at hand.

Students of Indian society have claimed that it can only be understood by employing the concept of "caste" in basically one of two ways: as a pan-Indian ideology that results in the variety of social behavior and relationships in Indian situations; or coming at the problem from the other direction, with a more Marxist perspective, as a dramatically exploitive socioeconomic order that is categorized and interpreted, or "mystified," as caste ideology. Although Leach (1962: 2) identifies these differences in approach as a central problem in Indian social research, stating that it "raises directly the question as to whether caste is best considered as a cultural or as a social structural phenomenon," both orientations assume that what is called caste is the underlying and crucial paradigm. These approaches compel the observer to search for and find data that shows the "fit" between model and reality.

Among the most influential writers on caste for Western social science are Max Weber (1958) and Louis Dumont (1970). Both base their assumptions on selected Indian texts which supposedly reveal the ideological justifications of the caste system.

For Weber, "caste is the fundamental institution of Hinduism" (1958: 29), and he finds that Indian social structure is regulated and explained by the concept of *karma*, the idea that one is reborn time after time into social positions determined by one's past actions. Weber is especially concerned, as was Marx, with relating the caste system to Indian economy, or more accurately, how the caste system has prevented economic progress in the Western sense. Caste to him is an irrational, repressive fact. On the other hand, and for this Leach (1962: 2) labels him "confused," Weber describes castes more generally as "closed status groups" in order to place Indian society in a broader comparative perspective. Some have suggested, however, that this latter approach led Weber to begin to consider some of the variation and discontinuities within the dominant system, which partially absolves his preoccupation with stereotypical aspects of caste.

Dumont commits himself totally to a structural model of caste that he insists informs all of Indian social life. Rather than finding its basis in karma ideology, Dumont proposes that caste is created and recreated by the ideological binary opposition of ritual purity and pollution, and inherent in his formulation is a concern for the subordination of power to ritual status. His work enjoins anthropologists to recognize a unity of these structural principles operating in South Asian society which are embodied in the classical Vedic *varna* theory. Dumont is most severely criticized for selectively reinterpreting classical texts and asserting that his interpretation is itself a conscious form available to Indian actors whose beliefs and actions it can describe and explain. Hawthorn (1982: 206) has boldly suggested that Dumont's characterization "starts from a false premise, misuses evidence, and in practice threatens to confine and distort the facts" and that his idea of an "encompassing conscious form . . . is not consciously held in all its aspects by anyone but him."

Although Dumont's structuralist depiction derives its components from what is essentially an idealized Brahmanical perspective, there are elements within it which should still be considered. Dumont does reveal some of the cultural resources that exist within Indian society although he ignores the fact that they may be variously internalized and only situationally invoked. The varna categories which he so meticulously investigates are not, as some critics have suggested, meaningless abstractions or simply all-Indian categories into which castes can be generally classified. As Lynch (1969: 71) has shown in his study of social mobility in Agra, they are "very important social categories which allow for some elasticity in what otherwise appears as a rigid hierarchy of castes. The *varnas* are open categories in which principles of recruitment are both ascriptive and achieved." Brahman, for example, is a varna category that is used in a variety of ways in Vrindaban. It must be considered in an analysis of social dynamics there, but its use by native or foreign actors does not necessarily indicate a concern for "caste."

Another point in Dumont's favor, although he insists on an invariable Indian "structure" in the Levi-Straussian sense, is that his model allows for variation within its encompassing structure. This is a recognition (if we read between the lines) that Hinduism is extraordinarily flexible and capable of absorbing an extremely wide range of human behavior and ideas—a fact that is widely accepted but seldom investigated. Furthermore, Dumont's identification of a central concern for ritual purity and pollution should not be overlooked, especially in any religious context, although it does not necessarily, as he suggests it must, always determine a Brahman-dominant status hierarchy. These things considered, nevertheless, it is his assertion of a phenomenological reality for his overarching, preexisting, unifying, textually derived "structure," which ultimately must be questioned. Dumont supposes that he knows what Indians *think*, and is not concerned with the fact that what they *do* may often not conform with his assumptions.

There are two more students of Indian society who should be considered for the impact they have had on contemporary analysis, both modifying and augmenting the approaches of Weber and Dumont. These are the anthropologists M. N. Srinivas and McKim Marriott.

Srinivas is credited, not without reason, for revolutionizing the standard conception of caste by pointing out that a focus on the textually based varna concept has "obscured the dynamic features of caste" (1966: 3). Essentially Srinivas attacks the idea that caste is a rigid phenomenon; that although hierarchy exists everywhere in India, who has the highest or lowest position is variable; there are processes that have always existed that allow for mobility and even change of caste. The Brahman, who must always mantain the superior position according to Dumont's scheme, may occupy any position in a local hierarchy (and hierarchy must be considered in situated contexts), including the lowest. Three concepts that Srinivas has introduced have found their way into the standard vocabulary of Indian specialists: dominant caste, Sanskritization, and Westernization.

Srinivas shows that the "dominant caste" in many villages—the kin-organized social grouping of inhabitants that own the most land and have the most prestige, power, and influence—may not be Brahman, or even "high caste." Furthermore, the caste which enjoys dominance is not necessarily fixed, and may give way to another. In a less than subtle way, he demonstrates that Dumont's textually derived model does not hold up in many villages (where most of India's population resides). He writes that "Manu would be a bad guide for field workers" (1966: 152), alluding to the fact that the "Laws of Manu" are a major source for Dumont's interpretation. At the same time, however, Srinivas also shows that in most cases, the caste that achieves dominance through secular factors such as land ownership, and the Western education of some its members (which probably means urban sources of additional income), also accrues high ritual status. This does not necessarily mean that Brahmans who lack secular dominance lose their ritual status, but rather that the group who enjoys secular dominance is also compelled to present themselves as ritually high as well.

There is indeed a pervasive concern for purity and pollution, but it does not always result in the formation of a hierarchy based upon opposition to Brahmans, who Dumont insists are always ritually the purest. Purity and pollution concepts are perhaps better seen as cultural resources that may or may not figure into the development and interpretation of social hierarchy. Kolenda (1981: 118) presents a striking example of this in an interview with an untouchable sweeper from a North Indian village. When asked "Will weavers, shoemakers, chamars [all low castes themselves] take water from you?" the sweeper replied, "No, as a matter of fact we are better off that they don't come to our well. It's purer without them. . . . We are the purest of all." For this untouchable, the concept of purity had nothing to do with his rank in the status hierarchy. In what is a reversal of the standard application of the concept, he reasoned that untouchables are "purest" because they don't have to deal with contamination from any other group. But he did not conceive that his "rank" had been elevated by his own evaluation of "purity"; rather, it was purely a personal concern.

Srinivas has also shown that evaluations of purity and pollution are as much a result of appearances as they are of birth-status. By codifying the concept of "Sanskritization," he has introduced into the anthropological literature an aspect of the caste system that is now considered undeniable fact; those proponents of the system's rigid lack of social mobility have been proven wrong. Sanskritization is a process by which a "low" Hindu caste, or other group, imitates customs, ritual, ideology, and life-style of an "upper" caste in order to claim a higher position in the caste hierarchy than traditionally conceded that group by the local community. The claim is usually made over a period of time, so that after a generation or two it is accorded higher rank.

This does not mean that the imitated caste must be Brahman. Rather, it is more likely to be the dominant caste of the village or regional area within which the attempt at status enhancement takes place. So again, the Brahmanical model of superiority is often irrelevant. The imitated model may in fact be *Kshatriya*, *Vaishya*, or even *Shudra*.

Yet, Srinivas is quick to point out that the mobility associated with Sanskritization results only in *positional changes* rather than *structural change*. The attributes of a particular caste may fluctuate, but for Srinivas the caste *system* remains the sociocultural fact of Indian reality. While he appropriates the idea that cultural resources may be manipulated by individuals in a caste, the only reason for doing this is to change the collective caste position.

In view of Srinivas's analysis it is tempting to analyze the integration of ISKCON in Vrindaban as an attempt at cross-cultural Sanskritization. But this would demand a view that the foreign devotees are attempting to win acceptance as a high-status caste group in a caste system, and, as I point out, in Vrindaban "caste" is neither an indigenously important nor analytically useful concept. Moreover, an individual's attempt at "Sanskritization" may have relevance for him apart from his own "caste" identity. Certainly many of the "traditional" concerns of Indian culture are of extreme importance in Vrindaban, but they are important in ways other than functioning to determine a caste-relevant hierarchy.

Another concept that Srinivas introduced is "Westernization." For Srinivas (1966: 46–60), Westernization is a process that began with the advent of the British, and involves the acceptance of Western dress, diet, education, technology, and above all, Western values. Although the process varies from region to region, Srinivas emphasizes that "the net result of Westernization of the Brahmans was that they interposed themselves between the British and the rest of the native population. The result was a new and secular caste system superimposed on the traditional system" (51).

This leads us to conclude that Westernization entails no deviation from the standard structural model of the caste system. Only the cultural symbols and life-styles which identified those who occupied the top rungs of hierarchy have changed. The traditional conception that India can only be understood in terms of caste is still maintained.

Almost parenthetically, Srinivas alludes to the fact that in some cases the concept of hierarchy is challenged or is not evident in a particular social environment. In this context he raises the question of the all-India importance of *bhakti* movements. Because of ideas externalized by bhakti saints and their movements, the concept of a "natural" Indian inequality was challenged. The aspects of Indian culture embodied in bhakti thought hold that the dignity of man is dependent upon actions, not birth; protest domination of society by priests; and stress that religious salvation is available to all. Untouchables, therefore, can and do become religious leaders, and Srinivas acknowledges that bhakti movements have always been a force subversive to ideological inequality.

Bhakti movements have historically been a part of the Indian socio-cultural landscape, providing interpretive resources that stand apart from "caste" ideology. Indeed, the concepts of bhakti that oppose the concept of caste are strongly operative in Vrindaban. Vrindaban culture is composed more prominently of categories and symbols derived from the Vaishnava bhakti texts and teachers than it is of traditional "caste" sources. These differences should not, I believe, be considered as opposing systems, but resources contained within a broader system of which caste is only one part and one possibility.

An all-India caste-based hierarchy based on ideas of purity and impurity is more properly seen as a foreign interpretation of Indian society and culture than one embraced and articulated by native informants. Marriott, and Ronald Inden, a historian well-versed in Sanskrit and Bengali, have therefore attempted to remedy this situation by attempting an "ethnosociology of the caste system" (Marriott and Inden 1977), and this has been followed up by their student Marvin Davis (1976). While some have criticized this approach for basically supporting Dumont's concern for purity and pollution (especially as opposed to a concern for power), I think their purported emic concerns reinforce several points that I have discussed.

Marriott (1968), in his early writings, emphasized that hierarchy can be determined by observing transactions between people, those that "give" being relatively lower in status than those that "receive." An interactional approach such as Marriott's, in the least, "brings out some of the more subtle and unnoticed patterns of individual motivation and group alliance which a formal ideology of caste rank would not predict" (McGilvray 1982: 5). His later attention to the fact that Indians believe some "coded-substance" is actually exchanged in transactions, reveals that a concern for purity is not always related to hierarchy, and may in fact not be associated at all with "caste." Marriott and Inden suggest that persons and *jatis* do not have fixed coded-substances, but that an individual's makeup may be improved or degraded by eating the correct food, performing the appropriate rituals, and learning. The concern is not, as in standard caste theory, which "caste" has the highest status, but how an individual attempts to improve his personal state of purity throughout life.

Marriott and Inden insist, as does Davis with his Bengali material, that the coded-substance idea is an emic one evident in both textual sources and informant accounts. It indicates that once we free ourselves from the intellectual limitations imposed by the ideas so long associated with "caste," we can better understand how Indians in various contexts actually construct their social reality. By associating with people and things that transmit "goodness" and avoiding those that are contagiously polluting, an individual is able to positively transform himself. "In this way," Davis (1976: 16) states, "individuals of the group and the birth-group as a whole become more cognizant of Brahma and lead a more uplifting, spiritual life." The concern for spiritual advancement, then, may be an overriding concern of Indian social life which takes precedence over more mundane and secular concerns of caste-based interaction.

The conceptions of Indian society held by many non-Indian observers, therefore, are incomplete, and perhaps even incorrect. To understand the Vrindaban situation, and other places in India as well, our thinking must go beyond the application of caste concepts and investigate the historical and cultural resources that are actually used to make sense out of everyday life. Students of Indian culture and social organization must be prepared to consider an almost unlimited variety of dominant and recessive themes and consider the flexibility of the system which they compose. What is needed is a sociology of Indian knowledge which seeks to understand people's experience, their social manipulation of symbolic forms, and the effects of both ideological and practical interests upon their cognitive processes.

Precedents for such an approach exist in Redfield's (1958) concern for the "social organization of tradition" and Singer's (1972, 1984) work which focuses on how elements of Sanskrit Hinduism are variously selected and understood throughout India. More generally, Geertz (1973) has emphasized that to understand man, the anthropologist must look at those situated aspects of society and culture that emphasize his uniqueness. In the Indian context, a similar concern would be helpful, for an understanding of "caste" is not an understanding of India. To accomplish this will entail many scholars studying the uniqueness of symbolic life in a wide variety of Indian contexts.

The task at hand, then, is to identify the cultural resources used by the actors in the situations occurring in Vrindaban. What are the significant categories and symbols used in everyday life? What are the referents of these symbols and how do they change in interaction? How do situational dynamics influence the development of relationships, the practical activities of daily life, and ideology?

Meaning, in the final analysis, exists only as a product of interaction. Accepting the potential variability of culturally embedded meanings, the observer must empirically discover what the meanings of symbols and objects are in specific situations and investigate how they are related. A description of the processes of meaning determination is therefore the primary subject of this study.

ORGANIZATION OF FOLLOWING CHAPTERS

The symbolic interactionist perspective directs attention to aspects of social reality and determines a research strategy; it also suggests how the final study should be presented. The organization of the following chapters is therefore structured by the primary concerns discussed thus far: the setting, the situations of interaction, the actors, and the meanings confronted and affirmed or modified.

Chapters 2 and 3 are concerned with the setting of Vrindaban as the symbolic locus of all the situations discussed in this book. Chapter 2 considers the historical and cultural meaning of the town, drawing from archival, textual, and informant sources, along with other pertinent literature, to establish its richness as an interpretive resource. Chapter 3 presents the town of Vrindaban as it is today, focusing upon its sacred complex of temples and sacred sites, its bazaars, and its people; especially considering those elements which help to compose the scenes of Western-Indian encounters.

Chapter 4 introduces ISKCON and its Vrindaban members. I briefly trace the organization's development from a 1960s American revitalization movement to a hierarchical institution with resources enough to embark upon a mission to revitalize Indian religion and society. ISKCON's career in Vrindaban is also discussed.

Chapter 5 is concerned with interactions between foreign devotees and pilgrims, considering the importance of the institution of pilgrimage to the overall context of interactions in Vrindaban.

Chapter 6 investigates interaction between permanent residents of Vrindaban and the Westerners, focusing especially upon explanations given by the Indian actors concerning the intrusion and acceptance of the foreign bhaktas there. It shows that in spite of the obvious changes that have occurred since ISKCON's arrival, the presence of foreign devotees has acted not so much as a disruptive force of change, but rather as an instrument of cultural continuity.

Chapter 7 outlines the ideal system of Krishna-bhakti which is the dominant cultural force in Vrindaban. I especially consider the understanding of mystical emotions, the central focus of this religious system, and show how appropriation of its different aspects by ISKCON devotees and Indian residents leads to conflict. The resolution of such conflicts through interactions results in a broader understanding of the total system by both sides, and leads to progressive acceptance of each other as valid members of a common cultural system.

The concluding chapter, besides summarizing the arguments presented in this book, considers discrepancies in the data, especially contradictions between written and verbal opinion and behavioral accounts. I suggest that this paradox actually points to the progressive transformation of cultural meanings through the dynamics of experience.

As a whole, this study attempts to show that significant interactions are occurring in Vrindaban, and have been since the first American devotees were brought there by Bhaktivedanta Swami in 1967. The establishment of the Krishna-Balaram temple complex in 1975 created a setting which has been accepted as a legitimate place of worship and pilgrimage, and wherein effective impression-management type interactions can be staged. In the larger arena of Vrindaban town, foreign devotees are now interacting with pilgrims and residents in all social spheres leading to subsequent transformations in the traditional symbolic system as they are incorporated into it. As such, it adds to the anthropological literature a concrete example of how interactional processes can transform symbols which express both the individual and cultural experience of history, mythology, society, language, and behavior.

Furthermore, this study raises particular questions concerning the functioning and importance of caste in India. The Vrindaban situation implies that some of our notions about Indian social organization must be reconsidered and perhaps revised. Not only must it be recognized that there are, and have likely always been, mechanisms for mobility within Indian society, but also that there are other ways that high status may be achieved. The fact that "outsiders" are being integrated into the Vrindaban sociocultural system should not be seen as simply a deviant case, but one that illustrates the functioning of indigenous cultural resources that are seldom noted as part of the Indian "system" by analysts. The resources that are operating in Vrindaban may not often be exploited, but their existence must be considered for a fuller understanding of social dynamics in India.

The Meaning of Vrindaban: Textual and Historical Developments

ISKCON has achieved integration in Vrindaban due to a conjuncture of historical, cultural, and social antecedents. Since the beginning of its development as a town about five hundred years ago, Vrindaban has, in retrospect, been preparing for the events occurring there now. Not only are the present situations of ISKCON-Indian interaction leading to the foreign devotees being incorporated into the town's traditional system, but they are having an impact upon how Indians view foreigners in general. Furthermore, transformations are occurring which affect how they perceive and intertact among themselves as well.

If an adequate understanding of these events is to be achieved, there must be an investigation of the setting which goes beyond a physical and demographic description. Vrindaban must be viewed as a symbolic object integral to all the situations occurring there, equal in significance to the actors and other objects which constitute the scene of each encounter. Indeed, without considering the complex meaning of this town, as do both its Indian and foreign residents, the situations, negotiations, and transformations which occur cannot properly be comprehended. Traditionally, this meaning exists on three distinct, interrelated levels, as Dimock (1966: 169) has accurately pointed out.

Not only does the word *Vrindaban* refer to the town located in the cultural and linguistic region of Braj situated on the banks of the Jumna River in present-day Uttar Pradesh, considered to be the location of Krishna's childhood and adolescence; Vrindaban also is the celestial realm where Krishna eternally conducts his transcendental lilas. Additionally, the ideal state of mind which is properly the goal of every Krishna bhakta is also called Vrindaban. The essential attribute of all these conceptualizations is the presence of the god Krishna and his retinue.

For both foreign and Indian devotees of Krishna, the terrestrial Vrindaban is identical with the celestial one; for, it is argued, Krishna does not exist separately from his mystical dham, the location of his activities and his full entourage. There is no doubt in the minds of devotees that Krishna himself "descended" to the earthly Vrindaban some five thousand years ago, but the equation between it and the spiritual realm rests upon more than his phenomenal presence there.

For the Bengal Vaishnava[1] tradition of which ISKCON is a part, De explains that Jiv Goswami—one of the "Six Goswamis"[2]—drew from scriptural sources to establish the identity between these two Vrindabans.[3] He writes:

> The terrestrial Goloka or Vṛndāvana is thus not essentially different from but really identical with the celestial Goloka or Vṛndāvana, and the Lord Krishna exists eternally in both places with the same retinue. . . . But the term 'terrestrial' must not be taken to imply that the earthly residence is phenomenal: it is as much non-phenomenal as the celestial abode, only it makes its appearance in the phenomenal world. . . . In other words, there is a mystical interlapping of the infinite and the finite, of the phenomenal and the transcendental. (1961: 334–35)

Vrindaban, then, is not perceived as just another sacred pilgrimage destination, or tirtha, one of the ideal locations to "cross over" into the spiritual realm; to be in Vrindaban is to be in the spiritual domain already. People living in the earthly Vrindaban do not see themselves as participating in normal activities, but rather taking part in an esoteric drama completely arranged by Krishna himself. Regardless of the reason one may find himself there, the full cosmic reality is that he is participating in Krishna's eternal pastimes.

One vairagi living on the riverbank at Chir Ghat[4] explained to me that "Krishna never leaves here. He is always present, and if you are

---

[1] *Vaishnava* means "worshiper of Vishnu." Since Krishna is an incarnation of Vishnu, Krishna devotees are also considered Vaishnavas. For Bengal Vaishnavas, however, Krishna is the supreme god and Vishnu is an expansion of Krishna.

[2] The "Six Goswamis" of Vrindaban were intimate disciples of Chaitanya Mahaprabhu who were sent there by him to establish the new sect's headquarters, develop the location as a pilgrimage center, and codify the religion's theology, philosophy, and ritual. By name they are: Rup, Sanatan, Jiv, Raghunath Das, Raghunath Bhatt, and Gopal Bhatt. The term *goswami* literally means one who is in control of cows, and by extension, of his senses. Goswami is also the name taken by priests in charge of Vrindaban's temples who trace their ancestry to the town's original founders.

[3] De lists the *Padma-purana* and *Brahma-samhita* as principal sources used by Jiv Goswami to establish dogma concerning the dham (1961: 334).

[4] A ghat is a place for bathing along a river, often with steps leading down to the water.

here also, then you are in his lila.'' Sripad Baba, [5] a key actor in for-
eign-Indian interactions in Vrindaban, put it this way: ''If you are in
Vrindaban, Krishna has called you.'' The fact that the bhakta sees
Vrindaban as not merely a sacred place, but as actually part of the spiritual realm, provides a powerful resource through which to interpret
and justify virtually any activity which occurs there.

It is an empirical fact of my research that all but a small percentage
of the total population of Vrindaban town see the physical surround-
ings, plants, animals, and people as part of the holy dham, and the
activities which occur there as part of Krishna's eternal pastimes.[6] Such
a firm belief often results in an interpretation of events based upon a
metaphysical logic which renders contradictions understandable and
violations to cultural rules acceptable. Simply put, Krishna and his lilas
are not bound by human conceptions and understandings. The bhakta,
therefore, has the option of accepting any events which occur in Vrindaban as caused directly by Krishna.

Beyond these two situated Vrindabans is the ''Vrindaban of the
mind,'' a psychological extension of Krishna's celestial and earthly
residences. Vaishnava texts indicate that one of the primary means for
achieving the perfection of human existence is to live in Vrindaban. If
a physical residence in the earthly Vrindaban is not possible, however,
then the cultivation of a psychological state wherein Krishna is the focus of consciousness is equally efficacious. Both physical residence in
the earthly Vrindaban, and achievement of the altered state of consciousness called Vrindaban, result in the soul automatically being
transferred to the celestial Vrindaban at the time of death. There the
devotee becomes part of Krishna's eternal entourage, never again to
suffer the pains of rebirth and death, and this is considered the ultimate
perfection.

For the ''pure devotee,'' this mental Vrindaban exists so that any
place can become Vrindaban-like. It is a state of mind which the bhakta
either possesses spontaneously or should be constantly striving for

---

[5] *Baba* and *sadhu* are terms that refer to ascetics, also usually perceived as holy men. A vairagi
is essentially a Vaishnava sadhu. Quotations from Sripad Baba are translated from a conversation
in mixed Hindi and English.

[6] This statement reflects the results of informal interviews, random surveys, and questionnaires.
In a questionnaire submitted to the merchants of Loi Bazaar, the main market area, all but 8
percent of the respondents (5 out of 66) agreed that Vrindaban was the same as Krishna's celestial
residence. In interviews, all but one temple Brahman from a sample of 22 (5 percent) agreed. The
one dissenter commented, ''When Krishna was here he kept the demons away. As soon as he left
all the big demons came back. That is who is here today, the big demons.''

through spiritual practices such as chanting, ritual worship, meditation, and study of the sacred literature.[7] ISKCON publicity materials emphasize the practicality of this approach since it negates the requirement of traveling to India in order to achieve perfection. Rather, devotees say that every temple is Vrindaban. Likewise, an Indian informant, a hereditary priest of one of Vrindaban's chief temples, expressed the same sentiment: "I never leave Vrindaban. Even if I am in Chicago or London, I am still in Vrindaban. So if I die elsewhere, immediately I am transferred."[8] This Vrindaban of the mind is what Bhaktivedanta Swami, ISKCON's founder, chose to call "Krishna Consciousness."

The complexity of Vrindaban's symbolic meaning must be considered in every situation, for it is certainly in the minds of all those who are actors in the encounters there. This meaning results from a prolonged development in Indian textual sources and in the historical development of the town. Though these two aspects are largely indistinct from the bhakta's point of view, I will consider each in turn. This will shed further light upon Vrindaban as a symbolic juncture which has allowed foreign elements to forge a penetration and integration into its traditional framework, winning acceptance as legitimate heirs to its cultural tradition, while simultaneously allowing the town to maintain an uncompromised aura of orthodoxy.

VRINDABAN IN TEXTUAL SOURCES

Especially in the Indian context, it is necessary to explore pertinent textual resources to frame data obtained from observation, interviews, and other methods of research. Marriot and Inden have explained that they "combine such diverse materials not because we suppose that one determines or directly influences the other, but simply because we find that they agree on certain major ways of defining the situation" (quoted in David 1977: 10). Indeed, the definitions of situations presented by actors in contemporary Vrindaban exhibit such congruence. But more than that, contained in the textual codification of cultural lore concern-

[7] There are basically two types of bhakti. One relies on a strict practice of formalized rituals and disciplined life-style to achieve a mystical loving relationship with Krishna (*vaidhi-bhakti*). The other is a "spontaneous" emotional relationship with Krishna that does not require strict practice since the devotee enjoys this transcendental consciousness "naturally" (*raganuga-bhakti*). The foreign devotees of ISKCON employ the ritual techniques, while many native residents of Vrindaban see themselves naturally engaged in a mystical relationship with Krishna due to their birth there. See chapter 7 for a more detailed discussion of these distinctions.

[8] Direct quotation in English from Srivatsa Goswami of Radha-Raman temple.

ing Vrindaban are many categories by which actors in the situations there construct their reality. It is not uncommon for them, in fact, to make direct textual references even during the most common of everyday activities in order to justify and explain behavior.

O.B.L. Kapoor, a resident of Vrindaban and *guru-bhai* (gurubrother, initiate of the same guru) of Bhaktivedanta Swami, claims that the first textual reference to Vrindaban can be found in the *Rigveda*, roughly datable to about 1200 B.C.[9] This reference is accepted by the Bengal tradition to which Kapoor belongs, and other Vaishnava *sampradayas* (sects, tradition) as well, although the specific name "*Vrndāvana*" does not actually occur there. Rather, an allusion to the *paramam-padam* (literally, "highest footprint") of Vishnu is considered an indirect citation. Kapoor (1977: 109) writes that "in the *Rgveda Vrndāvana* is described as the highest *Dhāman* (*paramam-padam*) of Vishnu." Linking Vrindaban to this early source elevates its importance in the hierarchy of places. It is interesting to observe how and why the Rigvedic paramam-padam of Vishnu has become equated with this study's setting.

The six original Goswamis of the Bengal Vaishnava sect went to extreme and effective lengths to find a basis for their theology and philosophy in the *Vedas*, *Puranas*, and other sacred texts. This effort to find such citations, beginning with the *Rigveda*, represents a technique of Indian scholarship used and accepted by many traditions, and its logic is clear within that context: in any argument or debate, especially one of a religious or philosophical nature, textual reference to the *Vedas* or other recognized scripture as a source of knowledge[10] is a point which cannot be contested. Moreover, if an idea can be traced to the *Rigveda*, there is a confirmation from the most ancient authority.

In personal conversations, Lee Siegel, a Sanskritist with the University of Hawaii's Department of Religion, suggested that while *pada* literally means foot, it also can be interpreted as a place marked or created by a footprint, in this case a cow's or bull's. The reference to cows in conjunction with this phrase is of primary importance because Vrindaban is the place where Krishna tends his cows and is often equated with Gokula or Goloka, the place of cows (*Go* being the Sanskrit root for "cow"). Furthermore, a cow's footprint (*goshpada*)

---

[9] Dates according to O'Flaherty (1975: 17–18). She has pointed out that dating of Indian texts is an "art" rather than a science. Her dates are conservative, especially for Indians themselves, but represent estimations generally accepted by critical scholars.

[10] The Sanskrit term for this category of knowledge is *shabda*.

made and then filled with water is an image that occurs throughout Indian literature as one process by which a tirtha, or place of pilgrimage, may be created.

Such correspondences in Sanskrit etymology are significant for Indian philosophical interpretations, and in this case provide the Bengal Vaishnava commentators with reason enough to identify Vrindaban with Vishnu's highest abode. Krishna and Vishnu are one and the same for them, and Krishna's heaven is Vrindaban. Both in this and other Rigvedic citations, the mention of Vishnu's realm being filled with cows, coupled with the subtle tirtha imagery, presents an effective and acceptable argument in Indian exegesis.[11]

While the Vedas and their commentaries comprise "revealed knowledge" for most Indian traditions, it is the *Puranas* which form the primary resources for extant Hindu sectarian religion, and in the *Puranas* references to Vrindaban become more numerous and detailed. For the *Gaudiya sampradaya*, the works of the Six Goswamis cite the specific *Puranas* important in the development of Vrindaban as a complete, unified concept. Alluding to sacred texts as a source of knowledge is seen by the founders of the Chaitanya school as the primary technique for legitimization of their ideas, and it is used to the exclusion of all other recognized methods (the others are perception, inference, testimony, analogy, postulation or assumption, nonrecognition, equivalence, and tradition), which they conclude to be defective in comparison (De 1961: 257). According to the Goswamis, the fully developed Vrindaban can be summarized as follows:

---

[11] The principal reference to Vishnu is found in *Rigveda* 1.154.1–6. Verse 6, cited here, is translated by Lee Siegel, professor of religion at the University of Hawaii, as follows (personal communication, parentheses mine):

> We desire to go to the place of both of you (Indra and Vishnu)
> where there are cows, many horned and swift;
> there the long striding bull (Vishnu)
> shines splendidly indeed.

Commenting on the use of pada, O'Flaherty says:

> Its primary meaning is foot (cognate with that word as with Latin *pes*, *pedis*); it then designates "step" (the foot's action) and footprint (the foot's after-image), as well as "stand" or "base" in the sense of dwelling place (later devotional Hinduism makes much of the fact that the lowest part of God is the highest part of the Universe). In the final verses, *pada* refers both to the actual place where men and gods dwell and the footstep which marks the place, in which the honey-fountain springs as water fills the mark made by a cow's hoof. (1981: 226)

Raychaudhuri (1975: 45) further notes that in *Rigveda* 1.22.18, Vishnu is called "Gopa" (cowherd), setting up the equation between this Vedic god and Krishna, who is also a cowherd.

1. Vrindaban is a manifestation of Krishna's energy, no different essentially than Krishna himself. It is "as good as" or identical to him. Since the earthly Vrindaban is the same as Krishna's celestial dham, living there puts the individual in direct contact with Krishna.

2. On a different level, but simultaneously, Vrindaban is the highest and most significant earthly location because it is where Krishna's *ras-lila* occurs. This event, his circle dance with the gopis, is the highest in the hierarchy of events, being the most symbolic and esoteric revelation of the relationship between man and God.

3. Since all objects in Vrindaban are part of Krishna, they each in their own way draw the person's mind—even against his will—toward meditation upon Krishna; and this ultimately delivers him from the bondage of the material world. Therefore, by living in Vrindaban and participating in daily life there, salvation is achieved.

4. Radha, Krishna's divine consort, is an essential element of Vrindaban. She is Krishna's bliss-giving energy, his *hladini-shakti* personified. Krishna manifests himself in this feminine form for two main reasons. First, he desires to experience his own beauty and capacity for giving pleasure. Secondly, Krishna allows man to witness Radha's incarnation as a separate object of devotion and as the ultimate model for man's own worship of the deity. It is Radha who can best please Krishna, and it is by imitation of her mood and actions that Krishna can be most appropriately worshiped. In Vrindaban it is a commonly expressed sentiment that Krishna is the only male; everyone else is female, relatively speaking. The ideal is "love in separation" (*viraha-bhakti*), a spiritually transformed passion that has its best analogy in a lover's all-encompassing desire for an absent beloved. Since Krishna is male, that transcendental passion is, by earthly criteria, naturally feminine.

5. Vrindaban attracts those who are at a certain stage in their spiritual evolution, automatically and beyond their conscious volition. The Vrindabanbasis say "Vrindaban calls," meaning that any person who comes to Vrindaban is there by Krishna's manipulation and for his purposes. Correspondingly, all events taking place in Vrindaban are part of his lila.

For the Goswamis, Vrindaban is the stage upon which Krishna acts; no other place is suitable. It is the frame within which the devotee can realize the highest *ras* (literally sap, juice), the highest devotional emotion in the mood of the gopis, especially Radha. Everything in Vrindaban is seen to inspire this mood: the Jumna River, groves, trees, flowers, creepers, clouds, breezes, birds, bees, cows, monkeys, and of course the gopis and *gopas* (cowherds) themselves.

Due to their meticulous citations, we know just which textual sources influenced the Goswamis' vision of Vrindaban, and the most influential work, without doubt, was the *Bhagavata-Purana*. This work, along with the *Bhagavad-gita*, form the two most popular texts for modern Hinduism and provide the central focus for all Krishna sects. The *Gita* deals with Krishna as God incarnate in the role of teacher and introduces the practice of *bhakti-yoga* as the supreme path of salvation, winning preeminence over the other types of yoga discussed. But in the *Bhagavad-gita* the details of devotional practice or *sadhana* are not explained, nor are there the vivid, detailed descriptions of Krishna as a child and adolescent which serve as the main objects of worship for his devotees. This full elaboration, which is inseparable from the contemporary image of Vrindaban, is first presented in the *Harivamsha-Purana*, an addendum to the *Mahabharata* of which the *Bhagavad-gita* is part, and further developed in other Vaishnava *Puranas*, including the *Bhagavata*.

The *Harivamsha*, dated to roughly A.D. 450, appears to be the first textual presentation of the Krishna myth including details of his Vrindaban lila. It should be remembered, however, that these texts are only the historical products of a complex cultural tradition, representing, as it were, only the tips of a vast iceberg of cultural knowledge. The importance of oral tradition among both the intelligentsia and the masses throughout Indian history should not be discounted, and some credence should perhaps be given to the popular sentiment of Indian people today that Krishna lived in Vrindaban about five thousand years ago and man's knowledge about him stems from that period. Even today much cultural transmission is facilitated by oral performances such as preaching, singing, dance, and drama. Whatever the case, the *Harivamsha* provides the first textual treatment of identity between celestial and earthly Vrindabans. As De (1961: 223) reminds us, for the devout "the Vṛndāvana-līlā is not a mere symbol or divine allegory, but a literal fact of religious history."[12] This *Purana*'s elaboration of the birth,

---

[12] See Raychaudhuri (1975: 62–118) for a detailed discussion concerning the historical evidence of Krishna's existence. He concludes that Krishna is a historical figure who "certainly lived before the Buddha . . . before 600 B.C." (64, 71). He also contends that there is good historical evidence to place Krishna's birth before 1800 B.C., and that a bhakti-type religion centered on Krishna worship flourished by the fifth century B.C. (20).

childhood, and adolescence of Krishna is presented as both historical occurrence and as the eternal lilas of the spiritual realm.

Later Vaishnava *Puranas* incorporate and elaborate upon the same themes. These include the *Vishnu-Purana* (A.D. 450), *Padma-Purana* (A.D. 750), *Brahma-Purana* (A.D. 900–1350), and the *Brahmavai-varta-Purana* (which falls between 759 and 1550 A.D.). However, it is the *Bhagavata-Purana* (A.D. 950) which eclipsed all the others in importance for the Goswami writers, probably due to its successful organization of vast amounts of information and its literary excellence. Hopkins (1966: 4) remarks that it is "the one Purāna which, more than any of the others, bears the stamp of a unified composition."[13]

While the *Bhagavata* is the primary and most quoted source for the Chaitanya school, it is interesting (and for some, problematic), that Radha is not directly mentioned in this text. For the Goswamis this does not present a problem, however, since Krishna does have a favorite gopi with whom he dances alone during the ras-lila, and they know without a doubt it is Radha. For direct textual citations of Radha's importance in the development of the Vrindaban complex, we must consult the *Padma-Purana* where her virtues are extolled, or the *Brahma-vaivarta-Purana* which presents her against a vivid background of sensuous imagery.

Chaitanya (1486–1533) was certainly inspired by the *Bhagavata-Purana*, as were his contemporaries, but his biographers maintain that a work often considered to be secular erotic poetry also had a tremendous impact upon him. This was the *Gitagovinda* of Jayadev, a twelfth-century work which portrays the full erotic imagery of Krishna and the gopis in Vrindaban, paying special attention to the Radha-Krishna relationship. So important was this work to the Chaitanya school, that it was elevated to the status of *rasa-shastra* (science of mystical emotions) along with the other recognized scriptural texts. The religious impact of the *Gitagovinda* was so great, especially in Bengal and Orissa, that it became integrated into the daily ritual of the Jagannath temple at Puri, where Chaitanya spent the last part of his life. By the time the Goswamis were writing their treatises at Vrindaban, therefore, the *Gitagovinda* was already considered canon, providing another rich source of imagery upon which they could draw to formulate their verses of mystical emotion and the ritual codes for the Chaitanya sect. Jaya-

---

[13] All dates according to O'Flaherty (1975: 17–18). See van Buitenen in Singer 1966: 23–40 for a discussion of the *Bhagavata-Purana*'s problematical dating.

dev's work influenced a group of poet-saints as well, whose works are also elevated to sacred status and continue to influence the popular image of Vrindaban.

At roughly the same time the Goswamis were establishing the significance of Vrindaban in Sanskrit, a number of these poet-saints were composing verses in the vernacular dialect of Braj-Bhasha which communicated the same meaning to the masses. These included Sur Das, Kali Das, Hari Das, Mira Bai, Nand Das, and Hit Harivamsha among others. Coming from various sampradayas, their works have also been elevated to the status of revealed knowledge for their respective traditions, as well as having broader, nonsectarian appeal.

Nand Das, one of the Ashtachap poets of the Vallabh sampradaya,[14] who lived in the Vrindaban area in the sixteenth and seventeenth centuries, sang of Vrindaban's mystical beauty in his *Raspanchadhyayi*, based on the five main chapters of the *Bhagavata-Purana*. Nand Das was a follower of Vallabhacharya, whose sect still flourishes in the Vrindaban area. It is this Vallabh sampradaya, along with the Radha-Vallabh sampradaya of Hit Harivamsha and the Gaudiya sect of Chaitanya, which combine today, as they did in medieval times, to present a unified complex of bhakti thought which includes the preeminence of Vrindaban. In the temple of Radha-Vallabh, established by Hit Harivamsha sometime in the mid 1600s, worship is still accompanied by the singing of appropriate verses written by the founder. A semiprofessional ensemble of musicians and singers called samaj extolls the glories of Krishna, Radha, and Vrindaban while the faithful file in and out of the temple for darshan. In his *Chaurasi-Pada* (translated by White 1977: 89–90), Shri Hit Harivamsha praises Vrindaban's essential attributes:

> First of all, according to my best judgement,
> I shall salute
> The very delightful Sri Vṛndāvana.

> Without the compassion
> Of Sri Rādhika
> It is unapproachable to the minds of all.

> The precious water
> Of the Yamunā irrigates
> Its eternal autumns and springs.

[14] Eight celebrated poets of the Vallabh sampradaya became known as the Ashtachap, literally meaning "eight seals," because they each "sealed" their work with a final signature phrase.

The perfumes of various
Kinds of flowers intoxicates
Whole clans of bees.

Cuckoos and parrots call
Amid the dark red
Tender mango leaves.

Tribes of peacocks dance—
Tremulous
With great bliss.

The pleasure-giving wind
Blows cool and gentle
And fragrant.
Red, blue and white:
The lotuses blossom
Everywhere.

The Crown of Lovers,
The Couple, Shyāma and Shyām
Play.

These poet-saints of Braj are taken as role models by some of the residents and sadhus of Vrindaban today. Composing their own lyrics, they speak of its celestial nature, insisting that this idyllic Vrindaban is the true Vrindaban, and available to all who take the time to purify their senses. One sadhu sang this impromptu stanza to express the feeling that "Vrindaban is. It cannot change":

Hari Das, Ram Vyas, Rupa, Jiv
Their Vrindaban still to see.
Celestial forest, not a town
Where Radha-Shyama's always found.
Jaya Radhe, Jaya Shyam, Jaya Sri Vrindavana dham.

The full image of Vrindaban, internalized today by local and foreign residents alike, sees its most complete development in the works of the Gaudiya Goswamis and the Braj poet-saints of the sixteenth and seventeenth centuries. The meaning elaborated by them follows two principal courses. The first centers upon the overwhelming physical beauty of the locale, which provides the only possible setting for the earthly pastimes of Krishna. The second focuses on the mystical qualities of the place: Vrindaban of the earth and Vrindaban of the heavens are identical, residence in the former serving as a positive indicator of a person's eternal participation in Krishna's cosmic drama. This attitude underlies all activities which occur in the town today, providing an explanatory resource often invoked to give meaning to behavior that would not otherwise be comprehensible.

These views of Vrindaban have their basis in the traditional literature, starting with the *Rigveda* and continuing through the Vaishnava *Puranas*, especially the *Harivamsha Vishnu, Brahma, Padma*, and *Brahmavaivarta Puranas*. It is in the *Bhagavata-Purana*, however, called by most Indians the *Shrimad-bhagavatam* or *Mahapurana* in allusion to its high ranking among the others, that we find the most organized and literary exposition of the full Krishna mythological complex. This text is considered by the majority of Vaishnava sects to be their primary source. In addition to these widely accepted traditional texts, the emotional component of the Chaitanya school was also highly influenced by Jayadev's *Gitagovinda*. Considered secular erotic poetry by some scholars, for Chaitanya and his followers, this work provided a rich source for the images of Krishna, Radha, and Vrindaban.

Since at least the time of the medieval revivalists, Vrindaban has been considered the epitome of earthly locales, but little factual information exists about the place before then. Many would say that the actual Vrindaban had been "lost," the exact location of Krishna's lilas forgotten as the present age degraded with time. Vaudeville (1976: 195–213) disagrees with this interpretation, asserting that no Krishna religion existed in the area before the Vaishnava reformers brought it there in the sixteenth century. She suggests, rather, that there was in fact a more indigenous worship of nature gods, incorporated within a *naga* (serpent) or shakti ritual structure dominant up until Chaitanya's time; therefore, there could be no question of loss or recovery, only the introduction of a new religion.

Vaudeville's opinion is summarily rejected by Vaishnavas, though it does serve to stress the importance of the medieval period for Vrindaban's emergence into a pilgrimage town of pan-Indian significance. The fact does remain that it was Chaitanya, considered an avatar of Krishna himself,[15] who decried the lack of concern for the dham, and

---

[15] More than being an incarnation of Krishna alone, Chaitanya is actually regarded as the dual avatar of both Krishna and Radha, his consort and energy of supreme pleasure. This perception of Chaitanya is traced by scholars to the *Chaitanya-charitamrita* of Krishnadas Kaviraj who wrote slightly later than the original Goswamis. Though this may be the first textual reference to Chai-

who according to tradition rediscovered the sites of Krishna lila by means of his psychic intuition. Although he did not reside for long in Vrindaban, he deputized his most intimate disciples to live out their lives there and not only codify the religion, but to also excavate the holy sites, establish temples, and generally develop Vrindaban into a town capable of supporting an active pilgrimage trade.

It is therefore to the development of Vrindaban as a town that I now turn. While little is known historically about the exact location occupied by present-day Vrindaban, some details are available concerning the wider linguistic and cultural area of Braj in which it is located.

EARLY HISTORY OF THE VRINDABAN AREA

The area included in the present district of Mathura has, over the centuries, been known by many names—Shurasena, Mathuramandal, Brajbhumi, Brajmandal, Braj—and today its residents still prefer Braj or Brajbhumi over the modern political classification. For the Hindu, Braj is conceived as a lotus with either Vrindaban or Mathura at the center, although neither is actually geographically central. While Mathura has historically been the political seat of the district that bears its name, at least since the construction of its first temples in the sixteenth century, most inhabitants of the region have considered Vrindaban to be its cultural center.

Archaeological Survey of India excavations near Govardhan, about twenty miles from Vrindaban proper, but still considered part of the total Vrindaban area, have yielded prehistoric stone implements and metal weapons. As with Varanasi, Mathura itself is considered one of the *mahapuris* (great cities) of India, one of the seven cities considered to be *mokhshada*, bestowers of liberation.[16] The city has likely seen the entire sequence of Indian civilization in Northern India from the Aryan conquerors, through the Mauryan, Kushan, and Guptan Empires, the Turkish and Afghan invasions, to the dominance of Mughul and British rule. Being on the silk route, it was crucial in the development of international trade, and saw its share of foreign visitors.

The first foreigner known to have recorded his visit to this region

---

tanya's duality, Dimock (1966: 32, 150) is of the opinion that even during Chaitanya's lifetime he was considered as such, and that Krishnadas in all likelihood received this idea from his teachers, who were in fact the Goswamis.

[16] Besides Mathura, Ayodhya, Hardwar, Varanasi, Kanchi, Ujjain, and Dwarka are also considered mokhshada (Eck 1982: 38).

was Megasthenes, Greek ambassador to the Mauryan court of Chandragupta at Pataliputra during the fourth century B.C. In his *Indika*, Megasthenes noted that "Heracles [Krishna][17] is held in especial honor by the Sourasenoi, an Indian tribe who possess two large sites, Methora and Cleisbora, and through whose country flows a navigable river called Iobares" (Joshi 1968: 27).

Growse states that General Cunningham of the British-run Archaeological Survey of India in the mid-1800s identified Cleisbora with Vrindaban, although Growse himself disagrees. He notes that General Cunningham felt "Cleisboro" was a Greek transcription of Kalikavartta, a name sometimes used for Vrindaban, meaning "Kalika's whirlpool"; Vrindaban is where Krishna fought the water serpent demon Kalika.[18] It seems that General Cunningham concluded that Vrindaban must have been a large settlement from ancient times due to its importance in his own time.

Though Mathura is now a primarily Hindu city, from both the archaeological and historical record we know that it has also seen periods of Jain and Buddhist dominance. The next available historical accounts by foreigners are provided in fact by two Chinese Buddhist pilgrims who evidently considered it one of the most significant Buddhist sites in India. Fa Hien visited Mathura around A.D. 400, and Hiuen Tsang in 634.

In the third century B.C. the Mauryan Emperor Ashoka became a great patron and devotee of Buddhism, doing much to spread this religion throughout Asia and establish its dominance in India. Under his influence, many stupas and pillars were erected, and the main sites of Buddhist pilgrimage, like Sarnath near Varanasi where Buddha preached his first sermon (the turning of the wheel of Dharma), were improved. No such significant event occured at Mathura, although according to legend Buddha did visit there. We do know from the accounts of these Chinese pilgrims, however, that Mathura was indeed a flourishing center of Buddhism during the fifth and sixth centuries,

[17] Preciado-Solis (1984: 23, 30, 59–60) summarizes the academic controversy concerning a proper identification of Megasthenes' Heracles in Mathura. His conclusion, shared by the majority of scholars (and accepted as general fact by Indians), is that "Heracles" is actually Krishna. Preciado-Solis shows overwhelming similarities between the the Indian and Greek hero-gods by convincingly comparing the two myths' distinctive features.

[18] Raychaudhuri (1975: 38) comments that according to his sources "Methora and Kleisbora are Mathurā and Kṛishṇapura. Now Megasthenes lived full two centuries before Patañjali. The name of the second city (Kṛishṇapura) mentioned by him is a certain indication of the early and inseperable connection of Kṛishṇa with the Sourasenoi (Śūrasenas or Sātvatas)."

with large monasteries that attracted monks adhering to both Hinayana and Mahayana doctrines.

Furthermore, the first image of Buddha may well have been sculpted in Mathura. According to Eck (1982: 62), the Buddha image was first produced there in the first century and represented the peak achievement of the "Mathura school" of sculpture during the Kushan dynasty which lasted until A.D. 300. The introduction of images into Buddhism by the monks and sculptors of Mathura altered the practice of that religion considerably from that time on.

The first of these Chinese pilgrims, Fa Hien, traveled to Mathura around A.D. 400, coming from Tibet through the Punjab. Mathura was the first major city Fa Hien encountered in India and he was impressed by its twenty monasteries situated along the banks of the Jumna River and by a population that was solidly Buddhist. Elements of the customs encountered and recorded by Fa Hien have a remarkably contemporary ring to them, and his description reinforces other evidence that a Brahmanical culture flourished there before Buddhism arrived.[19]

He described the people there as gentle, teetotalers, respectful of religious mendicants and monks, and eating a totally vegetarian diet that excluded onions and garlic. Today this is also the norm among the Hindu population there. While prohibitions against killing animals for food are logical considering the Buddhist doctrine of *ahimsa* (nonviolence), abstinence from onions and garlic is not so easily understood. Rather, this is a particularly Brahmanical prohibition which is usually explained in one of two ways. Hindus categorize food according to three "modes"—ignorance, passion, or goodness. Onions and garlic are considered to be in the mode of passion, and are therefore deleterious to religious practice. A more general explanation given today for excluding these items from the diet is simply that Krishna does not like them. Since this is the case, they cannot be offered to him, and therefore should not be eaten by man. It is a supportable Hindu hypothesis, therefore, that these restrictions survived from an earlier Vishnu-Krishna religious complex.

The decline of Buddhism in the Mathura area took several centuries before it was replaced by a resurgence of popular Hinduism, and this

---

[19] Growse (1979: 126) writes that "probably, the triumph of Buddhism was a mere episode, on the conclusion of which the city recovered a character which it had before enjoyed at a much earlier period; for it may be inferred from the language of the Greek geographers that Brāhmanism was in their time the religion of the country, while Hindu tradition is uniform in maintaining its claims both to holiness and antiquity."

is evidenced through the commentaries of the next Chinese pilgrim, Hiuen Tsang, who arrived there in 634. He found a Buddhist city with the same twenty monasteries, but they had a greatly reduced population of monks. Additionally, he reported that five "Deva" temples also existed with non-Buddhist adherents who lived scattered throughout the area. These temples represented the first markers of a popular revival of Hinduism which would result in an efflorescence that swept the district in the fifteenth and sixteenth centuries, creating the dominant culture that still exists today.

That neither Fa Hien nor Hiuen Tsang noted any other city of significance in the Mathura area tends to support the historical tradition that Mathura was the only urban seat in the whole of Brajmandal, other settlements being small villages. From an overall cultural perspective, however, it is the entire *mandal* (circle, circuit), not just Mathura, which is significant to the inhabitants of this area. The entire of Braj was and is composed mainly of forests and groves, rural encampments, and villages, some of which have now developed into small towns. These rural settlements and forested areas, along with the city of Mathura, are the dominant demographic and cultural landmarks, and none of these sites go unnoticed by the modern pilgrim.

A more recent outsider's description of the area, however, reflects the current perception of Vrindaban as the nexus of Braj culture. Monsignor Victor Jacquemont commented in 1830: "This is a very ancient city, and I should say of more importance even than Mathura. It is considered one of the most sacred of all among the Hindus, an advantage which Mathura also possesses, but in a lesser degree. Its temples are visited by multitudes of pilgrims, who perform their ablutions in the river at different ghats, which are very fine. . . . Next to Benares, Brinda-ban is the largest purely Hindu city I have seen. I could not discover in it a single mosque" (in Growse 1979: 188).

Traditionally, it is said that Braj is 84 *kos* (1 kos = 1 3/4 miles) in circumference—about 168 miles—and is composed of 12 main forests (*vanas*) and 24 smaller forests or groves (*upavanas*). These forests each mark in some way events related to the life of Krishna, and form the main points of a pilgrimage circuit which many devout pilgrims undertake. The precedent for a systematic pilgrimage journey to all these points (*Brajyatra*) is said by some residents to have been established by Krishna's great grandson, Vajranab (see also Vaudeville 1976: 200–201 concerning the yatra's antiquity). While Vrindaban (one of the 12 vanas) has always been considered part of the mandal, it was never a large settlement, or even a village, during most of the time that Mathura has been populated. Due to the events of the Krishna legend, it was traditionally a popular retreat for ascetics to be sure, but not until the early 1500s did its development as a town commence.

VRINDABAN AND THE BENGAL VAISHNAVAS

Today in Vrindaban there is a local organization—Shri Vrindavana Svarupotthan Paribhavana—whose Hindi slogan is *Shri Vridavana dhama ek vana hai, nagar nahi* (Vrindaban dham is a forest, not a city). Though its members have never experienced the place as a true forest, they desire its return to the "original state," or at least the prevention of its further development. They argue that a pilgrimage to Vrindaban should be a wilderness experience as it must have been until about five hundred years ago when Chaitanya initiated its development. Chaitanya had a much different vision of the dham, however, than the members of this modern organization.

Though it was never his intention to transform the place into a city, he and his followers took as their mission a development whereby the sacred sites of Krishna's lilas would become accessible objects of worship, where pilgrims would have adequate shelter during their yatra, and where temples for Krishna worship would be established. This in effect would open the holy dham to the masses, giving everyone the chance to receive its benefits. Concurrently, with the establishment of a permanent and flourishing Vaishnava community created around the Six Goswamis and their disciples, Vrindaban was to become the main organizational and intellectual center for the new religion.

These goals reflected the underlying structure of Chaitanya's movement, and its social implications were revolutionary. Access to God and the salvation which religion should provide was for Chaitanya not to be limited to Brahmans and those who had renounced society. Since religious emotions were for him superior to complex ritual, religion was therefore not dependent upon esoteric knowledge or education. As Hopkins (1966: 11, 18) has pointed out, the *Bhagavata-Purana* insists that religion should not be based upon qualifications of birth or status; a person's class should be determined by the characteristics he innately possesses or develops.

Likewise, the benefits of living in Vrindaban—a guarantee of salvation, *moksha*—should be available to all. Furthermore, even if a person could not permanently reside there, which was the ideal, at least he could come, stay for awhile, and leave refreshed and purified, confident that a start had been made on the path to spiritual perfection.

Presently Vrindaban is a town of about thirty thousand residents, with an influx of as many as one hundred thousand on the main festival days. Over the years it has grown in its capacity to handle visitors, but basically the sacred complex remains the same as it was after the initial development of the Bengal Vaishnavas. Therefore, before describing Vrindaban as it exists today, the events which initially transformed it from a forest retreat to a pilgrimage town should be considered.

In 1925 Kennedy wrote that "the development at Brindaban was the direct result of Chaitanya's own action. To all Vaishnavas, Mathura and Brindaban are holy sites because of their connection with the legends of Krishna. To a devotee of Radha-Krishna the scenes of Krishna's lilas at Brindaban must ever be of supreme sanctity" (1925: 65). De later commented that "the recovery of the sacred sites of Vrindaban by the Bengal Vaishnavas and its erection into one of the religious centers of Northern India form one of the most interesting events in the history of medieval Vaishnavism; for the modern Vrindaban, eclipsing today the glory of the adjacent city of Mathura by its fine temples, groves, seminaries, bathing ghats, is the creation chiefly of Bengal Vaishnavism" (1961: 65).

There are three early biographies of Chaitanya: *Chaitanya-charitamrita* completed in 1542 by Kavikarnapura, nine years after Chaitanya's death; Vrindavan Das' *Chaitanya-bhagavata* with a date no later than 1548; and the *Chaitanya-charitamrita* of Krishnadas Kaviraj completed in 1615 (dates from De 1961: 43, 48, 56). From these sources we know that at least from his early adult life, Chaitanya had formulated the idea of visiting and perhaps residing in Vrindaban.

Born in 1486, by the age of sixteen, Chaitanya was already considered a *pandit* (scholar-teacher) and had his own *tol* (school) with a large number of students, according to his hagiographers. During this early period he developed a reputation as a scholar in his hometown of Navadvip, which was then considered one of the primary seats of learning in Bengal. At this stage his behavior was suited to the academic status that he held, exhibiting no displays of religious fervor, though biographers do comment upon his forceful personality and physical beauty.

At the age of twenty-two, however, a marked change occurred in Chaitanya's life as a result of a pilgrimage to Gaya taken in order to perform *shraddha* (funeral rites) for his father. There he met the well-known guru, Ishvara Puri, who according to Vidyarthi (1961: 69) was the leading religious figure in Gaya, and jati-guru of the Gayawals, hereditary priests of the town. For reasons not entirely clear, Chaitanya was initiated by Ishvara Puri with a Krishna mantra, and this apparently transformed him from a dignified teacher into a Krishna-intoxicated ecstatic.

According to the legend, the content of Chaitanya's teaching shifted from the subtleties of Sanskrit grammar to discourses about the glories of Krishna. His school soon folded and his career as scholastic pandit came to an early end. Though modern scholars are reluctant to classify Chaitanya as a great intellect, his biographers and followers emphasize this early period as evidence of a highly developed rationality which, in spite of his ecstatic trances, would win many converts by logical debate, and serve him well as organizer of a significant new religious movement.

Yet it was his ecstatic personality which attracted the attention of established Vaishnavas of Navadvip who quickly gathered around him, creating the nucleus of a Chaitanya cult. At this time Chaitanya began to conduct *sankirtan* sessions in private homes. This congregational chanting, accompanied by musical instruments, dancing, and sometimes trance states inspired by Chaitanya's own ecstacies, is often cited as his main contribution to modern Indian religion, and it soon swept the entire town into a revivalistic fervor. Sankirtan became so popular, and Chaitanya became such a celebrity, that these meetings were not long confined to private homes, but soon spilled out into the streets.

Sankirtan so disrupted the normal life of Navadvip that the town's Muslim administration attempted to bar these public performances, but these restrictions ultimately had an opposite effect. In response, Chaitanya organized massive *nagar-kirtans* (kirtans involving the entire town), parading through the streets in a jubilant but organized defiance which some have cited as the original model for Gandhi's nonviolent civil disobedience campaigns (Chakravarti 1975: 35). The *kazi* (Muslim chief administrator) supposedly was won over by the sincerity of the masses and charm of their leader, subsequently authorizing nagar-kirtans by official proclamation.

Although it is usually argued that Chaitanya did not consciously initiate a movement, he apparently realized the significance of events occurring around him and began to take the role of religious leader seriously. It was his eventual decision, therefore, to enter the renounced order of life, *sannyas*, the status most suitable for guruship. Chaitanya's biographers depict this as a reluctant decision since it entailed leaving his family behind, but he nevertheless felt it was an essential step. By becoming a sannyasi, he automatically acquired increased legitimacy and respect; moreover, since for the sannyasi normal behavioral constraints are considerably relaxed, he could indulge in ecstacies without being labelled mad.

So at the age of twenty-four, Chaitanya became a sannyasi through initiation from Keshava Bharati and was given the name Sri Krishna Chaitanya, one who awakens the spirit of Krishna in the heart.[20] From the time of his Krishna-mantra initiation (diksha) from Ishvara Puri, Chaitanya had experienced trances wherein he would assume the mood of the gopis of Vrindaban, imagining that he was with Krishna along the banks of the Jumna River. It was natural for him, therefore, after being freed of family responsibilities, to decide to go to Vrindaban with the intent of establishing his hermitage there. However, due to the supplications of his mother, Chaitanya established his base of operations closer to home at Jagannath Puri in Orissa, and from there embarked on pilgrimages throughout India, one of which would finally take him to Vrindaban in 1515.

Chaitanya probably had in mind the establishment of some type of center at Vrindaban from the beginning of his religious activities. Both his diksha guru, Ishvara Puri, and sannyas guru, Keshava Bhararti, were in fact disciples of Madhavendra Puri, a Vaishnava who himself had propagated Krishna bhakti and foreseen the importance of Vrindaban to a revitalized Vaishnavism. Some writers would even give Madhavendra Puri credit for initiating the movement which Chaitanya would eventually inspire. Kennedy (1925: 65) states that some fifty years before Chaitanya, Madhvendra had "turned the thoughts of Bengal Vaishnavas toward the sacred sites of Vrindaban. He had established a small temple there and installed two Bengali priests as its custodians."

This temple—actually at Govardhan—was established for the worship of an image called Srinathji whose "discovery" is credited to Madhavendra, and it is indeed quite possible that Chaitanya received some form of direct instructions about going to the Braj area from his own gurus.

It is certainly Chaitanya, however, who should receive most credit for the development of Vrindaban. Although his initial plans for trav-

---

[20] Until the time of his sannyas initiation, Chaitanya was known either by his given name of Visvambar, or by Nimai, a nickname indicating his birth under a nim tree.

eling to Braj were cancelled at his mother's request, Chaitanya deputized a close friend and disciple, Lokanath, to go and live in Vrindaban, instructing him to discover and reclaim the sacred sites of Krishna's activities. According to Kapoor (1977: 29), Lokanath met with such success that by the time Chaitanya arrived in 1515, he was able to show his master many of the most significant locations. Lokanath is also credited with the founding of one temple, Gokulananda, and the initiation of one disciple, Narottam Das, who would become an important second-generation figure.

After settling at Puri and completing a difficult pilgrimage to South India, Chaitanya finally felt that the time was right to embark on his long-desired visit to Vrindaban. So in 1514, just after the finish of the rainy season, he embarked for the land of Krishna by way of Bengal. Chaitanya was accompanied by a large entourage at the insistence of the king of Orissa who had by this time fallen under his spell. In fact, Chaitanya was designated as "state god" of Orissa by the king (Das 1978: 137).

At Ramkeli, Chaitanya met two brothers, Sakar Malik and Dabir Khas, who were officials in the Muslim government of Hussain Shah, the nawab of Bengal. These men would become, after their conversion and initiation by Chaitanya, two of his most important disciples—Sanatan and Rup Goswami. When Sanatan saw the royal entourage, he suggested to Chaitanya that traveling in such a manner was improper for a sannyasi, and the master evidently agreed. So Chaitanya returned to Puri, and after an additional four months started off for Vrindaban again, this time with only one Brahman attendant named Balabhadra.

Although it is the opinion of some of his detractors that Chaitanya never actually went to Vrindaban, most scholars agree (Kennedy 1925; De 1961; Dimock 1966; Vaudeville 1976; Kapoor 1977; Majumdar 1978) that his biographers and the oral tradition are essentially correct. Following that assumption, we note that Chaitanya finally reached Braj, and after visiting Mathura, set out for Vrindaban proper; his entry into Vrindaban is a story relished and often told by Chaitanyites today. Kennedy (1925: 47) remarks:

> At Mathura, which is associated with Brindaban in the sacred legends of Vaishnavism, Chaitanya visited all the holy sites at twenty four different ghats. All the while, as he approached the scenes of Krishna's exploits, his emotions grew in intensity, until his companions became fearful of the results. Even the neck of a peacock was sufficient to send him into a swoon,

the dark colors reminding him of Krishna. On catching sight of Govardhan Hill, near Brindaban, he was so affected that he threw himself on the ground, clasping the very rocks in a frenzy. Finding two shallow pools in a rice field he bathed in them rapturously, thinking them the pools where Krishna dallied with Radha in the water. In this manner he visited all the holy sites round Brindaban, as far as they were discovered.

Bhaktivedanta Swami, in his translation of Krishnadas' *Chaitanya-charitamrita* (1975: 125) relates Chaitanya's entry into Vrindaban in this manner:

The Lord's ecstatic love increased a thousand times when He visited Mathura, but increased a hundred thousand times when He wandered in the forests of Vrndāvana. When Sri Chaitanya was elsewhere, the very name of Vrndāvana was sufficient to increase His ecstatic love. Now, when He was actually travelling in the Vrndāvana forest, His mind was absorbed in great ecstatic love day and night. He ate and bathed simply out of habit.

During his Vrindaban stay, Chaitanya was constantly entranced, and in that state he designated the locations of the legendary Radhakund and Shyamakund, ponds where Krishna is said to have swum and played with the gopis. This, according to Majumdar (1978: 28), was the most significant event during Chaitanya's visit, an accomplishment which his deputies had failed to achieve. This "psychic" discovery evidently gave considerable impetus to the religion's further development in Vrindaban, and the subsequent excavation and development of the Radhakund area produced one of the most important tirthas established there by the Bengalis, becoming a popular residence for many of them.

Not only are the "rediscovered" sites of Krishna lila important pilgrimage destinations today, but the places that mark Chaitanya's visit to Vrindaban are objects of adoration as well. Akrur ghat where he resided for that period, and Imli-tala, the tamarind tree under which he would do his daily chanting are especially revered. But at every place Chaitanya traveled around Vrindaban he was plagued by huge crowds seeking his darshan and blessing, indicating that by this time his fame had already spread far outside his native Bengal and adopted Orissa. These throngs concerned his companions who felt that their master's safety was threatened, and he was finally convinced to reluctantly leave Vrindaban earlier than planned.

On the return journey to Puri, Chaitanya stopped at Allahabad and

Varanasi. At these locations he held discourses with Rup and Sanatan respectively, not only commissioning them to develop the sect's written codes, but transmitting detailed knowledge concerning what should be contained in them. These two brothers would become regarded as great scholars, poets, and saints of the movement through their efforts at implementing Chaitanya's Vrindaban vision "to revive it as a Vaishnava pilgrimage center and as a headquarters for the movement, to build temples for the worship of Radha and Krishna, and to establish a scholastic and literary community there for the production of a systematic theology" (Goswami in Gelberg 1983: 232).

Therefore, by 1516, Vrindaban had been prepared by the reconnaissance of Lokanath and had received the first two of the "Six Goswamis" which Chaitanya would send there. It can also be assumed that by this time others had already settled there as well, and that a small community was beginning to form. Yet, Vrindaban could have still been little more than a forest settlement of ascetics at this point, since we know from the biographies that Rup and Sanatan both traveled to Mathura and neighboring villages daily to beg for food.

THE SIX GOSWAMIS AND THE SACRED PILGRIMAGE COMPLEX

Shortly after their arrival, Rup and Sanatan established the town's initial shrine to Brinda devi, a goddess who not only bore the town's name, but was considered an incarnate aspect of Krishna as well. In his *District Memoirs*, Growse (1979: 61) suggests that this shrine was located at the present-day Seva-Kunj, near the town's center. Local tradition, however, holds that the shrine to Brinda devi was built on the site that would later support the temple of Govindadev.

Growse further recounts the acquisition of two images, the deities of Govindadev and Madan-Mohan, which would eventually be housed in the first of the temples to be constructed. He states that Rup dug the image of Govinda from a cowshed in nearby Nandagoan, but local informants are a source of conflicting detail. By their accounts, the image was commissioned and installed by Krishna's own great grandson, Vajranab, and had been worshiped for centuries. During one of the Muslim invasions, however, it had been buried to prevent destruction and was subsequently lost.

One day, as Rup was wishing that he could locate this deity, a young boy appeared and disclosed that there was a hole in a nearby hill where daily a cow went and spontaneously deposited milk. Immediately Rup ran to the spot and discovered the image, relieved to know that even without human protection it had been "fed" by this cow (and presumably others over the years). The townspeople believe that this discovery was made at the future location of the Govindadev temple, near the spot of the original Brinda devi shrine. There is at least agreement between Growse and the local informants that the image was then installed in a hut on the hill where the Govinda temple now stands.

The image of Madan-Mohan was also by tradition established by Vajranab, who had placed Krishna deities throughout the Braj area. They, of course, by the time of Chaitanya had all been lost or forgotten, and it is generally thought that Chaitanya instructed his disciples to recover as many as possible in their reclamation effort. So the story is told that one day Sanatan dreamed of Madan-Mohan residing in the home of a poor Brahman at Mathura. The next day on his begging rounds, Sanatan visited the home of that Brahman and found the incidents of his dream to be corroborated. At first the Brahman refused to give up the image, but finally was instructed to do so by the deity himself, and Sanatan took possession of Madan-Mohan. He carried the image to another hill on the opposite side of town from Govindadev and established its worship in a small hut, again on the future site of a large temple, probably the first to be built in the town.

A wealthy merchant was taking his goods by boat to market at Agra when it became grounded on a sandbar just opposite Sanatan's hut. He sought out the local divinity for help and found Sanatan with Madan-Mohan, to whom he prayed for help. Soon the boat floated clear, the merchant successfully sold his goods at Agra for a large profit, and returned to Vrindaban where he gave most of the money to Sanatan in tribute to the god. Sanatan used this windfall to begin construction of a temple which was completed around 1580 and still stands today at the same location. These two temples, Govindadev and Madan-Mohan, stand on the highest elevations of the town, which for the most part is flat alluvial plain. It is said that on a clear day they could be seen all the way to Delhi, some ninety miles away.[21]

The sacred complex of Vrindaban was beginning to form, sprouting

---

[21] Local informants agree that the temple of Govindadev originally was either seven or eight levels high. The topmost three or four levels were destroyed by Aurangzeb, who was defeated in his attempt at complete destruction due to the temple's solid construction. It is said that a large butter lamp at one time burned nightly at the temple's pinnacle which could be seen clearly in Delhi at night. This nightly glow from Govindadev is attributed with so disturbing Aurangzeb that he vowed to destroy its Hindu source.

temple spires that would come to symbolize the town. During those early years, however, the religious pioneers were concerned not only with building new temples that signified the spirit; they were also hard at work constructing a literary foundation that would interpret their movement in the context of ancient traditions as well. Rup and Sanatan were joined by four other Goswamis (Gopal Bhatt, Raghunath Das, Raghunath Bhatt, and Jiv) over the next two decades to bring their number up to the revered complement of six. Although the dates of their arrival in Vrindaban are debated, as are the details of their backgrounds, the sketchy data concerning these key figures are significant to the history of Vrindaban.

Chaitanya probably encountered Gopal Bhatt, the son of a Brahman in whose house he was residing, on his South Indian pilgrimage. If Gopal was born in 1500 as his descendents in Vrindaban claim, he could have been no older than twelve at the time of Chaitanya's pilgrimage which lasted from about 1510 to 1512 (De 1961: 89–91). Whatever the case, the master was impressed by the piety of this young man who expressed a desire to join Rup and Sanatan in Vrindaban, and instructed him to go there upon the death of his parents.[22] There is no accurate accounting as to when this actually occurred, but he probably arrived in Vrindaban some years after Rup and Sanatan. It is known, however, that he codified the ritual aspects of the Gaudiya sampradaya in *Hari-bhakti-vilasa*, and established the temple of Radha-Raman for worship of the deity of the same name. This temple is considered today the highest seat of Gaudiya Vaishnavism outside Bengal, and is one of the sites of regular ISKCON-Indian interaction.

Raghunath Das was a companion of Chaitanya at Puri and attended him there until the master's death in 1533.[23] He remained in Puri until the death of one of his other teachers, Damodar Swarup, traveling then to Vrindaban in either 1535 or 1536. There he resided mainly at Ra-

[22] Concerning Gopal Bhatt, Dimock (1966: 76, 77) writes that "it should be noted here that the story, especially its chronology, about which the early writers had something of a cavalier attitude, is a bit confused. When Gopāla says that he is off to join Rūpa and Sanātana, Caitanya had not met those two Gosvāmins, much less sent them to Vṛndāvana."

[23] Chaitanya's death in Puri, though the date (June/July 1533) is not disputed, is shrouded with mystery. Gaudiya Vaishnavas recount that he merged with the deity of Lord Jagannath at the Puri temple; however, less supernatural explanations also exist. One account suggests that Chaitanya died (or some say was assassinated) while worshiping the Jagannath image and was buried within the temple compound. Priests subsequently propogated the myth that he had been physically absorbed into the image. Two other explanations are less mystical: one is that he drowned in the sea while in an ecstatic trance; the other that he died from a septic infection resulting from a stone cut on his left foot.

dhakund, a place today associated with him and Krishnadas Kaviraj, author of *Chaitanya-charitamrita*. Das Goswami, as he was called, produced a considerable amount of poetry on the Radha-Krishna theme and probably contributed much information incorporated into Krishnadas' biography of Chaitanya.

Raghunath Bhatt evidently was the only member of the group of six that left no literary contribution to the movement. Instead, he is remembered for his extraordinary asceticism, inspired preaching on *Bhagavata-Purana*, and beautiful singing voice. As did Gopal Bhatt, Raghunath Bhatt joined the Goswamis at Vrindaban after the death of his parents, sometime in the early 1530s, having met Chaitanya at the home of his parents in Benares during the master's trip back to Puri from Vrindaban.

The last of the Six Goswamis is Jiv, nephew of Rup and Sanatan. Jiv is considered the most philosophical of the group, his *Samdarbhas* being important contributions to Indian philosophy in general (Chakravarti 1969: 59). Jiv established the worship of an image called Radha-Damodar, supposedly sculpted by his uncle Rup, and built a temple of the same name to house it. This temple, though no architectural gem, is perhaps the most sacred of the Gaudiya temples in Vrindaban today because the remains of Rup, Krishnadas Kaviraj, and Jiv himself are there. It also contained one of the largest libraries of original Vaishnava manuscripts until they were acquired by the Agra University-affiliated Vrindaban Research Institute in 1976.

Furthermore, this temple is an especially significant object for ISK-CON since it was the residence of Bhaktivedanta Swami before his coming to the United States in 1965. Returning to Vrindaban in 1967 with his first American disciples, he established the initial Indian headquarters for the fledgling International Society for Krishna Consciousness there, and it has been a primary setting for ISKCON-Indian interactions since.

Although the precise dates of their arrival may be disputed, we know that by 1573 the Six Goswamis were present in Vrindaban and by then had established a wide acclaim for themselves and their sect. In that year the emperor Akbar, most tolerant of the Mughal rulers, visited Vrindaban specifically to meet these now-renowned saints. Akbar the Great, as he is known, was taken blindfolded into the garden called Nidhiban "where such a marvellous vision was revealed to him, that he was fain to acknowledge the place as indeed pious ground. Hence the cordial support which he gave the attendant rajas, when they expressed their wish to erect a series of buildings worthy of the local deity'' (Growse 1979: 241).

Akbar's visit, therefore, gave great impetus to the physical development of Vrindaban during its formative years, for it was in honor of this event that the rajas, under direction of the Goswamis, commenced the construction of the four original temples. Growse considers this temple series (Madan-Mohan, Govindadev, Gopinath, and Jugal-Kishor) not only of great importance for Vrindaban's own rise to importance, but also significant in the overall development of Hindu architecture. He comments especially that Govindadev ''is the most impressive religious edifice that Hindu art has ever produced, at least in Upper India'' (Growse 1971: 61).

The completion dates of only two of these temples can be accurately determined by their inscriptions: Govindadev in 1590 and Jugal-Kishore in 1627. Madan-Mohan was likely finished around 1580 according to local informants, and the Gopinath temple was also standing by the time Govindadev was completed. Shyamananda, a disciple of Jiv, is credited with establishing another important Gaudiya temple, Radha-Shyamsundar, sometime in the mid-seventeenth century. Though the present temple is of newer construction, its predecessor was at the same location.

Two contemporaries of the Goswamis who were influenced by Chaitanya personally or through his disciples, also established their own sects with images and temples in Vrindaban. These are Swami Hari Das and Hit Harivamsha. Hari Das was noted for his musicianship and is held in high esteem throughout India due to his being the guru of Tan-sen, Akbar's court musician. He lived most of his life at Nidhiban, the garden where Akbar met with the Goswamis along with, presumably, other notables such as Hari Das himself. According to local tradition, in this garden the image of Krishna named Bihariji appeared to the Swami, and today its worship is conducted in the temple of Banke-Bihari, statistically the most popular temple in the town. A date for the first Bihariji temple is not recorded, but informants report that a structure was built for the image in the early 1600s in Nidhiban, with the present temple being built in 1874.

Hit Harivamsha was a later contemporary of the Goswamis and founded the temple of Radha-Vallabh; the Gaudiyas claim that he was a disciple of Gopal Bhatt, though this is debated by members of his own sect. The image of Radha-Vallaba is said to have been given to Harivamsha by Krishna himself, and is one of the primary deities of

Vrindaban purported to have miraculous powers. The temple was built for its worship in the late 1600s and shares importance with Radha-Raman and Banke-Bihari as the most active traditional temples in the modern pilgrimage complex.

So by the mid-seventeenth century, the basic framework of Vrindaban's sacred pilgrimage complex had been established. This includes the original and architecturally significant temples of Madan-Mohan, Govindadev, Gopinath, and Jugal-Kishor, all built under the guidance of the Six Gosamis with patronage from Akbar. Two other temples initiated by the Bengali pioneers that still are in use are Radha-Damodar established by Jiv, and Gokulanand founded by Lokhanath. Though today there are newer temples with identical names near the original four except Jugal-Kishor, these old temples (now in various states of disrepair and under the protection of the Archaeological Survey of India) still draw devout pilgrims. Recently, the sanctums of Govindadev, Gopinath, and Madan-Mohan have been revitalized with the installation of Chaitanya deities (the original images all being taken to sites in Rajasthan to prevent their destruction at the hands of Aurangzeb).

The temples of Shyamsundar, Banke-Bihari, and Radha-Vallabh complete the list of early temples that existed in some form during the medieval period. This may not, however, be an exhaustive list, for then as now, Vrindaban supported a profusion of temples. Some were no more than private shrines, but nevertheless loaded with meaning for pilgrims there. These early temples just described are still components of the sacred complex today. Since they are also settings for many situations of interaction between foreign and Indian devotees, an attempt at understanding their meaning, which is ultimately linked to the past, is essential. Within their framework the modern sacred pilgrimage complex has developed, and along with it a social structure that is assuredly Indian, though in many ways unique to Vrindaban.

Today the sacred pilgrimage complex continues to expand. Perhaps Vrindaban's capacity to incorporate change while still maintaining its traditional continuity is best reflected by the temple of Krishna-Balaram, constructed by ISKCON and opened to the public in 1975. Although its priests and staff are mainly American and European devotees, Indian pilgrims and Vrindaban residents flood the inner courtyard daily to worship there. Indian pilgrims have ''voted with their feet,'' making Krishna-Balaram a significant new addition to the Vrindaban pilgrimage complex, coming a close second in popularity after Banke-Bihari. The Vrindabanbasis are quick to point out that Vrindaban has not changed by the incorporation of Western devotees; Vrindaban never changes, they say. Rather, for them the advent of ISKCON there simply confirms the attitude established by Chaitanya and the Goswamis that under Krishna, all people, regardless of their ascribed status, are equal; that the apparent culturally based meaning of Vrindaban transcends even ethnic and national boundaries.

The Sacred Pilgrimage
Complex

VRINDABAN was a place of pilgrimage long before it became a town, but until the time of the Bengal Vaishnavas the locations of Krishna's activities were visited only by the recluses who lived alone in the forests there. It was the desire of Chaitanya and the Six Goswamis, however, to make the experience of Vrindaban's spiritual power available to the masses of devout Vaishnavas, and the development they initiated there in the sixteenth century was toward that end. Anchored solidly upon their achievements, this development has been continued by a variety of Indian sects, holy men, wealthy individuals, and also by the International Society for Krishna Consciousness. In this chapter, I describe the sacred pilgrimage complex of Vrindaban as it is today.

As a descriptive device, I adhere closely to Vidyarthi's "sacred complex" formulation (1961, 1979), although in respect to Vrindaban a number of differences should be noted. In the towns analyzed by Vidyarthi—Gaya and Kashi (Varanasi)—there were distinct sacred and nonsacred districts within the municipal precincts, the adjective *sacred* designating boundaries of the sector which attracted pilgrims and within which the study was done. In Vrindaban, however, there is no such distinction between the secular and sacred in either geography or economy. No part of the town stands without sacred meaning; without temples, shrines, and other settings which compose its sacred geography.

Rather, Vrindaban is a unified symbolic entity with no demarcation between sacred and secular components as found in most other pilgrimage towns. It is a singular sacred space, perceived by pilgrims as the place of Krishna's activities or lilas. Therefore, as previously suggested, Vrindaban is a place which transcends the normal categories of sacred and secular in the mind of the bhakta. This conception manifests itself in a physical cohesion that is unique, as far as I am aware, among the places of Indian pilgrimage. Spatially, there is an integration of the temples, shrines, and other sacred sites into every street and alleyway.

Even the dust itself is considered spiritualized by virtue of its location, and the throngs that daily stream into the town touch it, rub it over their heads, taste it, and carry some of it home to be enshrined and worshiped just as they might do with an image of Krishna.

This integration exists in the economic sphere as well, for the residents of Vrindaban all make their livelihood either directly or indirectly from the pilgrimage trade.[1] The situation today is virtually unchanged from Hein's 1949 study (published 1972: 4) when he observed that "occupations related to spiritual and physical care of short and long term visitors dominate the economy in Vrindaban." This is not so exclusively the case in other pilgrimage centers. In Gaya, as studied by Vidyarthi (1961); Benares, reported on by Eck (1982) and Vidyarthi (1979); and Bhubaneswar by Miller and Wertz (1976), the sacred section exists in contrast to another, usually newer segment of the town which is primarily secular in its economy and physical development.

I have used the term *sacred pilgrimage complex* in describing Vrindaban rather than Vidyarthi's *sacred complex* to emphasize these differences, and to highlight pilgrimage's overall importance to the town. Without this institution Vrindaban would likely not have been developed, nor would it have survived in its present state. From the perspective of symbolic interactionism, the sacred pilgrimage complex concept provides an elegant heuristic device because it considers three components essential to the study of interaction: the physical settings, the activities that take place at these locations, and the actors who participate in them.

Vidyarthi includes as components of the sacred complex "the sacred centers, the sacred performances, and the sacred specialists . . . of a Hindu place of pilgrimage" (1961: xviii; 1979: 11). In my description, I expand these categories considerably in order to include all the interactions taking place in Vrindaban since none are without sacred or pilgrimage-related significance. Specifically, Vidyarthi does not allow the designation of any private shrine as a sacred center since the activities that occur in these places are not "public"; they are limited to interactions between family members and a close circle of friends. In Vrindaban, however, some private dwellings contain historic or renowned deities which draw pilgrims and local residents from outside the boundaries of kin and friendship networks. Some household shrines are well-known pilgrimage destinations equal in importance to institutionally

---

[1] See chapters 5 and 6 for details concerning Vrindaban's economy.

sanctioned temples and sites, and are essential components of the complex.

Within the sacred pilgimage complex, I also include the bazaars of Vrindaban where food, flowers, cloth, images, and religious paraphernalia—all necessities for worship and sustenance of pilgrims in the dham—are purchased. Besides the economic transactions enacted in shops and stands, other activities also occur there which are as significant in the context of religious pilgrimage as those in the temples. The bazaars provide settings for parades and processions, public recitations from sacred texts, encounters between gurus and disciples, interactions between saints and sadhus with the laity, spontaneous kirtans, and the worship of newly crafted images. In the tea stalls, shops, and on the streets, discussions of philosophy and religion seem to never end. Furthermore, every street in the town, including the bazaars, has a particular significance in Krishna's Vrindaban lila, making each one a sacred destination in itself; each has its share of temples, shrines, dharmshalas, and stages for the performance of the religious drama, ras-lila.[2]

This description of the pilgrimage complex provides a background for the specific cases of interaction to be discussed. I do not claim that the list includes all of Vrindaban's sacred components (it is said there are five thousand temples if the private ones are counted, and this may not even be inclusive), but it is my intent to list the major centers visited by pilgrims during their stay in town, the sites which residents consider essential for their own daily routine, and all those places where interaction occurs between Westerners and Indians. In many cases these three categories overlap; in others the separation is significant and will be considered in some depth.

Following Vidyarthi's distinction, it is useful to designate the main objects of pilgrimage or primary destination sites and the immediate space around them as pilgrimage *centers*. These centers include the various temples and shrines with their images, ghats along the Jumna River, specific trees that are worshiped, stages upon which the ras-lila is performed, tombs of saints, particular shops and stands, plots of ground where significant events in Krishna's life supposedly occurred, the places where saints reside, and the physical space immediately surrounding these locations.

Pilgrimage centers are often grouped together, forming pilgrimage *clusters* which can be distinguished from other such groupings. The

[2] See Hein 1972 and Hawley 1981 for a detailed discussion of ras-lila in Vrindaban.

proximity of the pilgrimage centers may be due to the development of an original site by a particular sect—such as a temple with a central image, tombs of saints in that particular lineage, secondary images, special trees and gardens associated with the temple, and the like. Or, the proximity may be only a random occurrence. In either case, these clusters serve to pattern the pilgrims' order of visitation and general flow of traffic in the town, with those sites clustered together being visited at one time, those farther removed at another.

Many types of activities take place at the pilgrimage centers in Vrindaban, ranging from highly orchestrated ceremonies to private devotions. These are all "cultural performances" in Singer's typology (1966: xiii), aesthetic forms which serve to transmit cultural knowledge and express normative social values. Vidyarthi refrained from using this term due to Singer's equating "cultural" and "religious" in the Indian context; Vidyarthi wanted to distinguish the religious cultural performances from the secular ones in the towns he studied. Whether or not there actually exists such a clear distinction in any nonurban Indian setting is debatable, but at least for Vrindaban a separation between sacred and secular culture would be artificial. All cultural performances there are undoubtedly sacred.

Although the types of activities at any pilgrimage center vary, they can be generally classified into three categories: those that require organization by specialists, those that are privately organized, and those that are situations of interaction outside an organized ritual context. In both organized categories it is possible to identify a specific object of ritual focus around which interaction occurs. If a specialist is required, the interaction will be directed or guided by him; if one is not required, an individual's personal culture provides the basic rules of behavior. In either case, the majority of participants perceive themselves as recipients of blessing or merit, as an audience receiving some transmission from a recognized sacred source. Outside the ritual frame, interactions that occur in the pilgrimage centers are not so formally structured and possess all the dynamic characteristics of any face-to-face situation regardless of its object or goal focus.

The cultural context of each of these activity types is purely Indian. Yet, today in Vrindaban there is a progressive integration of Westerners into the sacred pilgrimage complex. One of the primary pilgrimage clusters centers on ISKCON's Krishna-Balaram temple, and the cultural specialists who organize the performances there are predominantly American or European. Beyond that, members of ISKCON are now fulfilling other traditional roles such as guru, pandit, family priest, and sadhu, with their clients being increasingly Indian.

Moreover, since Vrindaban is a place of pan-Indian importance, the integration of ISKCON there has significance far beyond the town itself. Just as pilgrimage has historically served to incorporate the seemingly disparate elements of Indian culture and unify the Indian consciousness, the current situation acts to integrate ISKCON into that same heterogeneous tradition. These facts will be further considered in the chapter on ISKCON interactions with pilgrims, but are important to keep in mind as I describe the sacred pilgrimage complex.

SACRED GEOGRAPHY: SETTINGS OF INTERACTION

Appendix 2 lists the sacred pilgrimage centers and pilgrimage clusters in Vrindaban where interactions were observed and participated in during the course of my research (see appendix 1, p. 225, for their spatial arrangement). Although this listing does not include every place that pilgrims might visit during their yatra, most of the major sites are listed.

These pilgrimage centers fall into six basic categories: (1) the major traditional temples; (2) smaller temples or shrines found at sacred sites and in private dwellings; (3) sacred sites without any shrine or temple; (4) places associated with a holy man; (5) bazaar shops and stands; and (6) the ISKCON complex itself.

SACRED PERFORMANCES AND OTHER ACTIVITIES

At Traditional Temples

In the traditional temples and at many of the smaller sites and shrines, activities are organized by religious specialists, usually Brahman. Much of the ritual associated with the temple image is not for public display, but rather performed behind the closed doors of an inner sanctum. This is done in accordance with sectarian ritual codes in order to protect the deity's privacy and to prepare it for the public viewings which occur periodically throughout the day.[3] A high state of ritual

---

[3] The Krishna temples of Vrindaban, regardless of sectarian affiliation, generally observe a similar schedule of ritual associated with the images. The principal traditional temple of the Gaudiya Sampradaya, Radha-Raman, is typical, with minor alterations, of the other primary temples, as well as ISKCON's Krishna-Balaram temple. The day is divided into eight "watches," where the pujari bathes, dresses, and in other ways prepares the Krishna image (or in some cases Radha and

purity is required of any person who comes into direct contact with the image, this state being achieved in most cases by birth in certain Brahman lineages coupled with a ritual purification undertaken by the priest immediately before entering the deity's enclosure. Contact with anyone, including another priest, who has not undergone the purification ritual results in a pollution that must be rectified before image contact is again made. The state of high ritual purity is negated through any direct contact with a person not in that state, or when indirect contact is made through a simultaneously touched object.

This latter type of pollution is the most common and most guarded against by the priests, for the standard forms of public worship create the possibility of its occurrence. When pilgrims and resident devotees flood into the temple, typically three things occur. After entering into the temple's sacred space, their first intention is to have a glimpse of the deity—to receive darshan. Since the image is available for public viewing only during certain periods, the priests in effect control the flow of worshipers in and out according to a strict schedule. The temple fills with anticipation and joyful shouts ring out as the doors of the

---

Krishna) according to the time of day and his activities. The watches correspond to the activities that Krishna conducts during his typical Vrindaban day. After the private ritual preparations, the deity's chamber is opened and the actual *puja* (ritual offering) is done publicly, followed by darshan. The watches are:

1. *Mangal Arati.* The deity is awakened, usually around 4:00 A.M., and offered incense, water, and various things to pleasantly arouse him from sleep. This is considered the most auspicious time of the day, and the temples are usually filled even at this early hour.

2. *Sringar.* Krishna is fully and elaborately dressed for the day's activities and is offered a morning snack around 6:30.

3. *Raj Bhog.* Around noon, Krishna is served a large midday meal, after which the doors to his chamber are closed and he takes a nap.

4. *Utthapan.* Krishna is awakened from his nap and continues his activities.

5. *Sandhya.* Around twilight he returns home from his day of herding cattle, playing with friends, and resting.

6. *Vyalu Bhog.* Krishna is served his evening meal.

7. *Shayan Arati.* The last offering and darshan of the day takes place between 9:00 and 10:30 P.M., after which he is dressed for bed and retires for the night. Krishna is never bothered between this time and the *Mangal Arati*, for it is said that he often slips away to meet with Radha and the other gopis in the Vrindaban forest, and this is a most private affair.

Most offerings include, besides food, other items such as candle and ghee lamps, incense, leaves, flowers, and water. Each sect has its idiosyncratic method of conducting the puja, but it mainly varies according to objects waved and offered, or the order of their presentation to the deity. The secluded activities of the priest include bathing the image and dressing Krishna in silks, golden crowns, and jewels. Much of the temple wealth consists of gold and silver paraphernalia, expensive costumes, and jewels. At each watch Krishna is dressed in different clothes; and these vary appropriately in design, material, and color according to the season.

deity's chamber are opened. But darshan is not conceived as a simple viewing of the image; through direct eye contact between the worshiper and worshiped, a sacred blessing is transmitted. Without the establishment of that line-of-sight, the darshan does not occur. At this phase of worship there is no danger of priestly pollution, however.

The danger arises during transactions between deity and devotee where the priest must act as an intermediary. From the worshiper come offerings of flowers, food, and other objects which he wishes offered and sanctified. The devotee cannot place these objects in the vicinity of the image himself; only the purified priest can do this. Therefore, the worshiper must place the objects of offering into the hands of the priest without either of them being in physical contact with the object simultaneously. It is therefore dropped from hand to hand.

Similarly, after the object has been spiritualized by image contact, it becomes prasad, a sacred object returned to the devotee by the deity's "grace." Whether the prasad is something the worshiper has personally brought into the temple, or some object that has been used in ritual worship by the priest—usually food offerings, flowers, or *tulsi* (the sacred basil plant) leaves—the problem is the same: getting it into the devotees' hands without a transmission of pollution. Again this is done by dropping. In some cases, worshipers unaware of this ritual etiquette (such as some ISKCON devotees) grasp the prasad while still in the hands of a priest, thereby causing a considerable crisis. Rarely does the guilty individual repeat his mistake.

Apart from the performances organized by priests, much face-to-face interaction occurs in the temple between the worshipers while waiting for darshan, while listening to preachers in adjacent areas, and at other times when consultations or discussions are held with the temple's religious specialists. Furthermore, each traditional temple is the center of a larger pilgrimage cluster which usually includes subsidiary shrines, tombs of the lineage's saints, and numerous other sacred objects and plots of land. Activities at these places adjacent to the main temple are not so formally structured by priests and spontaneous interactions are frequent. All traditional temples in Vrindaban are visited by ISKCON devotees, and interactions between them and Indians from various statuses were observed at these locations.

At Smaller Temples and Shrines

At smaller temples and shrines, the rules of access are considerably relaxed. Since the smaller temples rely more on opportunistic donations from pilgrims, they are likely to be open for darshan whenever an individual or group demands it. At these temples, however, there is still the priestly interface between deity and devotee which in most cases prevents direct contact. Similarly, shrines located at sacred sites or scattered randomly throughout the town may also be owned or under the jurisdiction of a particular family, a member of which usually demands some payment before allowing the image to be viewed or before performing the particular ritual prescribed for that shrine.

On the other hand, there are many shrines which are freely accessible to any visitor without priestly mediation and where the ritual is performed by the worshiper according to his own private rules. These are often gathering places for pilgrims, residents, and sadhus which provide settings for frequent opportunistic interaction.

Sites Without Temples or Shrines

The same is true for sacred sites that have no shrine or temple associated with them. At these places, the standard ritual includes a circumambulation, or *parikrama* of the sacred tract or object (such as a natural formation or stones from other sacred locations placed there); worshiping the object by placing flowers, leaves, or money upon it; fumigating the object with incense; waving various types of flames around it; or by pouring holy water or milk over it. At the places where access and ritual are not formalized, face-to-face interaction may occur between members of a visiting group and between individuals and parties who meet there. At many of these locations will be found holy men who, though they are not ritual specialists, may still offer solicited or unsolicited advice to the worshiper. These sadhus, some of whom are considered enlightened beings by the pilgrims, may also engage the worshipers in religious and philosophical discussions. Sadhus are especially prevalent at the ghats along the Jumna River, where the primary performance is an ablution, or "holy dip."

However, even at places where access to the sacred object is not controlled by religious specialists associated with them, the pilgrims' routine still may be highly controlled by a guide. Many pilgrims making the rounds in Vrindaban hire pandas, members of Brahman jatis whose traditional role it is to escort pilgrims through the dham according to a prescribed order, and to assist with appropriate ritual at each place. In the past, it is said that specific panda families have had as clients members of the same pilgrimage family for as many as ten generations. While this is still the case in some other tirthas like Varanasi and nearby Mathura, the panda system in Vrindaban is no longer so organized. At every point of entry into Vrindaban will be found a variety of entrepreneurs who compete for the role of pilgrim guide, although they are considered by the traditional pandas to be unauthorized. The main advantage for the pilgrim in hiring a nonpanda guide is primarily a greater freedom of movement and freedom from paying fees at each of the sacred sites and temples visited. The pandas have long-standing agreements with proprietors at some sites to receive part of the donation. With the other guides, some of the less significant "pilgrim traps" will be avoided and the demand for money at the ones visited will be decreased.

At Places Associated with Saints

Some locations in Vrindaban are destinations for pilgrims because a recognized holy man lives there either permanently or periodically. Interaction with the more famous of these individuals is highly restricted, being guarded by an entourage of disciples. Just as darshan of the images is the primary form of public worship in temples, darshan of the saint is the principal activity that takes place at these sites, and it occurs only during certain periods of the day. Private audiences with such individuals are possible, but rare, and they involve convincing one of the holy man's close associates of a need to see him. Some holy men are in great demand by politicians, merchants, and wealthy industrialists who achieve close access by virtue of their high status or ability to make large donations. The masses of people, however, are usually content with a group darshan, some traveling to Vrindaban from distant places just for a brief glimpse. Since some holy men establish their compounds outside the main town, there is opportunity for interaction among pilgrims going to and from the site. This is especially the case with the compounds established across the Jumna, where access is dependent upon boat transportation during much of the year. As with the other locations, opportunities for interaction also occur during the wait before the main event which may sometimes be several hours.

In the Bazaar

In the early morning as pilgrims and residents begin to stir for their ritual baths in the Jumna and the temples' first darshans, the tea stalls and vegetable markets are hives of activity. But the bazaars in Vrindaban do not really spring to life until shops open for business, usually about 10:00 A.M. From that time there is a steady flow of people in and out of the shops and through the streets. The main activities are, of course, economic transactions between buyers and sellers, and many pilgrims who come to Vrindaban intend to return home with objects purchased there such as images, ritual paraphernalia, and clothing. But rarely are these interactions without more significant cultural importance.

Transactions in the cloth shops or places that sell images and decorations are serious events, with few purchases being made without inspecting most of the merchandise available, and this can take hours. During that time, information is traded about many topics: where the most famous holy men are residing; how much should be paid to pandas or priests at specific temples; which shops have the best merchandise at lowest prices; and gossip concerning people and events of the town. The shops of Loi Bazaar, the main market area, are also some of the best sources of information about ISKCON. Discussions with merchants may reveal which ISKCON gurus are in town, which devotees have been involved in praiseworthy or questionable affairs, information and gossip about all types of ISKCON-Indian interaction, facts about ISKCON's internal organization, and always a host of rumors—some plausable, some fantastic.

Interactions with members of ISKCON occur in many of the bazaar shops. ISKCON devotees who are long-term residents of Vrindaban frequent the bazaars almost daily for the same reasons that Indian residents do. They purchase food, supplies, clothing, and articles for their personal ritual life, and they engage in leisurely conversations with merchants. Over the course of ISKCON's Vrindaban career, some merchants have developed profitable relationships with devotees, and the shops of those who have profited the most reflect this. Some merchants have failed to capitalize on this lucrative source of income because of antagonism toward Western devotees; others have won patronage and then lost it due to a variety of conflicts and disputes. The dynamics of interactions occurring in the bazaar between ISKCON devotees and the various merchants provide a rich source of data concerning the movement's integration into Vrindaban's social and cultural system and will be considered in some detail in chapter 6.

Besides business transactions, conversations to pass the time in shops and tea stalls, and the events that transpire in temples located there, the bazaars are also settings for other cultural events that draw people from all segments of the population. On many days the bazaars are enveloped in a carnival-like atmosphere as pilgrims and residents alike celebrate the many festivals that occur throughout the year. Processions through the streets honoring holy men, living and dead, are common events. And periodically temple images are taken out for a stroll or moved to another location for the deities' amusement. All of these occasions are cause for public jubilation and provide opportunities for interaction. Similarly, organized and spontaneous kirtans take place as groups from various temples and sects, including ISKCON, take to the streets singing and chanting, encouraging others to join in. These activities occur well into the night, at least until after the final darshans which generally occur around 10:30. One of the most popular attractions in Vrindaban is the ras-lila, and many stages where troops perform this sacred drama are located in and adjacent to the bazaars. While the temples and sacred sites form the nucleus of Vrindaban's sacred pilgrimage complex, the bazaars function to link and integrate them into a unified entity, themselves becoming part of it.

At Krishna-Balaram Temple and the ISKCON Complex

Much that has been said about activities in the traditional temples of Vrindaban can also be said about ISKCON's Krishna-Balaram temple. Darshan is the main activity and it is regulated by priests who, just as in the indigenous temples, are concerned with ritual purity. The majority of the ISKCON priests, however, are not Indian, so the state of purity has no ascribed component, being dependent instead upon learned knowledge and ritual transformations.[4] Before and during periods of darshan, people mingle with others who are there for the same purpose, and the conversation is likely to center around the meaning of ISKCON. This may include discussion about the organization's founder whose tomb is located in the temple courtyard, the validity of foreign priests, or simply the beauty of the temple and its images.

The primary difference between cultural performances at ISKCON's temple and the other main traditional temples is that they are orches-

---

[4] ISKCON has three progressive initiations. The first is a mantra initiation, diksha, which the novice is given shortly after he becomes a devotee. The second is the Brahman initiation, given at the discretion of a guru or other high authority. This occurs after the devotee has demonstrated an adequate level of knowledge and has shown his intention to remain within ISKCON. Only after the Brahman initiation is the devotee allowed to act as a pujari. In the West, both male and female devotees may serve as temple priests, but in Vrindaban only male pujaris are used, in keeping with local custom. The third initiation is conducted if the devotee desires to enter the renounced order of sannyas. This occurs only after years of membership, and is available only to male members who then are considered swamis or goswamis. Presently there are only about forty sannyasis in ISKCON, out of a core membership of around four thousand.

trated and conducted at least in part to persuade Indians in attendance of the foreign devotees' legitimacy. The validity of the images are rarely questioned, for when they were installed, Bhaktivedanta insured that the ritual was done to precise specifications by the most highly competent and respected Indian ritual authorities available in Vrindaban and Mathura.

During periods before and between darshans, kirtan sessions are held by a samaj of ISKCON members, and prasad and literature are sold at the temple entrance by devotees, some fluent in Hindi and Bengali, who engage the pilgrims in discussion about the importance of Vrindaban and the meaning of ISKCON for the town. In other public areas well-produced films about Vrindaban and ISKCON's place in its traditional continuity are shown.

Before ISKCON's arrival in 1967, the location of its complex, an area called Raman-Reti, was removed from the main town by two kilometers of undeveloped land. Today, the stretch of road that connects ISKCON to the rest of Vrindaban is a vital part of the town and includes temples, ashrams, and dharmshalas that attract pilgrims. Numerous shops and stalls that attempt to capitalize on the pilgrim traffic have sprung up immediately around the Krishna-Balaram temple, and these places are settings for discussions about the events that transpire within the temple itself. As pilgrims sip tea and cold drinks or have a quick lunch, they will likely encounter ISKCON devotees there ostensibly for the same reason, although they are also likely to have the subsidiary mission of presenting a positive image to the pilgrims who are in the course of evaluating them.

Since ISKCON is the initial stop for many of Vrindaban's pilgrims due to its location on the town's main access road from Delhi, many of them will plan the remainder of their stay there and probably return one or more times before their departure. Some of the more affluent pilgrims may stay at the Krishna-Balaram guest house, advertised as having the best "international quality" facilities in town, and others will take at least one meal in the restaurant there. During none of these activities do ISKCON devotees miss the opportunity for presenting themselves and their sect in the most favorable light. Their acceptance in Vrindaban depends not only upon winning the confidence and support of the local population, but also upon so impressing the pilgrims that a good report will be taken home and conveyed to relatives and friends. Some of the pilgrims who can afford it will become life members of

ISKCON at a cost of around three hundred dollars, a plan that provides
the organization with its primary source of income in India.

THE PEOPLE OF VRINDABAN

As the *Mathura District Gazetteer* (Joshi 1968) indicates, most people
in Vrindaban, as in other parts of India, today generally see themselves
fitting into one of the traditional varna categories—Brahman, Kshatriya, Vaishya, or Shudra. However, the structure of Vrindaban society
is not quite so simple. In surveys, questionnaires, and interviews, the
people of Vrindaban indicated the following significant social categories, and generally agreed on their hierarchical order: (1) temple
Brahman (goswamis); (2) other types of Brahman (pandas and Brahman not peforming religious duties); (3) non-Brahman religious specialists (gurus, *acharyas* [noted teachers], etc.); (4) sadhus, *babas*,
sannyasis, and other nonattached holy men (varna classification of this
category and the preceding one is not generally questioned or of concern); (5) merchants (*vaishya*); (6) people who work in service occupations (washermen, rickshaw and horse-cart operators, builders,
potters, and other artisans); and (7) those who are considered
"untouchable." Although varna categories are recognized, they are not
the primary concerns when people engage in interaction. Vrindaban is
not seen as a place where normal social considerations are in effect,
and the perception of caste and hierarchy there differs considerably
from what is generally accepted for the Indian situation.

Caste and Hierarchy in Vrindaban

Weber (1958: 29) has stated that "caste is the fundamental institution
of Hinduism. Before everything else, without caste, there is no
Hindu." Although this is the dominant Western conception of Indian
society, since anthropologists first began fieldwork in India they have
known that the image of an inflexible, rigid order is not empirically
supportable. Rather, this image is based primarily upon a reification
created by the requirement of British censuses (David 1977: 18; Cohn
1971). Furthermore, that "caste" is not an indigenous term is a widely
known fact; neither varna nor jati, the two terms most commonly
equated with caste, adequately gloss this Western sociological concept.
    Srinivas (1966: 3) has stressed that the overwhelming concern for
varna by scholars has obscured the dynamic features of "caste." Berreman (1972) has furthermore shown that in urban India, varna and jati,

besides being considerably more flexible than usually understood, are in fact only two categories among others that are significant in the patterning of social interactions. The Vrindaban data fully support his findings,[5] providing an example where an individual's "caste" rarely operates to exclude him from interactions with others.

The academic focus on caste, in any case, has all too often considered only half of the Indian social system, as Uberoi (1967) and Turner (1974: 275) have pointed out. Rather, Hindu society is most accurately described by the Indian term *varnashram*, alluding to a complex interweaving of the individual and society. While varna refers to the hierarchical stratification of society, ashram is of equal importance, referring to the stages or statuses of an individual's life. As an integrating concept, varnashram does not present the image of a rigid, preexisting structure into which individuals automatically fit. Instead, the individual is an active agent in the processes which determine the course of his life.

It is in the fourth and final ashram—sannyas—that the person's capacity for free will is most clearly exhibited. In this stage he divests himself of all societal restrictions, achieving freedom to pursue the ultimate goal of life, spiritual perfection. Although sannyas is traditionally taken in old age, this step away from society can be practically taken at any time. Wherever there is a large mendicant population, a subsequent force of egalitarianism operates to loosen the rigidity of social structure. The large number of sadhus in Vrindaban, therefore, contributes another factor to the general de-emphasis of caste in social interaction.

Even for Dumont (1970), who bases his explication of Indian society upon an ideological conception of varna with its fundamental structure of purity and impurity, the opposition of "man-in-the-world" and "individual-outside-the-world" is also essential for understanding Indian culture. But his main point still remains that in Indian society there is a preeminent concern with hierarchy—for who has the higher status.

These factors lend support to my dual conclusion concerning the social reality of Vrindaban, especially as it relates to interactions between Western devotees and Indians: There does exist a tendency for the individual to determine the rank of a person with whom he interacts.

---

[5] In my Loi Bazaar questionnaire, response to the the two questions "What is your jati?" and "What other jatis are in Vrindaban?" yielded the following percentages: varna categories—45 percent; jati or subcaste groupings—12 percent; sampradaya—19 percent; linguistic or regional affiliation—7 percent; Hindu—8 percent; Sanatan Dharma—9 percent.

Simultaneously, however, there is a freedom for any individual to engage in social intercourse with any other, thus providing the opportunity to establish status based upon qualifications and consistent behavior.

In the case of ISKCON, a claim to the highest status (Brahman) is overtly presented. This claim is accepted without much reservation by many in the population; it is primarily with the town's Brahman community that conflict arises. Therefore, those situations which include Brahman actors are the most consequential for determining the devotee's ultimate position in the overall hierarchy, as I will show in chapter 6.

Although caste is not the primary determinant of social status in Vrindaban, as Weber has implied, his assumption concerning the operation of hierarchy is essentially correct: "the objective situation remains unescapable; that in the last analysis, a rank position is determined by the nature of its positive or negative relation to the Brahman" (1958: 30). While ISKCON at this time has not achieved full Brahman status in Vrindaban, this simply means that the Brahman community has not accepted its members as social equals. The term *social* is the key here. One Brahman informant states the matter clearly: "They may be as good as Brahman, but Brahman is a social category, not a religious one. I am a Brahman because I was born Brahman; no more, no less. The crucial questions are: Can the devotee eat freely with me, and can my daughters marry him? The answer to both questions is no, although personally he may be in every way better than a true Brahman."[6]

Indeed, the two factors of commensality and intermarriage are the primary anthropological determinants of caste superiority and inferiority. In Vrindaban there are numerous examples of devotees dining with Brahmans, and the data also reflect cases of Brahman fathers inquiring about ISKCON husbands for their daughters. These facts are empirically significant, although the verbalized position of most Brahmans remains uncompromising. Yet, it is my conclusion that ISKCON devotees do possess a high status *similar* to that of Brahman, which they have achieved by a subtle manipulation of the social system through interactions with its members. Specific cases of this will be cited in following chapters.

This has been done in a manner similar to the case described by

---

[6] Direct quotation in English.

Lynch (1969: 14), where an untouchable group in Agra changed the criteria for their status evaluation by refusing to identify themselves as untouchable. As he explains, "A Brahman can interact with both a ksatriya and an untouchable, but he cannot interact with a citizen since neither Brahman nor citizen is a counter status of the other. Brahmans can only interact with other castes in the caste system; citizens can only interact with other citizens in a democratic system."

Similarly, a devotee interacts with other devotees, not Brahmans and *shudras*. Few Brahmans in Vrindaban would concede that they are not also devotees of Krishna, and when pressed will even concede that "devotee" is their dominant status. Furthermore, there is ample support from Vaishnava texts, especially those of the Bengal Vaishnavas, for equating "devotee" qualitatively with "Brahman." In the temple offices of Goswami Brahmans, ISKCON has effectively debated using this scripturally based logic: a nondevotee is no better than a shudra, while a devotee is better than a Brahman. It is ultimately the opinion of the majority of Vrindaban residents, including most Brahmans, that in the town a person's status can properly be determined by the quality of his devotion to Krishna.[7] In effect, the structure of hierarchy in Vrindaban is not based upon a Brahman/non-Brahman opposition, but rather a devotee/nondevotee one. ISKCON has capitalized on this pattern by the successful presentation of its members in a variety of interactions, and the subsequent transformations have been felt throughout the town's sociocultural system.

A focus on the sacred pilgrimage complex emphasizes the fact that the principal formative components have been the religion of Krishna-bhakti and the institution of pilgrimage. Today every place, every actor, and every situation, and the very structure of interactions must all be seen in the light of these two factors if an understanding of them is to be gained.

[7] In response to the question "Who is higher—someone born a Brahman or a devotee of Krishna regardless of jati?", 82 percent of the total answered "devotee." The devotee response for the Brahman population alone was 71 percent. To the question "What makes one person higher than another?", 67 percent responded with an answer related to devotion to Krishna or personal characteristics. Thirty-three percent gave answers indicating status by birth.

ISKCON and Vrindaban

JUST as Krishna cannot be separated from Vrindaban, neither can ISK-CON. A. C. Bhaktivedanta Swami, ISKCON's founder, was himself a resident of Vrindaban for some ten years before embarking on his journey west, and in 1967 brought the first of his American disciples to this North Indian pilgrimage town as part of a sweeping vision to revitalize Indian religion and spread Krishna consciousness throughout the world.[1] From a modest beginning with two devotees at the temple of Radha-Damodar in 1967, the International Society for Krishna Consciousness has altered the cultural texture of the town, prompting one Brahman informant to declare the 1970s as "the decade of ISKCON in Vrindaban." The opening of the Krishna-Balaram temple complex in 1975 gave the Hare Krishna movement a major resource for completing the process of conversion and culture change of its members (see Brooks 1979), and simultaneously providing a base from which to stage interactions with Indian pilgrims and Vrindaban residents.

Before going into these events in some detail, however, it is necessary to put ISKCON in context by discussing its emergence as an American revitalization movement; its direct linkage to the Gaudiya sampradaya through Bhaktivedanta's guru, Bhaktisiddhanta Saraswati, and Bhaktisiddhanta's father, Bhaktivinod Thakur; and the movement's expansion back to the country of its cultural origin. Having done this, I will briefly discuss Vrindaban's historical relationship with foreign religious seekers, and that scene as it exists today with ISKCON being the dominant (though not the only) foreign presence in the town.

ISKCON'S EARLY YEARS

The International Society for Krishna Consciousness (ISKCON) is an American example of a class of sociocultural phenomena that Anthony Wallace (1956, 1966) has called "revitalization movements." According to Wallace (1956: 265), such a movement is any "deliberate, or-

[1] I am indebted to Satsvarupa dasa Goswami's six-volume biography of A. C. Bhaktivedanta Swami (1980a, 1980b, 1981, 1982, 1983a, 1983b), for much of the information concerning ISK-CON's early years.

ganized, conscious effort by members of a society to construct a more satisfying culture'' and includes such specific examples as the Iroquois Religion of Handsome Lake (Wallace 1970), the Ghost Dance Religion of the Sioux (LaBarre 1938; Miller 1959; Mooney 1965), and the cargo cults of Oceania (Belshaw 1954; Burridge 1960; Worsley 1968). Insight into the development of many of the ''new religions''[2] can be gained by viewing them as revitalization movements, and although it can be a dangerous assertion to claim that any one example typifies the general category, I believe that ISKCON closely fits Wallace's model.

Taking his cue from general systems theory, Wallace suggests that a society which provides most individuals with ways to resolve problems and meet their needs is in ''homeostasis,'' or ''steady state.'' In this condition, ''recognized techniques for satisfying needs operate with such efficiency that chronic stress within the system varies within tolerable limits'' (Wallace 1956: 265). However, in a sociocultural system where an increased number of individuals experience severe stress as a result of not being able to satisfy needs and desires by available techniques, a point is reached where these individuals begin a search for viable alternatives. When this occurs, it is the initial phase of a process leading to the eventual formation of a revitalization movement, a period that Wallace calls ''increased individual stress.''

As this stress affects more and more individuals, there is a gradual recognition by them that they are not alone in their dilemma, and ''deviant'' behavior which has to this point been individualized and piecemeal, now becomes a recognizable collective strategy. A subculture or counterculture forms in loose contradistinction to the dominant culture which is perceived by those in distress as ''the system,'' ''the establishment,'' or some other generally negative label which distinguishes between ''them'' and ''us.'' This is called a period of ''cultural distortion'' by Wallace, and at this critical stage other alternatives have failed; no solution seems to exist except the complete culture change offered by a revitalization movement.

---

[2] ''New religious movement'' is a sociological term used to describe religious phenomena that do not easily fit into traditional categories such as sect, cult, or church. Wilson (in Barker 1982: 17–20) has suggested that although the religions which they incorporate may not in fact be new, they emerge in a social context where other religious traditions are already established. He suggests that they generally fulfill the following requirements: They offer ''a surer, shorter, swifter, or clearer way to salvation;'' conduct an ''implicit assault on spiritual elitism;'' are available to a wider public than traditional paths of salvation; offer techniques that are accessible to the average man; facilitate spiritual mobility; and are therepeutic and generally life-enhancing for the ordinary individual.

The period in American history loosely bounded by the 1960s and early 1970s was such a period of cultural distortion and resulted in the formation of countercultural enclaves in New York's East Village, San Francisco's Haight-Ashbury district, and other major cities. The hippie movement was a result of mass cultural dissatisfaction which included the failure of available problem-solving mechanisms for a large number of people; yet, it was neither ideologically nor practically unified to the extent that it could effectively offer a lasting solution. A workable alternative must be relatively specific in its cultural and social organization, or at least have the recognizable potential for such development; it has to offer a coherent symbolic system that provides a new way of viewing and understanding the world, as well as a corresponding framework that provides guidelines for effective and satisfying social relationships.

As Judah pointed out in *Hare Krishna and the Counterculture* (1974), the hippie counterculture provided a rich supply of individuals actively searching for a cultural alternative, and for some the Hare Krishna movement was well suited to their needs. In fact, the timing was nothing short of perfect, for just as the flowering of the hippie movement was reaching its peak, A. C. Bhaktivedanta Swami appeared on the scene.

Bhaktivedanta Swami and ISKCON

Another crucial element in the development of a revitalization movement is a charismatic individual or "prophet" who himself has undergone a personal transformation, and is convinced that a similar transformation will provide "salvation" for others. The charismatic prophet actively pursues the transformation of others as a primary goal, in many cases believing that he is divinely empowered to effect such radical changes.

Bhaktivedanta Swami, known simply as "Swamiji" by his early American acquaintances,[3] had a long association with Vrindaban. Born in Calcutta on September 1, 1896, he first visited Vrindaban on pilgrimage in 1925. Having met his guru, Bhaktisiddhanta Saraswati, for

[3] Bhaktivedanta's given name was Abhey Charan De and became known as A. C. Bhaktivedanta Swami upon taking the renounced order of sannyas. During his early days in the United States, his friends and followers referred to him as "Swamiji" as most Indian gurus were called at the time. Later, upon learning that Bhaktivedanta's guru was called "Prabhupad," a title meaning "master at whose feet other masters sit" (ISKCON translation), they began referring to Bhativedanta by the same title. Therefore, the name by which he is known today is A. C. Bhaktivedanta Swami Prabhupada, his followers calling him affectionately "Shrila Prabhupad."

the first time in 1922, he received formal initiation at Allahabad in 1932. Bhaktivedanta again met his spiritual master at Radhakund near Vrindaban in 1935. Bhaktisiddhanta had organized the monastic and preaching organization, Gaudiya Math, around 1918 and had begun an annual circumambulation (parikrama) of the Vrindaban area as part of his mission. It was on this yearly pilgrimage of the Gaudiya Math that Bhaktivedanta met him for the third time. At each of these meetings, Bhaktisiddhanta had spoken directly to Bhaktivedanta about spreading the religion of Chaitanya to the West and the importance of writing and publishing books in English. At Radhakund, if there was ever doubt that this should be his life's mission, his guru inspired Bhaktivedanta to carry out the ''order'' at all costs, and the swami took this as Krishna's direct instruction through the medium of his ''personal representative.'' This perception was repeatedly confirmed throughout Bhaktivedanta's life through visions, dreams, and an overpowering mystical intuition that he was being guided by Krishna.

Finally, in September 1956, having left his family and societal responsibilities behind, he moved to Vrindaban to pursue the English translation, commentary, and publication of pertinent scriptural texts, especially *Bhagavata-Purana*; and to meditate upon how his guru's order to disseminate the message of Chaitanya could best be fulfilled. Vrindaban was Bhaktivedanta's main residence from that time until he embarked on his journey to the United States on August 13, 1965.

Current Vrindaban residents remember Bhaktivedanta from this period, but few suspected that he would be successful in implementing his dreams; he was only one sadhu among many living in the town. The head priest at one temple, acknowledging that he had perhaps ''misjudged'' Bhaktivedanta's potential, nevertheless points out the calm determination that the swami showed even in the late 1950s:

> Prabhupad was always trying to set up speaking engagements whenever there was some special event here. He was very persistent, but we always found some way to politely refuse. I took him as a bother, really. He spoke some English and wanted to speak in that medium, but our devotees spoke Bengali or Hindi, so what was the use? Yes, he would go on and on about how this industrialist or that wealthy person would sponsor his mission to America, but to me it was a child's fantasy—very innocent but improbable.

This priest, well-known throughout India, now reflects back on Bhaktivedanta's success with an explanation that has become very popular in Vrindaban:

He was not capable then of mounting such a movement. His intentions were there, but so naive. So how he was successful? This is the secret: On his voyage you know he received two attacks of the heart, it is said. But this was Krishna's work. This was Krishna entering Prabhupad for empowerment. So Krishna empowered, so how he can fail? It is like this: Krishna observed, "Oh, here is this old man that is determined, so I will use him, I will give the power." Of course only some real saint may receive it, so now we must admit he is saint. Such amazing success that thrilled all Vrindaban. But to have thought this old sadhu-baba (laughing).[4]

Others, especially in the merchant community, now proudly describe their early recognition of Bhaktivedanta's "power," although some of their friends laugh and remind them that at the time they were not so convinced. A seller of metal images and ritual items spoke in his shop with several other friends and family members:

Prabhupad is a great soul, very great. He was living at Vamshi-Gopalji, then took rooms at Radha-Damodar, so we met. Every day here he came and we talked. Very simple, but also very powerful, I could tell. All the time he is talking only Krishna and Chaitanya and Vrindaban. He would tell of his difficulties at publishing books in Delhi. Such difficulties, but . . . he said "I have temples already in America, and many people worship Krishna there. Only time now hides them from vision." He spoke like that and who was I to question. He had the manner of a *raja* (king), and I believed him.

(A friend breaks into the conversation, laughing) Perhaps you say this now, but then you thought he was a beggar. We were thinking: Why this old man has such fancy? He has no disciples.He is old and lives as Vrindaban sadhu, so he has reached life's goal. Why he was bothering with such fancy dreams to only disturb his mind? Of course now we say, "Oh yes, Prabhupad is my good friend for so many years. I encouraged his mission. I knew he was mahatma (great soul), and so forth." We were all fools. We could not see this old man was some future *jagadguru* (world-teacher)![5]

Bhaktivedanta's persistence paid off. After being rejected by many potential backers, he finally convinced Mrs. Sumati Morarji, head of Scindia Steamship Lines, to provide him free passage from Calcutta to New York on board the freight steamer *Jaladuta*. On August 13, 1965,

[4] Quotations translated from original spoken in both Hindi and English. Idiosyncratic English retained in translation.

[5] Quotations translated from original spoken in both Hindi and English. Idiosyncratic English retained in translation.

Bhaktivedanta Swami left Calcutta for the twenty-six-day ocean voyage. Along the way his diary entries reflect a deep attachment to Vrindaban. On September 10 he wrote:

> I am feeling separation from Sri Vrindaban and my Lords Sri Govinda, Gopinath, Radha Damodar. The only solace is Sri Chaitanya Charitamrita in which I am tasting the nectarine of Lord Chaitanya's lila. I have left Bharatbhumi just to execute the order of Sri Bhaktisiddhanta Saraswati in persuance of Lord Chaitanya's order. I have no qualification, but I have taken up the risk just to carry out the order of His Divine Grace. I depend fully on Their mercy, so far away from Vrindaban. (Goswami, Satsvarupa 1980a: 3)

After one month's stay in Butler, Pennsylvania with the son of an Indian patron who arranged for initial sponsorship in the United States, Bhaktivedanta moved to New York where he stayed for a time with Dr. Ramamurti Misra, a teacher of *hatha yoga* (the path of spiritual realization which includes body postures and breathing control) to a decidedly upscale clientele. While Misra treated the swami with respect, they were on opposite ends of the Indian philosophical spectrum,[6] and Bhaktivedanta's desire was to be independent so that he could preach his own form of bhakti-yoga. It soon became apparent to Bhaktivedanta that the people most interested in him were not the well-to-do West side clients of Misra, but the "bohemian" types whose life-styles were in sharp contrast to those attracted to hatha-yoga. It was members of this bohemian group, not even known as "hippies" at this time, that persuaded Bhaktivedanta to join them. One of the swami's early admirers explains:

> I think most of the teachers from India up to that time had older followers, and sometimes wealthy widows would provide a source of income. But Swamiji changed right away to the younger, poorer group of people. The next thing that happened was that Bill Epstein and others began talking about how it would be better for the Swami to come downtown to the Lower East Side. Things were really happening downtown there, and somehow they weren't happening uptown. People downtown really needed him.

---

[6] Misra followed *advaita* philosophy, the impersonal, nondualistic interpretation of the *Upanishads* and *Vedanta-sutra*, especially the nontheistic system presented by Shankara. Vaishnavas are generally united in their distaste for advaita philosophy since it precludes the dualistic conception of Krishna as supreme god and man as his devotee.

Downtown was right, and it was ripe. There was life down there. There was
a lot of energy going around. (Goswami, Satsvarupa 1980b: 66)

Soon Bhaktivedanta was indeed free to preach on his own. After two
months of sharing small spaces in the lofts of sympathetic "hip"
friends in New York's Bowery district—an experience that was incon-
venient for all parties concerned—he finally moved to Second Avenue
in the East Village where the International Society for Krishna Consciousness first got off the ground. In a storefront apartment that displayed the sign "Matchless Gifts," a survival from a curiosity shop
that had previously occupied the building, Bhaktivedanta soon added
another that announced "International Society for Krishna Consciousness, Inc.; A. C. Bhaktivedanta Swami; Lectures on the Bhagavad
Gita; Krishna As He Is; Daily Morning Class 7 A.M." It was now July
1966, and with a group of sympathizers who knew little about the swami's ideas and ambitions, the International Society for Krishna Consciousness was officially incorporated as a tax-exempt religious organization.

By the summer of 1966, thousands of young people disenchanted
with middle-class American culture were walking the streets of the East
Village and occupying most of the available housing. It was the first
wave of the hippie movement, and they were actively searching for an
alternative. Bhaktivedanta found them the most receptive group that he
encountered in his ten months in the United States, and on September
8, the day celebrated that year as Krishna's birthday, the swami asked
the small group that had formed around him to fast; the next day he
initiated his first eleven disciples in a ceremony that none of them really
understood. The previous year Bhaktivedanta had marked Krishna's
birth alone at sea, and now he had small temple in New York City, the
curious interest of the entire East Village community, and a small
group of disciples; he felt that his mission to spread Krishna consciousness to the West had truly begun.

When one of his first disciples moved to San Francisco and sent a
ticket with the message that he and his wife had rented a storefront in
Haight-Ashbury for a temple, Bhaktivedanta decided to leave immediately. This shocked his East Village devotees who had come to think
of him as their own, and of ISKCON as an East Village phenomenon.
But the swami saw it as only the small beginning of a worldwide movement. So in January 1966, Bhaktivedanta arrived at San Francisco airport as fifty greeters, including Allen Ginsburg who had been a fre-

quent visitor to the East Village temple, chanted "Hare Krishna." Although Ginsburg disagreed with many of the swami's required prohibitions, he had encountered the Hare Krishna mantra in India and often sang it publicly as part of his eclectic philosophy. He was enchanted that now a real swami was trying to spread the mantra in America and enjoyed Bhaktivedanta's company despite their differences. Bhaktivedanta himself was glad to receive the publicity and support provided by one of the main figures of the counterculture, tolerating the misconceptions and bad habits of this countercultural hero just as he did those of his early followers.

Ginsburg had been one of the leaders of a "meeting of the tribes" at Golden Gate Park a few days before the swami's arrival, one of the events that ushered in the San Francisco hippie movement in earnest, and he wanted to incorporate Bhaktivedanta into that scene. Although his New York disciples objected to the swami's participation, the San Francisco devotees with Ginsburg's assistance arranged a "Mantra-Rock" concert at the Avalon Ballroom on January 29, 1967. With some three thousand in attendance to hear the Grateful Dead, Moby Grape, Big Brother and the Holding Company, Jefferson Airplane, and other rising San Francisco bands, Bhaktivedanta entered from the rear of the hall as the audience stood and cheered. After Ginsburg's introduction, "Swamiji" led a kirtan for two hours to the accompaniment of a psychedelic light show as everyone sang and swayed to the sounds of "Hare Krishna" in an atmosphere filled with marijuana smoke. Bhaktivedanta was pleased with the reception and the fact that around two thousand dollars had been raised for the temple, but remarked to one of his disciples as he exited immediately after the chanting, "This is no place for a *brahmacārī* [celibate]" (Goswami 1980b: 15).

Nevertheless, the swami had been introduced to the hippies of San Francisco. Allen Ginsburg had told the crowd at Avalon Ballroom that the Krishna temple was providing a valuable community service for people coming down from LSD who wanted to "stabilize their consciousness on reentry" (1980b: 41); and this brought a new crowd to the early morning services at the Hare Krishna temple. Interest continued to grow and the devotees chanted and distributed prasad at any important event that was happening, usually with the swami in attendance.

Bhaktivedanta's fame and the popularity of the Haight-Ashbury temple continued to grow. The swami became a cult hero to most of the hippie community whether or not they appreciated the details of his philosophy and the life-style restrictions that he suggested. The mantra and dancing had been adopted by all levels of the counterculture there; it at least provided a loose commonality for the hippies' often chaotic eclecticism. More than once "Hare Krishna" had transformed a violent scene into one of reconciliation. Even the Hell's Angels respected the swami, and his chanting more than once defused violence that they had instigated.

The group of core devotees continued to grow. More initiations were held with individuals and couples committing themselves full-time to the routine Bhaktivedanta proceeded to implement. He introduced the worship of Jagannath deities, perhaps the most abstract, bizzare-looking images in popular Hinduism,[7] and gave the name "New Jagannath Puri" to the San Francisco center; these images immediately became a psychedelic hit. The swami knew that he would be highly criticized in India for not upholding the proper standards of purity and ritual stricture, but he was firmly convinced that it was all Krishna's plan and prayed that Krishna would forgive the offences taking place in his temple.

All this had happened in the space of two-and-a-half months since his arrival in San Francisco, and again the swami was encouraged that his mission was continuing to be successful. But the devotees in New York were spiritual neophytes and needed his personal guidance, and they begged him to return there. Moreover, they had proven to be incompetent in handling the financial operation which included plans to buy a larger building, so his presence was definitely needed in New York. With his new followers in tears, Bhaktivedanta Swami left San Francisco and returned to New York.

Shortly after his return to New York, Bhaktivedanta suffered a mild heart attack and was hospitalized. He had told the devotees simply to chant and pray that he be saved since the mission was not finished, and chanting went on around the clock on both coasts. Alienated by the modern medical treatment he received in the hospital, the swami talked of returning to India, to Vrindaban, for Ayurvedic treatment (the indigenous Indian medical system) and to benefit from sun and heat. He had said this heart attack had been the appointed time for his death, but that

[7] Jagannath is considered a form of Krishna worshiped throughout India, with the main temple in Puri, Orissa. Abstract in appearance, the image has large circular eyes and short arms that project perpendicularly from its rounded body. Jagannath, which means "Lord of the Universe," is worshiped alongside similar figures representing Subhadra, Krishna's sister, and Balaram, his brother.

Krishna had spared him due to the devotees' prayers. His strength gradually returning, Bhaktivedanta traveled back to San Francisco for a short visit, and then decided to leave for India via New York. He had established temples in New York, San Francisco, and recently some followers had opened one in Montreal; at the airport he asked that one be opened in Los Angeles. Along with the swami went one of his disciples, Kirtanananda. On August 1, 1967, Bhaktivedanta arrived back in Vrindaban, but this time with his American disiciple. Soon Kirtanananda was given the sannyas initiation, becoming Kirtanananda Swami.

Kunj Bihari is one of many cloth merchants in Loi Bazaar. On the wall of his shop are pictures of ISKCON Radha-Krishna deities, Bhaktivedanta Swami, and Kirtanananda Swami. In August of 1967 he was barely twenty years old, gradually assuming the full responsibility of running his father's cloth business; he was a sincere devotee of Krishna. He remembers the first ISKCON devotee that he met in Vrindaban vividly:

> Actually I could never leave from Vrindaban, but I was a restless young man. I thought, "let me have some experiences, let me travel, let me see modern things." One day my father told me, "Bhaktivedanta Prabhu has returned from America. He made some disciples of Harinam (holy name of Krishna), and one has come." It was spoken that on Janmashtami (Krishna's birthday) at Damodar mandir he would take sannyas and there was much talk. This we could not believe, an American sadhu in Vrindaban. So I went and saw Kirtanananda Maharaj first time. Not only he looked like sadhu, I thought, but Mahaprabhu [Chaitanya] also—golden skin. So he was walking Loi Bazaar, Keshi Ghat, all around, with *danda* (staff carried by renunciate) and always chanting with hand in the bag. Everyone laughed. . . . But everywhere also he would speak of Krishna, so everyone was amazed how this could be. . . . Then I felt Vrindaban will give my experiences. Something will happen here to make big experiences, and yes, ISKCON made big experiences and I don't leave Vrindaban.[8]

Today pictures of Kirtanananda can be found in several shops, and in some, pictures of other ISKCON gurus as well. Only two Vrindaban residents have become disciples of Kirtanananda by formal initiation, but six people in Vrindaban claim him as their guru. One is Krishna-Saranam, an elderly man living in a small dharmshala room, who rev-

[8] Direct quotation in English.

erently worships the American devotee's picture daily. He once was employed by ISKCON but had run-ins with the devotees because he smoked cigarettes, a habit that he claims Kirtanananda cured:

> I wanted to serve Prabhupad, but I was working at the *goshala* (dairy and place for cow-protection) and addicted to tobacco, so devotees said I must stop or leave. I went to Prabhupad and said, "Oh Maharaj, how I can think of Krishna when I only think of cigarette?" Prabhupad said, "My students are eager. Just chant and then smoke when you must if it disturbs your mind. Gradually it will fall away." So I met with Kirtanananda Maharaj and he showed his mercy on me: "Take these beads and wash off hands before every time chanting." So he chanted the *mala* (rosary) and gave me from Radhakund some *tulsi-mala* (beads made from the wood of the tulsi plant) and I said, "Maharaj you are my guru." His shakti is in the beads, so after one year only I had only desire for japa and no more smoking. So my guruji delivered me this offense. Now he has such big, big temples and many disciples too. But always he comes back to Vrindaban and always to Krishna-Saranam.[9]

After returning to the United States in December 1968, Bhaktivedanta resumed his normal schedule of translating, opening temples, and initiating disciples. He sent devotees to Boston, Sante Fe, West Virginia, Columbus, Ohio, and London, and encouraged them to fan out over the globe opening new temples, even if it was done by only one or two of them. He traveled to as many of these new centers as possible, and by the time he flew to London in September 1969, ISKCON counted fifteen temples to its credit.

Bhaktivedanta's prestige continued to grow as the press gave him and his disciples increasing publicity, most of it positive. London was especially a challenge to the swami since his own guru, Bhaktisiddhanta Saraswati, had sent an emmisary there in the 1930s to test the water for Krishna consciousness. The extent of his success had been a few photographs taken with members of the royal family and one initiated female disciple who was given the name Vinoda-vani dasi. The conclusion of the Gaudiya Math hierarchy in India was that it was all but impossible to convert Westerners to Vaishnavism; the prediction by Chaitanya that the names of Krishna would be chanted "in every town and village" remained a conundrum; perhaps this only meant every

---

[9] Quotation translated from original spoken in both Hindi and English. Idiosyncratic English retained in translation.

town and village in India. So Bhaktivedanta was e̶
new disciples had early success in London.

Following the swami's instruction, these devotees appea̶
streets to chant—the men shaven-headed in orange robes, the ̶
in saris—and they immediately attracted attention. The newspaper̶
carried headlines like "Krishna Chants Startle London" and "Happi-
ness is Hare Krishna," and Bhaktivedanta pronounced that his neo-
phyte followers had succeeded where his austere, scholarly god-brothers had failed. Indeed, he concluded, "every town and village" meant
every town and village in the world.

In London, ISKCON received an additional boost due to the sympathetic relationship the devotees there developed with the Beatles, especially George Harrison. Harrison helped them clear legal and financial hurdles to purchase a downtown building which they converted to
a temple, and during the renovation period John Lennon allowed them
to stay at his country estate. Collectively the Beatles produced and
played on a record of Krishna chants which sold seventy thousand cop-
ies the first day of its release. "Hare Krishna Mantra" soon became
the number one song on the English music charts, and had similar success in West Germany and Czechoslovakia. Also, Harrison donated the
money to publish the first volume of Bhaktivedanta's *Kṛṣṇa* trilogy.
The swami visited England from September to December 1969, where
he officially opened the temple there, then returned to the United States
to visit the Boston center before settling in at Los Angeles for five
months. In L.A. the first temple that ISKCON actually owned was
opened, and Bhaktivedanta intended to make it a showplace and world
headquarters for his movement. From there he traveled back to India
for the first time in almost three years with an entourage of ten American sannyasis, and twenty more devotees would join him within the
month. Bhaktivedanta had returned to India to initiate a new phase of
his movement, with visions of monumental temple complexes in Bombay, Mayapur in Bengal (the birthplace of Chaitanya), and Vrindaban. The ISKCON group was a rage from the moment it arrived in Calcutta.

Before considering the history of ISKCON's relationship with Vrindaban, however, I wish to consider an important element that links this
movement to the Indian Gaudiya Vaishnava tradition, giving it its distinctive revivalistic and expansionist zeal. Important to any claim of
"tradition" in India is a person's or group's spiritual genealogy. In
India it is said that no tradition can be transmitted fully by simply

e full knowledge must be handed
guru to disciple. It is, then, a key
ed by most people in India as a bona-
linked to his own teacher. Therefore,
ISKCON's *param-guru* (guru of the guru)
nd his father, Bhaktivinod Thakur, it be-
are Krishna movement is a culmination of
ize Chaitanya Vaishnavism after a lacuna of
nd to interpret it as a universal religion that
ly expansionist in scope. It is their spirit of re-
onism that ISKCON appropriated and continues.

Bhakti.   r and the Western Expansion of Chaitanyaism

Born in 1838, Bhaktivinod received an English education and gradu-
ated from a Christian college. On his own the *thakur* (master, respected
teacher) studied law, and after passing the law examinations became a
civil servant with the government of Bengal, a position that he held
until retirement in 1894. He also was appointed by the Indian government as overseer of the large Jagannath temple at Puri in Orissa. As a
result of his training and employment in the British system, Bhaktivinod was well-versed in Western philosophy and Christianity, imbibing
the prevalent attitude of his day that Indian religion and philosophy was
relatively inferior.

However, he maintained a keen interest in the Vaishnava tradition of
his own family and sought to learn more about its subtleties in order to
compare the two systems. With much difficulty he finally obtained cop-
ies of *Chaitanya-charitamrita* and *Bhagavata-Purana* in 1868, and this
was a transformative event for him. He was surprised and over-
whelmed by the depth of philosophical and theological teachings presented by these two key Vaishnava scriptures, and soon dedicated himself to actively promoting the religion, an effort that led to a
revitalization of Chaitanyite Vaishnavism.

By the mid-seventeenth century, the religion initiated by Chaitanya
had lost its ecstatic zeal and had come to be primarily identified with
one its offshoots, the *sahajiya* sect. Tracing their inheritance to Chaitanya, the sahajiyas integrated tantric aspects into their spiritual practices, ritual sexual intercourse being primary. A Gaudiya Math publication states: "Vaishnavism was almost abandoned by the educated
section of people. Its literature was hardly read. Kirtana was looked
upon not as a form of prayer, but as means of gratification by people of

loose morals. Most of the Vaishnava followers of the period lost their high standard of morality; they ceased to love asceticism, intellectual superiority and devotional fervour which were the main characteristics of the previous Vaishnava masters'' (Yati 1978: 39).

In this context Bhaktivinod burst upon the scene, translating the Vaishnava texts into various languages including English, writing his own commentaries, and founding a journal to disseminate the teachings of Chaitanya to a broad public. Another accomplishment for which he is also noted is the ''rediscovery'' of Chaitanya's exact birthplace which apparently had been forgotten over the years. Just as Chaitanya had mystically rediscovered the places of Krishna's activities in Vrindaban, Chaitanya's birthplace was revealed to Bhaktivinod in a vision. Planning to move to Vrindaban after his retirement, he was dissuaded by the celestial voice of Chaitanya himself saying, ''There is much work left out in Gaudamandal [the area in Bengal where Chaitanya lived] to be done by you. Refrain from going to Vrajamandal [Vrindaban]'' (Yati 1978: 33). What happened after that is narrated by Bhaktivinod in his life history:

> Thereafter every Saturday I visited Navadvip and enquired about the places connected with my Prabhu (Gaurānga) but the local people knew nothing, steeped as they were in their own selfishness. One night I got upon the roof of the house. It was at about 10 o'clock at night. While the sky was heavily clouded, I saw towards the North on the bank of the Ganges a palace-like building beautifully illuminated. Next morning I once again observed that palace from the roof and found a tall palm tree marking the spot. . . . On enquiry the grand old man of the place informed me that that was the Birthplace of Srimān Mahāprabhu. (Yati 1978: 33)

Being a man of letters, Bhaktivinod realized that the general population would not accept his vision as valid proof that this site was indeed Chaitanya's birthplace. Therefore, he carefully researched all available maps, records, government documents, and scriptural descriptions for verification until he had compiled a convincing argument that corroborated his vision. In 1894 a public meeting was held where Bhaktivinod's research was accepted by historians and government officials as valid. On that site Bhaktivinod then constructed a temple which still stands today.

Besides this accomplishment, which had the effect of revitalizing interest in the worship of Chaitanya throughout Bengal and Orissa, Bhaktivinod was also a prolific writer, publishing books, articles, and periodicals in Sanskrit, Bengali, Hindi, and English. His intent was to widely disseminate the religion of Chaitanya, and he wrote, "Oh, for that day when the fortunate English, French, Russian, German and American people will take up banners, mṛdaṅgas and karatālas and raise kīrtana through their streets and towns. When will that day come?" (in Goswami, Satsvarupa 1982: 189). Some of his English essays were also sent to colleges and universities in the West, where they have been on library shelves since at least 1896.[10] As Hopkins (in Gelberg 1983: 121) has pointed out: "It was he, more than anyone else, who made possible the resurgence of Gauḍīya Vaishnavism in late nineteenth century India, and it was he who set in motion the chain of events that led to the establishment of the Krishna consciousness movement in America in the next century."

Bhaktivinod laid the groundwork for the resurgence and spread of Chaitanyaism, and his son Bimala Prasad, later known as Bhaktisiddhanta Saraswati, took the helm after his father's death in 1914. Bhaktisiddhanta would found the Gaudiya Math, a monastic and preaching organization, establish temples throughout India and in some foreign countries, and initiate a new generation of Chaitanyite disciples, including Bhaktivedanta Swami.

Bhaktisiddhanta Saraswati and Gaudiya Math

Bhaktivinod refused to acknowledge caste distinctions and had burned the physical signs of his upper-class status, including the "sacred thread" (upanayana). His son internalized this anticaste belief from his father and other Vaishnava pandits during his childhood, gradually taking over with organizational efficiency the movement that Bhaktivinod inspired. Well-versed in the Vaishnava scriptures and in the commentaries of the Madhva and Ramanuja schools, as well as his own Chaitanya sampradaya, Bhaktisiddhanta argued convincingly that Chaitanya had preached a pure Vedic philosophy and religion. And just as his father had done, Bhaktisiddhanta preached the paramount belief that status was dependent not upon birth, but upon the quality of one's devotion to Krishna.

In 1900, Bhatisiddhanta took initiation from an illiterate holy man,

[10] Bhaktivedanta Swami dedicated *Teachings of Lord Chaitanya* to Bhaktivinod, "Who Initiated The Teachings of Lord Chaitanya in The Western World (McGill University, Canada) in 1896, The Year of My Birth" (Bhaktivedanta 1968: vii). According to one informant, it was in 1896 that Bhaktivinod sent a copy of his English essay, *Jaivadharma*, to McGill.

Gaurkishor Das Babaji,[11] whom his father had known and respected for many years, in order to balance his scholarly nature with a devotional attitude; upon Bhaktivinod's death in 1914, he actively began to structure an organization that would continue his father's goals. His first step was to establish a printing press for the dissemination of his writings. Many times during the remainder of his life, he would emphasize that writing and publication were the primary tools for preaching at that time in history, a principle that Bhaktivedanta Swami would continue to follow.

Interestingly enough, Bhaktisiddhanta utilized a symbolism to de-emphasize caste that was just the reverse of his father's. Rather than insist upon the removal of caste indicators, he taught that anyone properly trained in devotional service was in fact a Brahman, and deserving to wear the sacred thread. He therefore instituted a system of initiation whereby his disciples would be awarded the sacred thread, in essence transforming them into Brahman, regardless of their birth-status. This practice was taken one step further by Bhaktivedanta when he began initiating his own Western disciples as Brahman.

Until his death in 1937, Bhaktisiddhanta traveled throughout India preaching and opening temples. He also sent disciples to England, Germany, and Japan, where small missions were started, but without much success. The Gaudiya Math became the first organized monastic institution within Vaishnavism and was highly criticized, especially by the hereditary priests in Gaudiya Vaishnava temples since they perceived it as a threat to their superior status. Eventually, however, it became accepted that the Gaudiya Math was another branch of the religious tree that Chaitanya had planted, and today it is recognized as such.

After Bhaktisiddhanta's death—as often happens with a movement centered upon a charismatic personality—there arose disputes concerning ownership of Gaudiya Math properties and distribution of his spir-

[11] Among Gaudiya Vaishnavas there is a great deal of controversy and dispute concerning Bhaktisiddhanta's initiation from Gaurakishor. Apparently, Bhatisiddhanta never received direct initiation, but rather experienced it in a dream or, as some say, initiated himself before a picture of the babaji. For some, this is a breakdown in the direct guru succession (*parampara*), and is used to argue against the validity of the Gaudiya Math institution. Subsequently, if the Gaudiya Math is not legitimate, then neither is ISKCON. Critics of both organizations consider this an important point; however, most Vrindaban residents take the position of one informant who explained, "The proof is in the pudding. What if the initiation was in a dream? In my mind a mystical initiation is cent percent better." Some former ISKCON devotees have left that organization because of this parampara controversy, and have affiliated with gurus who can prove their direct guru-succession.

itual and institutional authority. To this day some of the disputes have
not been resolved, and the once unified Math is now divided into factions—a state of affairs that has considerably tarnished its reputation.
Although he was initiated by Bhaktisiddhanta in 1932, Bhaktivedanta
was not involved in these power struggles, but instead set out to work
alone for the implementation of his guru's instruction, in spite of criticisms from the others.

As a result, some of his god-brothers (other disciples of Bhaktisiddhanta) have been critical from time to time about the method and final
content of ISKCON. In the final analysis, however, it has been difficult
for any of them to substantiate their criticism of Bhaktivedanta, for he,
out of all of them, was capable of fulfilling their guru's ultimate
dreams, adapting the religion to a Western context without deviating
from its basic content. The final evaluation of his own peers was perhaps best exhibited as five of Bhaktivedanta's remaining god-brothers
gathered around his bed several days before his death in 1977. Satsvarupa Goswami (1983b: 415–16) describes the scene in his biography of
Bhaktivedanta:

> When Prabhupāda began asking his Godbrothers to forgive him, they
> protested. "You are the eternal leader," one of them asserted. "You rule
> over us, guide us, chastise us."
>
> "Forgive all my offenses," Prabhupāda repeated. "I became proud of all
> my opulence."
>
> "No," said Purī Mahārāja, "you never became proud. When you started
> preaching, opulence and success followed you. That was the blessing of Śrī
> Caitanya Mahāprabhu and Śrī Kṛṣṇa. There cannot be any question of your
> being offensive."
>
> When Śrīla Prabhupāda presented himself as *mahā-patita*, greatly fallen,
> Purī Mahārāja did not accept it. "You have saved millions of people around
> the world," he said. "Therefore, there is no question of offenses. But you
> should be called *mahā-patita-pāvana* (the great savior of the fallen)."

Indeed, those Indians today most critical of ISKCON frame their criticisms not in terms of that movement's innovations, but rather within
the context of its Gaudiya Math inheritance. The dynamics caused by
subtle tensions that persist between the Gaudiya Math and a few of the
hereditary Gaudiya goswamis in Vrindaban, therefore, paradoxically
serve to aid in ISKCON's Indian acceptance strategy. ISKCON's Brahman
critics evaluate the movement as so true to its Gaudiya Math inheritance that they attribute its perceived defects to the parent organization,

primary among these being the challenge to hereditary Brahman riority. In this way ISKCON's claim to guru-succession through Bha siddhanta and Bhaktivinod is actually strengthened.

For the majority of people in Vrindaban, a community that has confronted and adapted the egalitarian ideals of Chaitanyaism for five centuries, ISKCON's legitimacy is rarely questioned. Brahman criticisms, if they have any impact, serve to endear ISKCON devotees to the non-Brahman population rather than estrange them.

ISKCON IN VRINDABAN

By the time Bhaktivedanta returned to India in 1971, he had established temples in most major American cities, in Toronto, Montreal, London, Paris, Amsterdam, Tokyo, and even had several Russian disciples working undercover in Moscow. His goal, especially in the United States, was to distribute as many books as possible while maintaining the deity worship in temples for the advancement of his disciples. Now he was ready to implement the second, equally important thrust of his overall vision: to bring ISKCON back to India in force, capture the attention and fascination of Indians by the phenomenon of Western devotees, and attract India back to what he saw as its original religious consciousness. One essential element of this plan was the construction of elaborate temple complexes in Bengal, Bombay, and Vrindaban on a scale that had not been done in India in recent times. Each of these temples had a particular symbolic significance: Mayapur in Bengal was the birthplace of Chaitanya, and Bombay was the center of material decadence, but there can be little doubt that for Bhaktivedanta the temple in Vrindaban was symbolically most important.

From the time of his return to Vrindaban in August 1967, the swami had talked of having an "American House" there for his disciples. He remained in India for four months, regained his health, and again departed for the United States. Leaving behind two senior disciples to begin groundwork for the Indian centers, he instructed them to begin the search for suitable properties. Bhaktivedanta did not return to Vrindaban until November 1971, although a few devotees had lived there since 1967. This time, however, he was accompanied by an entourage of fifty international devotees, and they took the town by storm. He was given an official welcome by prominent citizens and when it was his time to speak, he directly told the assembled dignitaries that they should accept his foreign disciples without question:

ıder that Kṛṣṇa is Hindu or Indian. Kṛṣṇa is for all.
taking to Kṛṣṇa consciousness by understanding that
As long as one is Hindu or Muslim or Christian, there
ṣṇa consciousness. . . . So these boys and girls, or la-
, who have joined me, they have given up their desig-
o longer Americans or Canadians or Australians. They
nselves as eternal servants of Lord Kṛṣṇa. . . . When
ınced they are given the sacred thread, *upanayana-sam-
skāra*,[12] following the path of instruction of my Guru Mahārāja, His Divine
Grace Bhaktisiddhānta Sarasvatī Gosvāmī Prabhupāda. According to the
śāstra [sacred texts], they should not be considered as coming from families
of *mlecchas* and *yavanas*—they should not be considered like that—because they are now purified. (Goswami, Satsvarupa 1983a: 20–22)

He concluded his address by appealing for a donation of land, emphasizing that since Vrindaban was now becoming famous the world
over because of his movement, a beautiful temple and guest house
should be available so international visitors who were sure to come
would appreciate Krishna's and Vrindaban's importance. Immediately
afterwards, a local landowner came forward to offer a parcel in Raman-
Reti, about two kilometers from the center of town.

However, Bhaktivedanta knew that not everyone in Vrindaban
would automatically accept his disciples as legitimate. The caste goswamis especially, he felt, feared ISKCON because it threatened their
hereditary social preeminence, just as they had earlier felt threatened
by Bhaktisiddhanta's Gaudiya Math. Thus he communicated an ad-
monition to his followers that whenever they were in Vrindaban they
had to be on their best behavior, emphasizing the proper etiquette for
living there. He emphasized, ''In the holy *dhāma*, if one of my disciples drinks from a jug incorrectly and he contaminates that jug, everyone will notice it. Don't be criticized for uncleanliness, or I will be
criticized. It is the duty of the disciple to follow these etiquette habits
very austerely. I am putting so much energy into this party in India
because I want to train you how to live here'' (1983a: 30). ISKCON's
acceptance and integration in Vrindaban, Bhaktivedanta was keenly
aware, depended on the devotees' proper presentation of self in public.

---

[12] *Samskaras* are rites of passage conducted in India at important stages in a person's life.
Especially important are the rituals associated with birth, marriage, death, and for the male, reaching the age that allows him to fully participate in the religious system. This last mentioned rite of
passage, called upanayana, is when the ''sacred thread'' is given.

During this period Bhaktivedanta traveled throughout India to establish his three main projects, leaving behind a group of devotees in Vrindaban to acquire the land that had been promised. This was not an easy task, however. After announcing his intent to give the land to ISKCON, the donor had been bombarded by requests from other organizations and individuals for it, causing him to have second thoughts. Finally, one of Bhaktivedanta's representatives demanded that a decision be made, only to find reluctance on the owner's part. Since he was troubled with indecision, the donor and his wife decided to place the matter before their Radha-Krishna deities. In front of the ISKCON devotee left in charge, the owner's wife took two slips of paper, writing "yes" on one, "no" on the other, and placed them before the images. She then asked the devotee to select one of the slips, and in the presence of Radha, Krishna, the owner, and his wife, the devotee unfolded the slip upon which "yes" had been written; the decision had been made by Radha and Krishna themselves. Elated by this news, Bhaktivedanta returned to Vrindaban to sign the deed and conduct a ground-breaking ceremony in March 1972.

As he did with all the properties acquired in India, Bhaktivedanta directed that construction start as soon as the deed was signed since it was not uncommon for owners to construct the document of sales so that if details were not meticulously carried out within a specified period, the land might be reclaimed. The swami's logic was that occupation of the land, and at least a symbolic start of construction would make it difficult for reclamation to be carried out. Therefore, two days after the final transaction, he held a large festival on the property, invited dignitaries from Vrindaban and the surrounding Mathura district, and held ground-breaking ceremonies.

To initiate the construction of each of his Indian temples, Bhaktivedanta ceremoniously placed a golden image of Ananta Shesha, the multiheaded serpent deity upon which Vishnu reclines, in a fifteen-foot pit situated in the center of the temple site. Everything went well during this ritual, and the residents of Vrindaban seemed supportive, but later that night the pit was dug up and desecrated by someone throwing garbage and human excrement into it.

It was soon discovered that this incident did not reflect opposition by the general Vrindaban population, but rather the jealousy of a female sadhu who lived adjacent to the property. She had herself been trying to convince the owner of this property to give the land to her, and had vowed that if she could not have it, no one else could. The police were notified and shown the deed, apprehending the perpetrators when they returned later that same night; no similar incident occurred after this. The woman responsible now denies that she was involved in the incident in any way. She explains:

> I love the foreign bhaktas. This is a vicious rumor someone jealous to me started long ago. I have always supported, and was so glad that Balaram mandir was going up there. I also have disciples in England, Australia, and when they see me they dance and sing in ecstasy. I am guru also, you see. There will be many opinions as there are many classes of men. The good people who have true vision will welcome. It is good fortune and we see the foreign presence here the flowering of a lotus. Others can only see thorns. Don't be concerned with these fools.[13]

After my discussion with this woman ascetic, she offered a type of brittle sugar-candy as prasad, immediately calling for water from one of her female servants to wash her hands. With me were several ISKCON devotees, and one inquired if the water was for purification. She replied, "Yes, purification from sugar-dust. I take your dust on my head for real purification." Perhaps this lady was cynical in her praise of the foreign devotees, but this and other conversations with her indicate that her acceptance, at least now, is genuine. Common knowledge, as well as police records, however, confirms her implication in the desecration incident and her desire to see the foreigners gone. Her present attitude, then, reflects a transformation over the course of her living next to the ISKCON complex now for some ten years, having to interact daily with the devotees. In the beginning she disavowed the possibility of foreigners becoming Vaishnavas, much less Brahmans; but following the example set by Bhaktivedanta, she now awards the sacred thread to her own Western followers.

Bhaktivedanta hoped that the Vrindaban temple would be completed by Janmashtami in August 1973, and charged the devotees living in Vrindaban with that task. One group lived at the Radha-Damodar temple while others were scattered around town, but they were inexperienced in conducting business in India. Repeatedly they would be cheated, and each time Bhaktivedanta came to their rescue. There were also unavoidable delays caused by the scarcity of cement and marble along with the bureaucratic system involved in procuring these commodities. The 1973 opening date passed, and Bhaktivedanta was dis-

---

[13] Translation from interview in Hindi, April 7, 1982.

appointed with the slow progress, but accepted it. At a festival held on the land during the Janmashtami celebration, vows were made to hold the official opening at a similar festival the following year.

Problems continued to plague the temple project. The land's donor tried to reclaim fifty feet of the property facing the road to build shops and a gas station. The devotees immediately erected a high wall completely around the parcel, lawyers agreeing that ISKCON had full ownership, and the situation was eventually resolved. Throughout 1974 Bhaktivedanta traveled around the world, but communicated almost daily with his Vrindaban representatives, as well as the ones in Bengal and Bombay. Each time the Vrindaban devotees would be optimistic about the grand opening in August, so Bhaktivedanta was confident that the temple would indeed be ready this time, and invited devotees around the world to join him in Vrindaban for the August festivities. He also directed that formal invitations be sent to politicians and other prominent individuals from all over India.

Bhaktivedanta arrived back in Vrindaban on August 4, about a week before Janmashtami 1974, to find the temple only half finished, and he was thoroughly enraged. Immediately he directed that invitations be cancelled and devotees worldwide be notified not to come. No festival was held and he developed a fever that would last for the two weeks he remained in town. Although weak, the swami daily contacted politicians and businessmen, trying to arrange shortcuts for the delivery of construction materials and imploring them to help his foreign disciples build the temple that he so desperately wanted open before his death.

The Krishna-Balaram temple was officially opened on April 20, 1975, the day celebrated that year throughout India as Ram-Naumi, the festival of Rama.[14] For the eight months that Bhaktivedanta had been away from Vrindaban, workers had labored day and night in a prolonged marathon to complete the three-domed temple and four-story "international guesthouse." On the opening day, six hundred ISKCON devotees from around the world were present, along with several hundred Indian life members and representatives from all levels of the Indian government. The population of Vrindaban and the surrounding

---

[14] In general Vaishnava theology, there are ten avatars, or incarnations, of Vishnu that are "saviors" who descend in particular epochs to correct specific problems. The list of ten is as follows: Matsya, Kurma, Varaha, Nrisimha, Vamana, Parashurama, Rama, Krishna, Balarama, and Kalki. Besides these, other avatars are included by various sects. Buddha, for example, sometimes appears after Rama and before Krishna. All these avatars have already appeared except for Kalki, who will come at the end of the present age to destroy this creation and usher in a new cosmic cycle of time (see Klaustermaier 1984 for a detailed discussion).

countryside also turned out in such force that the large courtyard and grounds surrounding the temple could not accommodate them. Police had to be called in to direct traffic flow through the temple so that everyone could get a glimpse of the ritual proceedings.

Bhaktivedanta was aware that if the Vrindaban temple was to be accepted as legitimate by all segments of the society, the ritual installation of the images had to be done according to rules that would satisfy even the harshest potential critics; therefore, he arranged for well-known Brahman ritual specialists from Mathura and Vrindaban to conduct the ceremony. Apparently he did not personally consider these pandits a necessity for Krishna to be "called down" into the images, but he was overwhelmingly concerned with what the Indian people considered proper. An ISKCON devotee involved in the opening preparations at Krishna-Balaram comments:

> I was helping to make all the arrangements with these Brahmans, these pandits who were installing (the deities) . . . anyway, we went through a whole thing, Prabhupad went through a whole thing—should we have these men? Actually he said there is no need for these men, we can install them . . . but because they will make some politics, and people will be influenced, they won't come to the temple. "Let them do their thing," he said, "and we'll chant 'Hare Krishna.' That's the real installation, the chanting of 'Hare Krishna,' but let them come and chant all their mantras." He said otherwise they will make politics outside and they'll try to prevent people from coming. But Prabupad was not very much into it at all. Anyway, he took that attitude here and he also did that in Bombay, but in Mayapur he didn't. There's no need for this in Mayapur. No one considers that there at all, and the people come to our temples.[15]

Although Bhaktivedanta had instructed his disciples generally to not mingle with Vrindaban residents, his purpose for this restriction was to avoid what he saw as the potential for doctrinal contamination. Believing that he had transmitted a "pure" form of the Chaitanya religion, he was concerned that idiosyncratic and "heretical" Indian interpretations would confuse his spiritual neophytes and possibly draw them away from ISKCON with promises of mystical powers and other forms of spiritual adventurism. But he was most concerned with positive community relations and took every opportunity to encourage relation-

[15] Direct quotation, Bhavananda Goswami Vishnupad, ISKCON guru for Vrindaban, August 9, 1982.

ships especially between prominent Vrindaban residents and the devotees. One such attempt is reflected in an accommodation to the merchant community at the Krishna-Balaram temple.

A number of merchants from Loi Bazaar, the town's principal market area, had recognized that the new temple would be a powerful attraction for the thousands of pilgrims that swarmed into town each day, and they wanted to capitalize upon this ready market. Aware of this fact, the temple administration began to make plans for the inclusion of five shops in the *gurukula* (school) building that was under construction. They reasoned that if these shops were located within the temple precincts, they could be controlled, and the development of a commercial area adjacent to the temple could be avoided.

When the gurukula opened in 1977, shops were allocated to a set of highly selected clients, and they enjoyed success for a number of years from both pilgrim and ISKCON clientele. In 1982, however, the decision was made by a new temple administration that businesses were an improper utilization of temple land, and the merchants were asked to leave. Having become dependent upon the income these shops were generating, however, several of the shop owners refused to leave, claiming that their tenure there (over five years) gave them the right to remain. Ultimately, negotiations between the merchants and ISKCON failed, and a legal resolution of the dispute is still in progress. (This event will be discussed in chapter 6.)

Regardless of this later development, the original decision to integrate the merchant community into ISKCON's temple scene represented a general attitude of accomodation with the local people. Certainly, the intuition of the merchants was correct, and the ISKCON temple soon became one of the main attractions in Vrindaban. Its drawing power was only increased after Bhaktivedanta's death on November 14, 1977, since tombs of saints often become objects of veneration and pilgrimage themselves, and this was certainly the case with Bhaktivedanta's.

The morning after his death, Bhaktivedanta's body was taken on one last parikrama of Vrindaban, and most of the town's population turned out to pay their last respects. Vrindaban had lost one of its own, and Bhaktivedanta's passing only served to endear his institution to them even more. His surviving god-brothers conducted the funeral rites according to Vaishnava ritual, and his body was placed in a deep pit in the courtyard immediately in front of the temple. Bhaktivedanta had chosen the spot himself, and had instructed that an elaborate *samadhi* (tomb) temple be constructed over the site. One of ISKCON's architects, himself a devotee, commented:

> Prabhupad was not concerned for an elaborate memorial for himself, but he knew how the Indian people loved him. He told me that an elaborate samadhi of marble should be built here, and one *pushpa samadhi* ("tomb" containing the funeral flowers) at Mayapur, with large bronze murtis of His Divine Grace. He said it wasn't for his glorification, but that it would increase the temple's attraction. It would add to the sanctity of the temple in the minds of the Indian people. Of course for us it is the most holiest site because his holy body is there in samadhi. And of course he was correct. Even though it is taking so long for construction due to marble difficulties and the slow work on the fine craftsmanship, people from everywhere come to see him. When it is completed it will rival the Taj (in Agra some forty miles away) as the best attraction in North India.[16]

Although this devotee was perhaps overstating the point, one of the merchants who is involved in the legal battle over ISKCON shop space, agreed: "The samadhi will bring us increased business even in Loi Bazaar. Even now, more are coming, and when it is complete, it will be a good boon to our business."

Bhaktivedanta's instruction concerning the gurukula also established another setting for interaction between Indians and devotees. The American and European administrators thought that the school would be only for children of ISKCON devotees, but when their guru heard this idea, he reprimanded them. The gurukula headmaster in 1983 commented:

> We were showing Prabhupad this building before it was opened, discussing where the administrative and teachers' offices would be, and although he was very weak, close to death, he became enlivened with a guru's kind rage. "You are thinking about offices, but what of the students? Don't waste energy on 'this room is mine' thinking. Bring at least five hundred students here," he said. When we said there weren't five hundred children in ISKCON, he said, "ISKCON, FISKCON. Educate the intelligent Indian students also. Solicit from the best families and educate true Brahmans from the Indian society at large." So that is our policy—to of course bring the ISKCON children, but to provide quality spiritual education and the basics to promising Indian children also. And we have so many applications that we can't handle them, although we still aren't up to the five hundred number.

[16] Direct quotation, Surabhi Swami, ISKCON architect, August 12, 1982.

Around one hundred only, about half ISKCON and half Indian, some from wealthy families, but also bright kids on scholarship that could not otherwise afford it.[17]

Today in Vrindaban, ISKCON devotees conduct no planned schedule of sankirtan through the streets of Vrindaban, although this event does take place whenever a large number of devotees gather for special festivals. However, part of the gurukula curriculum requires the students to participate in a daily sankirtan procession, an event that is enjoyed by residents and pilgrims. As the ethnically mixed crowd of children dance and sing through the Vrindaban streets, many onlookers join in and comment upon the positive effect it has on the mentality of the town. The sight of Western children participating along with Indians in this cultural performance has created a significant impression. Some informants have cited it as one of the main reasons they have come to appreciate ISKCON, and see it as an encouraging symbol of international cooperation.

Today the presence of ISKCON in Vrindaban is obvious even to people who visit for only a few hours. The temple is visited by practically every pilgrim, and many residents go there regularly. Most well-known or well-to-do Indians stay at the guest house because of its reputation for having the best facilities in town. At the gurukula, there are around fifty young Indian boys as boarding students who, along with their parents, come into close contact with foreign devotees.

The operation of such a large temple complex necessarily brings ISKCON devotees into daily contact with Vrindaban merchants, and the temple's public relation strategies force interactions with most segments of the community. Furthermore, any devotees that reside in Vrindaban for any length of time are drawn into the daily ritual cycle of the town, visiting other temples and sacred sites. Face-to-face interaction with Indian pilgrims and residents are frequent in all these settings, and even when devotees are not present, they and their organization are favorite topics of discussion. On any day in Loi Bazaar, it is not difficult to obtain information concerning which "famous" devotees are in town or coming, what special events are happening at the temple, what problems or projects the ISKCON organization is dealing with, and through a variety of rumors ranging from the almost-true to the fantastic, the current attitudes concerning daily interactions with devotees can be discovered.

[17] Direct quotation, Dhanurdhara Swami, ISKCON gurukula headmaster, December 3, 1982.

The devotees of ISKCON, however, are not the only Westerners in town, nor are they the first Westerners of the Gaudiya sampradaya that the residents have encountered. In order to further place the current events occurring in Vrindaban in context, I will briefly describe an important historical precedent for the Western devotees, and then comment upon the other types of Westerners also living in the town.

THE CASE OF SRI KRISHNA PREM

In 1930, Jagdish Lal Goswami was about twenty years old, and his father, Bal Goswami, was well known throughout Vrindaban as a priest at Radha-Raman temple, artist, and guru. Jagdish, now in his seventies, recounted how the famous English sadhu, Krishna Prem, came to be a disciple of his father, and therefore part of the Gaudiya Vaishnava sampradaya. The following information is derived from interviews and informal conversation with Jagdish Goswami, who now operates his deceased father's photography and art studio at Radha-Raman temple, and from a series of letters exchanged between his father and Krishna Prem. Gaps in the chronolgy have been filled in by reference to the biography of Krishna Prem by Dilip Kumar Roy (1968).

In the early 1920s, Ronald Nixon, a former fighter pilot in the British Royal Flying Corps, moved to India to become a professor of English at Lucknow University. Besides his studies of philosophy and literature at Cambridge, Nixon had developed a fascination with the Pali language, and became well versed in the various schools of Buddhism, as well as becoming something of a practitioner. At the end of his Cambridge studies, he wanted to find some way of living in India in order to learn the more practical aspects of Buddhism from experienced teachers, and after interviewing for the job in London, Nixon accepted a post as Reader in English at Lucknow University.

He was taken under the wings of the university's vice-chancellor, Dr. Chakravarti, who sympathized with Ronald's spiritual quest (Chakravarti was himself a member of the Theosophical Society), and invited the young instructor to reside permanently in his home. Rejecting the standards of expected British behavior, Ronald did not mingle with the British establishment, but instead became quickly Indianized, making many friends in the local community. Chakravarti was a Bengali who shared Nixon's spiritual inclinations, impressing the Englishman with both his knowledge and spiritual depth. However, it was the vice-chancellor's wife, Monica, whom Nixon accepted as his guru in 1924.

After Chakravarti's retirement from Lucknow in 1926, he, his wife, and Nixon moved to Varanasi. After eighteen months there, however, Mrs. Chakravarti was advised by her doctors to live in a cooler climate, which she agreed to do; however, her husband felt that he could not make a move due to a bad heart. Chakratvarti, therefore, acting as her guru, initiated his wife into the Vaishnava mendicant order of vairagis, in essence releasing her from marriage and family responsibilities. She moved to the hill station of Almora in Northern Uttar Pradesh to construct an ashram, named Uttar Vrindaban, which included a temple to Radha-Krishna, and at each step of the way Ronald Nixon was with her. She in turn initiated him as a renunciate, giving him the name "Sri Krishna Prem."

Mrs. Chakravarti, who took the renounced name of Yashoda Mai, began to live strictly by the ritual codes of the Gaudiya Vaishnava sampradaya, which she also imposed upon her disciple. Although Krishna Prem fully acknowledged Yashoda Mai as his diksha guru, and was completely dedicated to her, he desired more detailed instruction than she could provide. Upon his request, therefore, Yashoda Mai took Krishna Prem to Vrindaban in search of a more traditional teacher.

Jagdish Lal Goswami first met Krishna Prem and Yashoda Mai on their guru-finding mission to Vrindaban. Yashoda Mai had a long history of interaction with the temple goswamis at Radha-Raman, but Krishna Prem insisted on searching the entire town for the best teacher, regardless of sectarian affiliation. As Jagdish recounts, they lived at one of the ghats for several weeks (where he photographed them), publicizing the fact that a foreigner was searching for a spiritual teacher: "Every sampradaya was after him. All the gurus and fake gurus came also." Eventually Krishna Prem decided that Bal Goswami, Jagdish's father, had the best answers to his questions. Correspondence with him, and several return trips to Vrindaban for discussions, culminated in a ceremony at Almora that formalized the teacher-student relationship. This had considerable implications for the present attitude of Vrindaban toward Westerners.

According to Jagdish, and confirmed by the available letters, Krishna Prem actually requested another diksha initiation from Bal Goswami, but because Yashoda Mai had already conducted the diksha ceremony, it was considered poor etiquette. Since Krishna Prem demanded some formal ties to the Gaudiya sampradaya, and especially the temple of Radha-Raman, it was decided that Yashoda Mai would take direct initiation from Bal Goswami, and as part of the same ceremony, she would formally initiate Krishna Prem into the same parampara. This made Bal Goswami Krishna Prem's param-guru, from whom he could legitimately take instruction.

Yashoda Mai had already invested her disciple with a sacred thread at the time of their renunciation ceremony, in effect making him Brahman. I therefore asked Jagdish if his father would have done the same, had this not already taken place. "Maybe, maybe not," was his reply. "More important than the thread were the *kunti* beads (neck beads of tulsi wood) and *shikha* (lock of hair on the back of an otherwise shaved head)."

This initiation is the first instance of a Westerner being accepted as a disciple, albeit indirectly, by any traditional Vrindaban guru, and it raised a number of serious questions. On his next trip to Vrindaban, Krishna Prem was escorted into the temple by Bal Goswami, and although no one said anything at the time, shortly thereafter the guru was notified that he had been excommunicated by the temple authorities, the consensus being that rules of ritual purity had been violated. This situation was later taken before a full council of temple priests who, after searching the sacred texts for a final solution, decided that if an individual met required standards of knowledge and cleanliness, he could be admitted to the temple, and any priest could accept him as a disciple. Bal Goswami was thereby reinstated, and the reaffirmation of the underlying principle of noncasteism already implicit in the Chaitanya religion set the foundations for this temple's future attitude toward the foreign Vaishnavas of ISKCON. Other sects in the town have also adopted this precedent established by the Radha-Raman priests as the basis for their own policy. As Jagdish put it, "Krishna Prem had intellectual capacity for understanding the knowledge, and he was so careful about his purification habits also. Only in such cases can we accept, so it is person to person only. ISKCON, not-ISKCON, that is not the point. With Indian persons the same is also. The person-quality, that is what counts."

Krishna Prem's evident intellectual and inspirational qualities gained him wide fame and many disciples in India, as reflected in numerous books on his life and teachings (see Roy 1968; Sri Krishna Prem 1976; Kaul 1980).[18] After Yashoda Mai's death in 1944, he took over her

[18] Interestingly, none of these sources say anything about either Krishna Prem's or Yasoda Mai's Vrindaban connection.

ashram where he lived until his own demise in 1965. While there are few people in Vrindaban willing to make any personal comparisons between the devotees of ISKCON and Krishna Prem, his example is often cited as a precedent for their acceptance today.

FOREIGNERS IN VRINDABAN TODAY

There are other foreigners in Vrindaban besides the devotees from the International Society for Krishna Consciousness. While occasionally some Westerners that are not involved in any religious search come and stay for a short time, most longer-term foreign residents of Vrindaban are there for professed spiritual reasons and affiliated with a temple or guru. Some are former ISKCON members who have left the organization due to various disputes or for study under other Indian teachers, something that ISKCON does not condone. Tables 1 and 2 detail the average compostion of the foreign population during the period of my field-work.[19]

Table 1. Distribution of Foreigners in Vrindaban (ISKCON)

Place	Male	Female		A	B	F	G	D	L	J
Temple	27	11		10	9	6	4	4	4	1
Gurukula	45			21	12	7	2	1	2	
Goshala	5			4	1					
Kishor Ban	2			1	1					
Vraja Academy	2			2						
Other	6	3		6	3					
TOTALS	87	14		44	26	13	6	5	6	1

A=American	B=British	F=French	G=German
D=Dutch	L=Latin American	J=Japanese	

[19] It should be noted that the Vrindaban gurukula enrolls only male students. Other ISKCON schools at places such as Dallas and New Vrindaban, West Virginia, have both male and female students. The usual explanation of this by ISKCON devotees is that life in Vrindaban is too ''austere'' for girls of such a young age.

These figures are averages from five surveys taken periodically during the course of fieldwork. There was little deviation from period to period except during two ISKCON festivals when the number of Hare Krishna devotees increased considerably for about one week. During early April, around two hundred additional devotees arrive in Vrindaban from Mayapur where every year they celebrate the birth of Chaitanya in late March. A similar number arrive the last week in November to celebrate the day marking Bhaktivedanta's passing. Although these two periods are significant times for the Vrindaban community, figures collected during them were not averaged into the totals. The tables, therefore, reflect the number of foreign residents that are present in Vrindaban during most of the year.

As noted, some ISKCON devotees live away from the Krishna-Balaram complex, but usually attend ritual activities there daily. Those living at Vraja Academy are employed as translators or do secretarial work in exchange for accomodations. The sadhu in charge has been a quiet supporter of ISKCON devotees since their arrival. For both ISKCON and non-ISKCON, the "other" place category includes dharmshalas, nonaffiliated guest houses, and private residences. Three non-ISKCON residents, however, are sadhus, and consistent with the Indian ideal,

Table 2. Distribution of Foreigners in Vrindaban (Non-ISKCON)

Place	Male	Female	A	B	F	G	D	L	J
Vraja Academy	3	3	2	1		2	1		
Nim Kiroli	2	2	4						
Harikhan Baba	4				2	2			
Radha-Raman	2	1	3				1		
Jagannath Temple	1			1					
Other	5		2	1			1		1
TOTALS	17	6	11	3	2	4	2		1

A=American   B=British   F=French   G=German
D=Dutch   L=Latin American   J=Japanese

do not have a permanent residence and are included in the "other" category in table 2.

With the exception of one scholar and his wife who lived in an apartment at Radha-Raman temple, all other non-ISKCON foreigners were affiliated with some guru or religious organization. Vraja Academy is an institution established by Sripad Baba, a well-known sadhu, and the individuals living there profess at least an informal student-teacher relationship with him. For the ISKCON residents there this is a very informal relationship without any "guru" implications. Nim Kiroli Baba was a famous saint who died in 1976, and his tomb is located at the Vrindaban ashram run by his organization. Harikhan Baba is considered an avatar of Shiva by his followers, which include a large number of foreigners. Four lived at his ashram in Vrindaban, and during occasions when he was personally present in town, as many as twenty more would be in residence.

However, the overwhelming foreign presence in Vrindaban is ISKCON. Even foreigners who show no outward signs of religious dedication or inclination are assumed to be Hare Krishna devotees, and it requires a considerable amount of work to convince some Indian residents otherwise. As buses arrive at the Vrindaban bus stand, and rickshaw drivers clamor for business, their cry to any foreigner is always first "Krishna-Balaram?" If they are finally convinced that this is not the desired destination, a hierarchy of places will then be recited until the appropriate one is found: "Nim Kiroli? Sripad Baba? Harikhan Baba?"

Extended residence in Vrindaban, as it is for any place in India, is problematic for foreigners who are not citizens of British commonwealth countries. For this reason, those having the longest tenure in Vrindaban are British, their stay not being limited by law. Americans and others are normally limited to six months, the extent of a tourist visa, which can only be renewed by leaving and reentering the country. Due to ISKCON's connections with the government and business sectors, however, some devotees are given "entry" visas which allow for a longer period, usually one year. In one case, an American devotee has been granted Indian citizenship, normally considered impossible to obtain.

The specific situations discussed in this book are ones which most clearly show the transformative dynamics occurring between foreigners and Indians. Of all the situations observed, approximately one-fifth included non-ISKCON foreigners.

SUMMARY

The International Society for Krishna Consciousness is an American revitalization movement that formed in 1966 around A. C. Bhaktivedanta Swami, an Indian monk of the Gaudiya, or Bengal, Vaishnava sect. Founded by Chaitanya Mahaprabhu in the sixteenth century, this religious system was revolutionary in the Indian context because it sought to incorporate all levels of society, regardless of caste affiliation. One of its primary tenets was that an individual achieved Brahman status not by birth, but by personal qualities developed through devotion to the god Krishna.

After Chaitanya's death, the Gaudiya religion experienced a gradual decline in influence until it was revitalized in the early twentieth century by Bhaktivinod Thakur, a district magistrate in Bengal. Bhaktivinod "rediscovered" the birthplace of Chaitanya in Bengal where he erected a temple, using this event as a centerpiece for reviving interest in both religious and philosophical aspects of the sect. He published works in a number of languages, including English, to disseminate the teachings, and concluded that the religion of Chaitanya was a universal religion that could transcend cultural differences, predicting that eventually it would include communicants of all nationalities.

Bhaktivinod's son, Bhaktisiddhanta Saraswati, continued his father's mission by establishing the Gaudiya Math, a monastic preaching institution. Bhaktisiddhanta established temples throughout India, as well as centers in England and Germany, and initiated a large number of disciples whom he charged with spreading Chaitanyism. To his disciples, regardless of caste background, he gave the "sacred thread," indicating that they had been transformed into Brahmans. One disciple was A. C. Bhaktivedanta, who came to the United States in 1965 on the order of his guru, and extended the practice of Brahman initiation to foreigners, considered by most Indians to be ritually impure, and therefore "untouchable."

After successfully implanting his Hare Krishna movement in the United States, partially due to wide acceptance by the hippie counterculture, Bhaktivedanta took his foreign disciples back to India to establish large temples in Bengal, Bombay, and Vrindaban. His strategy had been a dual one from the beginning. By spreading Krishna consciousness to the West, he was helping to save his disciples from the dangers of materialism and atheism. Beyond that, however, he reasoned that if Indians saw Western Vaishnavas, they would be motivated to reconsider and accept their own religious heritage, saving India from encroaching Westernization.

Throughout his life, Bhaktivedanta maintained a close relationship with Vrindaban. In 1954, he moved there, establishing a permanent residence where he would translate Indian scriptures into English, meditate upon Krishna, and plan how to spread his religion to the West. It was to Vrindaban that he brought his first American disciple in 1967, and there he opened the temple of Krishna-Balaram in 1975. Since that time there has been a permanent ISKCON presence in Vrindaban. Bhaktivedanta died there in 1977.

The information presented in this chapter and the others preceding it, frames the present-day reality of Vrindaban. This historical and textual context provides the resources by which both foreign and Indian actors make sense of the situations that they are participants in. Similarly, these same resources provide the observer with the interpretive resources necessary to analyze the dynamics of these interactions.

The following chapters focus on specific situations of interaction and their significance. In chapter 5, I will discuss interactions with pilgrims to Vrindaban; chapter 6 considers the impact of interactions upon the resident population of Vrindaban; and chapter 7 looks specifically at the emotional components of the Chaitanya religion as a focus of interaction in everyday situations taking place between ISKCON devotees and both pilgrims and residents of the town.

Pilgrimage Processes: Aspects of Pilgrim-ISKCON Interactions

PILGRIMAGE was a unifying force in Indian society long before the country's diverse regional, linguistic, religious, and ethnic groups were politically united. Today the institution of pilgrimage still functions to unite people from far-flung regions and is serving to bring yet another group, ISKCON, under the common cultural umbrella of Hinduism. For this study, the attributes of pilgrimage combine with the concept of Vrindaban as a celestial space and the egalitarian ideals of Vaishnava Hinduism to provide the resources for understanding the dynamics of social flexibility and cultural integration in the town. Since the opening of the Krishna-Balaram temple in 1975, pilgrims have made the ISKCON complex one of Vrindaban's most popular pilgrimage destinations, establishing it as a primary setting for interaction between Indians and foreign devotees. In situations of interaction between pilgrims and ISKCON devotees, the meanings of traditional cultural symbols are being extended, manipulated, and transformed as Indians come to accept foreign devotees as part of a common religious system.

Turner (1974: 167) suggests that the inherent attributes of the pilgrimage phenomenon in long-established places of pilgrimage articulate "in some measure with the environing social structure," and this is certainly the case with Vrindaban, a town that was established primarily as a pilgrimage destination. Furthermore, due to the flow of information via the pilgrims themselves, the effects of interactions occurring in Vrindaban can be seen to extend far beyond the boundaries of Braj, back to home villages, towns, and cities of the pilgrims.

Turner has concluded that pilgrimage is a "liminal" phenomenon, one that exists outside or between the normal states and categories of social structure, and wherein transitions and transformations can easily occur. For the pilgrim, there is a state of spontaneous or existential *communitas* that reigns during the pilgrimage journey, a condition that relaxes the constraints of normative social structure. In this state of

106

communitas, there is a "direct, immediate, and total confrontation of human identities which tends to make those experiencing it think of mankind as a homogeneous, unstructured, free community" (1974: 169). Interactions in this mode, then, are more apt to be less patterned, and open to the possible emergence of new relationships and meanings.[1]

The force of face-to-face interaction even in normal everyday situations makes it comparatively difficult to impose rigid patterns and establish unequivocal meanings. And when such situations occur in the pilgrimage context, the transformative potential of face-to-face interaction is considerably augmented. For ISKCON devotees in Vrindaban, this creates an environment ideally suited for the successful employment of acceptance strategies based upon presentation of Vaishnava and Brahman identities.

Pilgrims to Vrindaban anticipate the possibility of transformative personal religious experiences due to their understanding of Vrindaban's mystical nature. Their encounters with Western devotees are also affected by this mystical context, predisposing them to effective persuasion by the foreigners; they come with an "anything can happen" attitude. ISKCON capitalizes on this mystical belief in a variety of ways, including the distribution of fliers down to the village level throughout India with words such as: "VISIT HOLY DHAM VRINDABAN Where Lord Sri Krishna is performing His eternal pastimes. WE WELCOME YOU to join in His intimate pastimes with His devotees of INTERNATIONAL SOCIETY FOR KRISHNA CONSCIOUSNESS at Sri Krishna Balarama Mandir and International Guest House."[2]

---

[1] Morinis (1984) criticizes Turner's analysis of pilgrimage as a "grand scheme" which does not hold true for his own data on Bengali pilgrimage. Morinis, however, takes only a narrow view of Turner's notions of "liminality" and "communitas," suggesting that since among Bengali pilgrims "maintenance of inequality occurred" (257), it is not liminal. While it is certainly true that pilgrimage neither competes with nor destroys the structural significance of hierarchical stratification in normative society, still, it does uniformly provide the opportunity for the formation of new relationships and an environment wherein new meanings may be discovered.

Morinis focuses on the fact that Turner applies the term *liminality* to pilgrimage, a term that Morinis himself feels should only relate to rites of passage. In that vein he concludes that pilgrimage is not a liminal phenomenon because "pilgrimage is frequently not initiatory and does not necessarily mark a change in the social status (prestige or station) of the pilgrim" (259). Turner, I think, does not use the term in such a limited sense. Rather, pilgrimage is a liminal event precisely because it does remove the pilgrim from his everyday routine of structured activities and relationships. The pilgrimage journey places him in an environment that is full of possibilities for social, symbolic, and mystical transformations because it exists "between" or apart from the time and space constraints of everyday life.

[2] Flier distributed by ISKCON Vrindaban in spring 1982.

In all but a few instances, interactions with ISKCON devotees confirm for the pilgrim the reality of foreign Vaishnavas, and this is a minimal outcome. Indeed, for some pilgrims, especially members of the urbanized upper classes, their ISKCON experiences provoke a dramatic revival of faith in a traditional belief system that has been rejected in favor of a scientific world view. It provides for them a type of resolution for the conflict that they perceive exists between Hinduism and modern reality—a viable integration of East and West.

There are numerous examples from my data where pilgrims, through a series of interactions with Western devotees, have transformed negative perceptions about ISKCON into an evaluation that it occupies a legitimate place in the overall structure of contemporary Hinduism, an interpretation that has pan-Indian significance beyond the sociocultural boundaries of Vrindaban and the sectarian limitations of Vaishnavism. In this chapter I will present examples that represent the range of situational types wherein the pilgrimage frame combines with other contextual components to produce transformative interpretations. Specifically, situations between ISKCON devotees and villagers, Indian residents from small towns, and Westernized individuals from urban centers will be discussed. The cases presented here may appear one-sided to the reader since none reflect situations which result in negative evaluations by the pilgrims; although I searched for negative examples, none apparently existed. This is perhaps due to the limited amount of interaction time between pilgrims and ISKCON devotees which might have limited any opportunities for contradictory events. As chapter 6 will demonstrate, the resident population does not exhibit such uniformity. The empirical evidence, nevertheless, suggests that ISKCON has so mastered its impression management techniques with pilgrims that they are practically 100 percent effective.

THE YEARLY DISTRIBUTION OF PILGRIMS TO VRINDABAN

Although pilgrims from all over India arrive in Vrindaban throughout the year, some periods are more popular than others with certain regional groups. These pilgrimage patterns—although probably developed over long periods of time due to multiple factors such as agricultural cycles and family traditions—reflect the belief that one season of the year is more appropriate and beneficial than others for their particular "type" (jati).[3] Similarly, some periods that have more religious festivals than others, especially those associated with Radha and Krishna, draw many more pilgrims than others. This is important information for a community that relies primarily on pilgrimage as its chief economic resource, as well as for ISKCON which must be well prepared to present the desired front in the face of demands caused by large masses of people. Figure 1 presents these two distributions for the fieldwork period which, according to informants, were typical years.

This figure contains several types of information. India traditionally uses a lunar calendar, with each month beginning on the day after the full moon. Mid-month, therefore, is marked by the new moon. There are four days—*amavashya*, the day of the new moon; *purnima*, the day of the full moon; and the eleventh day of each fortnight, *ekadashi*—which are considered the most auspicious. In Vrindaban, local residents and people from surrounding villages visit temples in the largest

Figure 1. Yearly Distribution of Pilgrims by Month

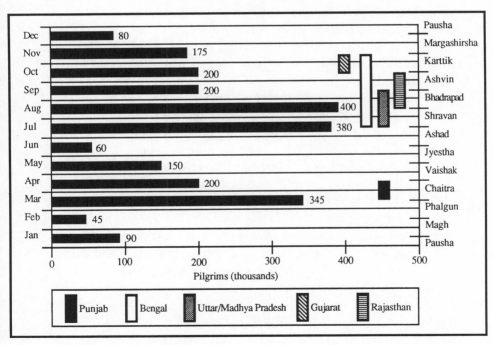

³ As indicated in chapter 3, jati does not necessarily refer to "caste." In Vrindaban the word is often used in a broader sense, meaning "type" or simply "group." Therefore, you may belong to a language jati, a region jati, a religion jati, etc.

numbers on these days in any month, excluding days of specific festivals. The month of Shravan, for example, begins after the full moon day of July and ends on the full moon day of August. The waning period of the moon is the "dark" fortnight, and as the new moon waxes, it is the month's "bright" fortnight. Days of the month, then, are numbered to indicate their position in the dark or bright half. Shravan is the month that usually ushers in the rainy season after a hot, dry summer, and in the temple of Banke-Bihari, the beginning of this season is ritually marked by a festival that begins on *tij*, the third day of the dark fortnight. On this night the "swing" festival (*jhulan*) at Banke-Bihari attracts around one hundred thousand pilgrims.

I have determined the number of pilgrims coming into Vrīndaban each month by a combination of techniques. First of all, toll gates are located at the two main entrances into the town, and all vehicular traffic is required to stop. The total number of people in buses, cars, and horse carts are counted, and a "pilgrim's tax" assessed according to that number. I was able to inspect records at these toll stations which are kept for a one-year period. Based on personal experience, the guards here are very conscientious in carrying out their duties, so I feel their records provide a good approximation of total numbers. However, there are many pilgrims who walk into Vrindaban, or enter the town in other ways. I therefore conducted monthly samples at the primary pilgrimage destinations to determine a rough estimate of attendance, especially on festival days. Assistants counted attendance at the same locations, and these figures generally coincided. After the toll gate data were compared to and adjusted by the sample results, these figures were discussed with key informants who agreed that they appeared correct.

While I trust the accuracy of the numbers reported in figure 1, the more important information is represented by the distribution patterns they reveal when considered over a full year, and these patterns are consistent with government surveys conducted in the past and with the information possessed by residents who know which periods are the busiest. One government survey conducted by the Uttar Pradesh Department of Tourism (1973: 44) shows a similar distribution. However, the numbers reported in the 1973 survey are roughly one-third the totals for the 1982–1983 period. ISKCON's Krishna-Balaram complex was opened in 1975, an event that both local people and the head of the Mathura tourist bureau credit with most of the increase. For example, the Antai Navami festival on the third day of the bright fortnight of

Karttik in November drew twenty-five thousand to Vrindaban in 1973. That evening in 1982 saw seventy-five thousand people pass through the doors of Radha-Vallabh temple alone.

The horizontal bars in figure 1 represent the total number of monthly visitors to Vrindaban in thousands. By the Western calendar, August has the highest influx of pilgrims, with July close behind. This, by far, is the most popular season of the year, falling as it does during the month of Shravan which extends from the full moon of July to the full moon of August. Included in this month is the festival of Janmashtami which celebrates the birth of Krishna. The fewest pilgrims come to Vrindaban during February and June, which are respectively the coldest and hottest months of the year.

The vertical bars show the predominant regional distributions of pilgrims during various times of the year. Throughout the year pilgrims from virtually every region of India, as well as some from Nepal, Pakistan, Bangladesh, and Sri Lanka can be found in Vrindaban. However, during specific periods, the dominant composition is as indicated. During Chaitra (March–April), many Punjabis (including Sikhs), arrive in Vrindaban. Gujaratis prefer Karttik (October–November), and Rajasthanis Bhadrapad (August–September) and Ashvin (September–October). Pilgrims from southern Uttar Pradesh and northern Madhya Pradesh are in evidence during Shravan and Bhadrapad. As might be expected, since the town of Vrindaban is largely a creation of the Bengal Vaishnavas, Bengalis make up a large portion of the pilgrim population over the longest period, extending from Shravan to Margashirsha (July through December). Figure 1 reflects that the month with the highest degree of overlap between regions is August, when the largest number of pilgrims visit Vrindaban.

ECONOMIC IMPORTANCE OF PILGRIMAGE

Since Vrindaban is a pilgrimage town, its economic vitality is directly dependent upon the pilgrims visiting there. This is not to discount the importance of agriculture in the surrounding area, nor other industries such as construction, crafts, and the provision of services, but these too rely heavily on pilgrimage for their viability. Vrindaban has primarily a market economy that fluctuates according to the number of pilgrims coming into town, and all segments of the population are affected by the pilgrimage flow, including beggars, merchants, craftsmen, dharmshala proprietors, rickshaw drivers, boatmen, priests, and other religious specialists. I have not undertaken a detailed economic analysis to establish the validity of this conclusion, nor are there any other private or government surveys that consider Vrindaban as a separate economic entity. Nevertheless, there is no doubt that the quality of life in Vrindaban depends directly on its continued popularity as a pilgrimage destination, and this correlation is illustrated by some economic data.

This type of information was the most difficult to obtain due to the fact that residents were always wary that I would use it to inform the government of unreported, or ''black market'' income. I cannot, therefore, confirm that the information presented here is completely accurate; yet, it does indicate that monthly income varies with the number of pilgrims present. The following data were derived from a questionnaire given to Loi Bazaar merchants and augmented by formal and informal interviews with them. Similarly, I obtained information about income from discussions with priests at six temples and proprietors of four dharmshalas. These individuals all agreed to discuss income provided that specific amounts, their names, and their establishments remained confidential. Figure 2 shows that there is a significant variation in the income averages for all three categories according to the number of pilgrims in the town.

The months of February, June, and August were selected because, as already noted, they represent the extremes: February and June are

Figure 2. Percentage of Yearly Income for February, June, and August 1983

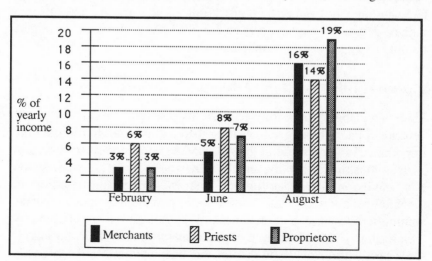

months with the least pilgrims, and August the most. It is evident from figure 2 that income does not correlate directly with the numerical distribution of pilgrims. If it did, we would expect the income for August to be almost seven times greater than June's, and nine times the amount for February. Obviously, there are many other variables which affect monthly income besides number of pilgrims. Still, the figures show that for the month of August there was a considerable increase in income over the other two months. For merchants, February income was one-fifth of August's, and June's was one-third. August income for priests was about double the amount taken in for both February and June. The largest difference was reported by dharmshala proprietors, whose August income was over six times the income for February; for June it represented almost a threefold increase.

Figures 1 and 2 convey the scope and importance of pilgrimage in present-day Vrindaban. For ISKCON, however, pilgrimage takes on more than economic significance. Through interactions with large numbers of pilgrims from all over the country, a process is initiated through which ISKCON devotees are achieving wide acceptance in Indian society. Demanding a considerable alteration of preconceived notions concerning the potential for the participation of foreigners in the Indian sociocultural system, this integration implies symbolic transformations of historical importance. In the remainder of the chapter I will describe situations of interaction that specifically demonstrate how these transformations are occurring, illustrating in the process how actors on both sides come to interpet the changes as continuous with their cultural traditions and personal identities.

SITUATIONS OF ISKCON-PILGRIM INTERACTION

There are numerous examples where pilgrims, through a series of interactions with Western devotees, have confronted the existence of ISKCON for the first time, or have been challenged to alter their conceptions about it and its place in the overall structure of contemporary Hinduism. Furthermore, through these situations some pilgrims have found a resolution of the perceived conflict between Hinduism and modern reality. This does not happen casually; rather, the pilgrims must be open to change, and the devotees must be perceived as correct and truthful in their intentions.

The motivation and disposition to engage in an activity and evaluate it as personally meaningful is established in the course of learning to engage in it. Consequently, the problem becomes one of describing the set of changes in the person's conception of the activity and of the experiences it provides him.

Learning through participation in the interactions associated with cultural performances and their related situations has long been a standard means of education and socialization in Indian society, especially for the rural majority. Hein noted in his 1949 study of the indigenous ras-lila dramas of Vrindaban and Mathura that whereas "continuity in other stable advanced cultures has usually rested upon well-developed institutions of formal education," in Hindu culture this process rests "upon another base . . . the existence of old, non-literary forms of Hindu education, through which the children of each generation have been trained in the lore fundamental to their culture " (Hein 1972: 1).

The Hindu temple, with its associated cultural performances, is one of the primary settings for the transmission of knowledge about Indian culture and society. Since the ISKCON temple exhibits enough congruence with the image of a traditional Hindu temple, the pilgrim is usually at ease within it, despite the administrative and ritual leadership of foreign priests. For the Indian, in other words, the setting appears to be a "normal" one.

The importance of normal appearances for the initiation and successful completion of situations of interaction cannot be overemphasized. This normalcy includes not only the perception of correctness in the physical setting, but also the perception that the other actors involved are not cynical or manipulative in their presentation.

Only when the conditions of normalcy are met can the devotees expect to conclude the temple situations as they intend, and considerable work goes into establishing an environment conducive to the pilgrim's feeling at ease. Yet, even if the Indian actors appear to behave in a receptive manner, their ultimate evaluation of the experience may be negative if they sense that these conditions have not been met. When this occurs, their final evaluation of the foreign devotees will likely be one of rejection rather than acceptance. An analysis of the actual outcomes, therefore, requires not only the observation of appearances, but an inquiry into the opinions of the Indian actors after the situation's completion as well.

In this section I will discuss three representative cases of interactions between ISKCON devotees and pilgrims. The first involves pilgrims from a rural village in north-central Uttar Pradesh near the Nepal border; the second concerns a family group from a town in Rajasthan; and the final one describes the experiences of a Westernized pilgrim from New Delhi.

Situations with Rural Pilgrims

During the course of his life, the rural pilgrim is likely to visit a wide range of religious shrines, some not belonging to any component of "great tradition" Hinduism. These may include sites and objects sacred to Sikh, Jain, Buddhist, or Muslim traditions, but due to the capacity for pilgrimage to integrate diverse elements into a coherent framework, no contradiction is sensed by those visiting them. As one Indian anthropologist commented, "The key paradigm of India's Hindu majority, mainly the village people, is 'cover your bases.' If there is a chance of benefit, visit any shrine, propitiate any god or saint, regardless of religious affiliation. Hinduism at this level can incorporate them all."[4] Extending this line of reasoning, then, visiting a temple or shrine established by foreigners has the potential for yielding just as potent an experience as a visit to an indigenous one, provided the site is interpreted as sacred by the devout pilgrim. At least there is nothing lost in the effort.

Consequently, the rural pilgrims who visit the sacred sites and temples of Vrindaban come to the Krishna-Balaram temple with an innate reverence for the deities there because the images appear correct and because they have been told by numerous authorities that it is a sacred place. This in itself does not confer respect and acceptance upon the foreign devotees, however; the pilgrims must be convinced of this by their experiences with the foreigners. If the experience at the ISKCON temple is a positive one, not only does a reinforcement and reaffirmation of their own cultural values and institutions occur, but the pilgrims are also compelled to consider the status of the foreigners who created and maintain the sacred site. The presence of Western religious specialists is a fact that can be learned and reconciled by the pilgrims—provided other expectations of normalcy are confirmed and no suspicions to the contrary are aroused.

On several occasions, I walked from Mathura to Vrindaban along with pilgrims, primarily from rural areas, who out of necessity or preference were traveling the last leg of their journey on foot. On one of these occassions, I set out from the Mathura Cant station with a large crowd of pilgrims who had just disembarked from the second-class cars

---

[4] Personal communication, Dr. Indra Singh, Department of Anthropology, Delhi University.

of a morning train. With me was a young Vrindaban sadhu, a key informant with long, matted hair who wore nothing but a loincloth, and carried his only possession—a handled wooden bowl. Upon sighting the "holy man," many in the crowd of several hundred put down their meager bundles and respectfully approached him, touching his feet, and saying "*dandavat maharaj*" ("I prostrate myself to you, great soul").

By this time I had become accustomed to walking barefoot, as the majority of local residents do, and due to the heat wore little more than my sadhu friend. Obviously, the crowd was curious about my presence, and questioned the sadhu at length. When he replied "We are guru-bhais," several then tried to touch my feet too, although most continued to regard me with polite curiosity. The sadhu was fully aware of my project in Vrindaban, and as we walked, both of us talked in Hindi to the pilgrims about their home villages, reasons for the pilgrimage, and the logistics of their journey. Eventually we settled into a discussion with a foursome from the village of Pallia near the Nepal border in north-central Uttar Pradesh, and before we reached Vrindaban it was agreed that the sadhu and I would accompany them during part of their Vrindaban pilgrimage, a visit that was planned to last three days. They explained that it was not good for average people to stay in a holy place for more than this length of time because they might unwittingly commit offenses that would be detrimental to their spiritual well-being. They also explained that it was difficult to handle the mystical intensity of such a sacred place for a longer period. So after three days in Vrindaban, their plan was to move on to Barsana, Govardhan, and Nandagoan—nearby villages associated with Radha and Krishna—before returning home.

These four pilgrims were lifelong friends from the same village—two married couples in their sixties who considered themselves to be in the retired order of life (*vanaprastha*). They explained that only now in their old age could they leave farming duties and family responsibilities behind and go on an extended pilgrimage, although they had visited other sacred sites closer to home, and one had visited the Himalayan holy place, Badrinath. Now their sons could manage their plots and look after their few buffaloes while they fulfilled religious vows. All four walked without shoes, dressed in well-worn, unbleached cotton clothing. The women both wore heavy silver wrist and ankle bangles, and the men had gold earrings in each ear. Their small bundles contained a few utensils, flour and rice to last them the entire journey, dung cakes for fuel, return railway tickets from Mathura, and about one hundred rupees between them.

The mid-June sun beat down on the pilgrims as they shuffled along the dusty road, lined now with dry, dead-looking trees and bushes, waiting it seemed, along with the local inhabitants, on the life-giving rains due to come in about a month. The crowd headed for Vrindaban, however, sang songs about the beauty of Braj, its lush forests, flowing river, dancing peacocks, and lustful maidens. And they sang of Krishna and Radha, someone shouting every few minutes *"Bansiwale ki jai"* ("Glory to the Flute-player [Krishna]"), *"Giriraj ki jai, Hari, Hari bol"* ("Glory to the king of Govardhan, Hari, shout the name of Hari"), or *"Jaya Radhe, Jaya Shyam, Jaya Shri Vrindavana dham"* ("Glory to Radha, Krishna, and Vrindaban"). Their mood was joyful and playful, but full of devotion for Krishna. It was a mood inspired by their understanding of Krishna's own "personality": as God he is both a mischievous, playful child, and an unmerciful destroyer of the demons who attack his devotees.

The pilgrims talked and joked among themselves, revealing that they had no idea about where they would stay when they reached Vrindaban. Maybe they could stay for free in some dharmshala, for none had enough money for accommodations; it was the hot season anyway, and the town should not be crowded. If not, surely they could sleep on the steps of a temple, at a ghat along the river, or perhaps somewhere on the parikrama path. Either way, they were not very concerned. Their plans for the three days in Vrindaban were just as open, but one thing was sure—they would be searching for Krishna wherever he could be found: "We will walk along the parikrama path looking for that flute player in every kadamb tree, and we will see him in every temple."

"Also at the Angrezi mandir (ISKCON)?" asked the sadhu. Laughing, one of the men from Pallia said, "We have heard only of this place. Maybe we will see for ourselves. If Krishna is there, we will find him; if not, why waste our time?"

As they passed the toll gate marking the entrance into Vrindaban, both women stopped, collected a handful of dust and tied it into the corner of their saris. They reprimanded their husbands for walking on, and demanded they stop and rub some of the dust over their foreheads before proceeding. This ritual, they argued, would ensure an auspicious stay in the town, and the men complied. Mizrapur dharmshala was about half a mile down the road, and they had decided to stop there to inquire about accommodations. No rooms were available without

paying one rupee per day, but they were welcome to stay in the courtyard along with a large number of pilgrims who were taking advantage
of the same offer. It was mid-afternoon by now, so they decided to stay,
and the men ordered the women to prepare a meal while they bathed
and rested.

In a baked mud oven provided by the dharmshala, one of the women
lit a couple of dung cakes and started to boil water for rice, and mix
dough for chapatis. The other walked up the road to a vegetable vender
and purchased a few potatoes and bitter melons. By six o'clock the four
pilgrims from Pallia had eaten, freshened up, rested, and were anxious
to begin their search for Krishna. The sadhu had declined an invitation
for the two of us to share their meal, but he promised to return in the
evening to guide them to the main temples and show them around
town. They had discussed hiring a panda, but decided it would be too
expensive, especially if the sadhu would show them around for free.

Around 6:30, my friend and I returned to Mizrapur dharmshala
where the four villagers waited on the steps, along with ten other pilgrims from a neighboring village that they had met during the afternoon. Banke-Bihari was the first temple they wanted to visit, and it was
also the first stop on the tour the sadhu had planned for the evening.
Although this was a relatively quiet time for Vrindaban, still the steps
of Banke-Bihari were crowded with pilgrims and residents pushing
their way in for the evening darshan. One of the women stopped to buy
a few flowers to offer the image, giving them to the sadhu who knew
one of the priests officiating that evening. He would give the flowers
directly to the priest who would give them special prasad in return. As
the sadhu left the group to find the priest, the pilgrims jostled for position before the image so they could have a good view when the curtains
were opened.

Since it was the hot season, the image of Banke-Bihari was taken
from his dark inner sanctum and brought forward on the raised stage at
the temple front. This was a cooler place for the deity whose altar was
lavishly decorated with complex designs created from jasmine blossoms. As the priests threw back the curtains, shouts arose from the
crowd and worshipers stretched their arms toward the image, ''capturing'' his blessing in their hands which they then touched to their foreheads, eyes, and chests. Some threw coins and flowers, and a spontaneous song that everyone seemed to know echoed throughout the
cavernous temple. All too soon, however, the curtain was quickly

closed, but only for a few seconds, then opened again, and this was repeated for about fifteen minutes.

"They are teasing us with such short glimpses of our Love," one woman cried. An off-duty priest offered an explanation to her for the "teasing" caused by the opening and closing of the curtain. Some pilgrims feel it is done to protect them from the intensity of the image's stare, but actually this ritual was implemented "to keep him in the temple." It seems that during one darshan long ago, one saintly worshiper gazed at the image with such pure devotion that Banke-Bihari followed him from the temple. Drawing the curtain every few seconds, therefore, prevents such a strong mystical bond from occurring, and consequently keeps Krishna where he belongs. "He is our child," the priest explained, "and it is our duty to protect him like this. What choice do we have for such a naughty boy?"

Our sadhu guide returned loaded down with several bowls of sweet prasad, and scores of hands clamored for it. Finally, he was able to get most of it into the hands of the pilgrims from Pallia, who gazed upon it reverently. The men soon devoured theirs, but the women only took a small taste, securing the remainder, again, in the folds of their saris, to be taken home and used sparingly. And then we were off to other temples for similar darshans.

One temple along the way was Radha-Damodar, and the pilgrims wanted especially to see the tombs of Rup and Jiv Goswami. They acknowledged no sectarian affiliation, yet wished to worship at the tombs of these Bengal Vaishnava saints. At this temple there is also a stone that contains several impressions said to be Krishna's footprint and the point of his staff, and we all waited in front of the altars while the priest unwrapped this holy relic—but not until several rupees were produced. On one of the courtyard walls hangs a large picture of Bhaktivedanta Swami who had once lived there, and it was noticed by all four pilgrims. Inquiring about him from the sadhu, our guide briefly told the story of how this Vrindaban babaji had gone to America and returned with foreign disciples to build a beautiful temple.

Before we left, several ISKCON devotees entered the temple, and the pilgrims stared intently, whispering among themselves. Finally, one of the men told the sadhu that they wished to visit the Angrezi Mandir next. Since it was getting late, however, he suggested this be put off until morning, and this provoked another discussion. Finally, their spokesman said, "Very well, we will go with you there for *mangalarati*, then we will do parikrama and see other places where Krishna can be found.'' Since mangal-arati is the first ceremony of the day, held between 3:30 and 4:30 every morning, the sadhu was not overjoyed at this suggestion, but agreed to take the villagers there anyway. We concluded our temple tour, made a quick inspection of Loi Bazaar, and said goodnight to our companions. It was already ten o'clock, and morning comes early for the pious pilgrim to Vrindaban.

Around 3:00 every morning, temple bells start to ring, signalling the morning services that awaken the deities. The exact time varies from temple to temple so that worshipers may attend several in a single morning, and for over an hour the bells create a haunting counterpoint to the early morning stillness. Although most residents and pilgrims have slept for only a few hours, many rise at this early period, considered to be the most spiritually charged time of day. As we walked towards the Krishna-Balaram temple at Raman-Reti, the pilgrims from Pallia talked energetically about their plans for the day.

The ISKCON complex faces Chhatikara Road, renamed Bhaktivedanta Swami Marg several years ago, and is situated just inside the toll gate that most visitors coming from Agra or Delhi pass. A high wall surrounds the entire compound which includes the temple, Bhaktivedanta's tomb, guest house, school, and living quarters for most of the devotees. Over the wall can be seen three high domes that mark the same number of altars in the temple below. Entry is gained by way of a side gate which brings one into a large, landscaped open area in front of the temple, and in one corner rises the ornately carved marble tomb of Bhaktivedanta. Actually, ''tomb'' does not properly describe this structure, for it is a temple itself, capable of holding several hundred people on three different levels. Incense wafted from the samadhi's interior where several devotees were conducting the first of seven daily ceremonies to their guru.

A uniformed Indian stood before the temple entrance pulling the rope which tolls a bell continuously during every ceremony. Large marble elephants stand guard on either side of wooden doors which open into a spacious interior courtyard paved in a black and white marble checkerboard pattern. To the front right of the courtyard, just before the raised deity area, a huge *tamal* tree grows through the marble floor. It was the largest, greenest tamal tree, a species sacred to Krishna, that the villagers had seen in Vrindaban, a place famous for such trees. One of the women commented, ''Krishna could not stay out of such a tree as this one.'' French crystal chandeliers illuminated the temple's interior with bright yellow light, dimmed now and then by billows of smoke rising from large pots of frankincense. Just in front of the images, about fifty young boys dressed in yellow and saffron dhotis played cymbals and drums as they danced and sang. "Here is surely *Golok* (Krishna's heaven)," one of the men commented as he stood and gazed at the spectacle.

In all, about one hundred ISKCON devotees, including the boys, were present in the temple for mangal-arati, the one ceremony a day they are required to attend without fail. But the temple can hold over a thousand, and it was nearly full at four o'clock that morning with Indian worshipers. The pilgrims made their way through the crowd past the lifelike image of Bhaktivedanta, whose feet they touched, and stopped before each of the altars gazing into the eyes of the images. On the left stand images of Lord Chaitanya and his associate Nityananda;[5] on the central altar are Krishna and his brother Balaram; and on the right altar are Radha and Krishna. All the images were clothed in yellow and red silk, wearing golden crowns, and draped with jewels. As they made their way back into the crowd, the pilgrims passed an American woman in an unbleached white sari, about the same color as their own clothing, who offered them a few flowers and some tulsi leaves. A Frenchman, the chief priest, emerged from the deities' sanctum, tossed holy water above the crowd, and distributed sweets that had been just offered to the deities to eager hands, including the four villagers. In response they folded their hands in respect and smiled widely at these two ISKCON devotees; one of the men touched the pujari's feet, who returned this gesture with a slight bow. No words were spoken, and the group kept silent until we had walked several hundred meters away from the temple along the parikrama path.

At this point, I wish to reflect upon the situation in the Krishna-Balaram temple just described. During the course of this study, I have analyzed the "situations" by considering five interrelated components: the actors, the scene, acts occurring, the actors' purpose or motivation, and symbolic agencies used. (The relationships between these components are diagramatically presented in appendix 3.)

The scene is the full context which frames the activity within a situ-

---

[5] One of Chaitanya's key assistants, and his primary disciple that remained in Bengal rather than Vrindaban, Nityananda is also considered divine. Bhaktivedanta taught that Chaitanya and Nityananda were identical to Krishna and his brother Balaram. Consequently, one of the reasons for establishing the temple in Vrindaban was "to broadcast to the world that worship of Gaura-Nitāi [Chaitanya and Nityananda] is the same as worship of Kṛṣṇa-balarāma" (ISKCON Vrindaban Newsletter, April 1983: 3).

ation, and is the creation of each individual actor. When individuals come into each other's presence, a situation begins if there is some mutual agreement—stated, assumed, or emergent—concerning a goal or object focus, and at that point each actor ''generates'' his scene. It consists of all the resources the actor draws upon to help him understand the situation and interpret its meaning. It is the ''world'' the actor is in for the duration of the situation.

The pilgrims from Pallia are *jats* by ''caste,'' farmers by occupation, and their religion is an integral part of their daily lives. They propitiate various gods for different purposes, some being only local deities, others the main gods of Hinduism including Shiva, Ganesh, Durga, and Krishna. For this pilgrimage, their mind is focused upon Krishna, although they do not necessarily consider him the ''supreme god.'' Rather, he is only one of the forms through which the Godhead may be worshiped, albeit a major one. They know how a temple should look, where the images should be placed, and what type of activity should go on.

The devotees of ISKCON have constructed their temple, furnished its interior, and act within it by standards which coincide closely enough to the villagers' expectations for the setting to seem normal to them. Therefore, the scenes generated by both parties—the villagers and the devotees— are largely consistent. In other words, they generally agree that the physical aspects of the temple setting are appropriate, correctly placed, and meaningful; they interpret Vrindaban as a mystical location; and they accept the revitalizing potential of the pilgrimage experience. ISKCON devotees conceive of Krishna as the ''Supreme Personality of Godhead'' and wish to convince others of this, but in the pilgrimage setting they usually must settle for less. If the situation arises, they will make their case for the supremacy of Krishna, but it is not necessary for the pilgrims to share this view for temple worship to occur. Most temples are sectarian with the priests affiliated with them often seeing their particular deity as the highest, but the debate is ultimately between religious specialists and does not often concern the pilgrim.

The actors themselves are objects of the scene for the other actors in it. For the villagers, foreign priests are a novelty. They have no previous experiences with them on which to base an evaluation, and are not convinced initially of their ''correctness.'' The main variable, then, is the meaning of the foreign actors. Following the situation scenario, therefore, there is basic object agreement; the scenes generated by all actors coincide sufficiently. Likewise, there is meaning agreement for all objects except the foreign actors, and as the situation proceeds, evaluations, interpretations, and reinterpretations will be going on in the pilgrims' minds concerning them.

The ISKCON devotees are keenly aware of such interpretive dynamics, and their goal is to achieve positive results. It is not a purpose openly stated or suggested to the villagers, for they have no need to be aware of it for the situation's successful conclusion by ISKCON's criteria. So in this sense, it is a "manipulation" on the devotees' part. It should be noted, however, that the foreign actors have other purposes as well, one being to worship the deities correctly for the mystical and practical benefit it may provide; and this is also a purpose—the primary one—for the Indian actors.

No conversation took place here between the ISKCON devotees and pilgrims, yet the situation was concluded in a manner that has significance for all the actors in it; a manner that was not predetermined, but resulted from the developments over its course. For both the Indian and foreign actors, changes occurred during the situation that made their worlds a little different than before. For the villagers, it incorporated the foreigners into the Indian cultural category of Hindu priest. For the ISKCON devotees, it expanded their world of "significant others," those individuals who contribute to and reinforce (positively or negatively) the foreigners' self-conceptions.

We can discern two distinct phases of activity in this situation, a type that regularly occurs at the ISKCON temple. First of all, there are elements that do not include any actual person-to-person encounter and do not depend on any communication, tacit or spoken. Rather, the different parties establish a feeling of normalcy and trust as each observes the other as the situation progresses. Goffman (1971: 5) states that "as the two parties approach each other, each provides progressive evidence to the other, a small step at a time, that each is adhering to a proper course of action and to the one he has been indicating." As long as there is no apparent attempt at trickery, disruption, or confusion, an evaluation of normalcy and trust will be sustained. This aspect of the situation is not simply a matter of individuals properly playing their respective "roles," but rather is a process consisting of a progressive series of detailed actions, observations, and interpretations, one predisposing and leading into the next.

Each step the pilgrims took after entering the temple compound successively and increasingly sustained the positive impression of foreign devotees and priests correctly performing as they would expect Indian devotees and priests to do in an Indian temple. The setting and performances, of course, were staged by the ISKCON personnel to accomplish this very outcome. Moreover, part of ISKCON's "back stage" strategy entails the creation of a "spectacular" effect by a display that is considerably more opulent than the Indian pilgrim, especially the villager, is expecting. Consequently, the situation did not simply appear correct to the villagers, but the experience was magnified to such a degree that they felt it was something extraordinary—from Golok, Krishna's perfect realm.

Every situation requires a minimal amount of this type of activity in order to establish trust and a perception of normalcy. Actors that are familiar with each other require less of this type of work, but in a situation where the actors have no prior relationship, and especially if there is reason for some actors to be suspicious of others, this behavior is essentially preparatory to any actual face-to-face communication.

The other discernable type of activity in this situation was an actual face-to-face encounter between the Indian actors and ISKCON devotees, and communication occurred although no words were spoken. The devotees' presentation of leaves, water, and sweets to the pilgrims was more than a religious performance because it resulted in an interpersonal response from the pilgrims. It was a "supportive interchange," to use Goffman's terminology—a brief, interpersonal ritual that establishes a mutual bond of good will and appreciation. Another type of ritual was also going on in the temple, a ritual between man and the supernatural; but the ritual which occurred between the Indian and foreign actors was not essentially different since "ritual," in the most general sense, is any conventionalized act through which an individual demonstrates his respect and regard for some object of perceived value to that object or its symbolic representation.

Not only did this situation establish for the pilgrims that foreigners could perform correctly as priests, and that the temple had a supernatural aura about it, but it went further than this by establishing a personal connection between the actors, something that does not always occur between worshipers and religious specialists in most Hindu temples. Usually, the distribution of prasad is handled by intermediaries between priest and worshipers, or if the priest gives it directly to them, it is dropped or tossed from within the deities' sacred enclosure which is often on an elevated stage. In Krishna-Balaram, however, the priest not only approached the pilgrims at eye-level, but also met them outside the deities' enclosure. As I later discovered, this increased proximity did not decrease the foreigners' status in the villagers' eyes, but augmented it by demonstrating a personal concern for them. The villagers could have rejected the presentations, or simply walked away without affect. Instead they smiled broadly and touched the foreign priest's feet, which he acknowledged with a bow. Superficially this brief interchange may appear unimportant, but for the villagers it was a crucial initial step in the transformation of their personal symbolic systems to incorporate the concept of non-Indian Hindu priests. Furthermore, when the similar experiences of hundreds of thousands of pilgrims that visit this temple yearly are considered, their consequences for ISKCON's integration into Indian society become considerable.

Walking on along the river as the sun began to rise, the villagers commented that this experience had been a fitting one to begin their first full day in Vrindaban. The conversation dwelt not so much upon the fact that foreigners were in charge of the temple, but on how beautiful the temple was, and how contented Radha and Krishna seemed to be there; that obviously the deities liked the treatment they were receiving from ISKCON. One of the men concluded that if the deities accepted the foreigners, then so should they. The women wondered about the American girl they had encountered. She wore a widow's sari, one thought, and regretted that one so young must live without a husband. The sadhu suggested that perhaps her husband had just taken sannyas, and the women replied, "It's the same thing."

The parikrama path winds its way along the river to Keshi Ghat, the most popular spot for bathing on the Jumna, and all four decided to have a "holy dip." As the first rays of sunlight pierced the horizon the pilgrims shouted "jai ho" ("glory to it") and uttered appropriate mantras as they entered the cool water. Bathing in a sacred river, especially the Jumna or Ganga (which are seen to be essentially the same since they merge at Allahabad), is a core ritual for all devout Hindus and its importance cannot be overestimated. The river absorbs and removes past sins as it flows away. Its flow is analogous to the circulation of blood through the body, and bathing in it "tunes" the circulation. The Jumna is also "liquid shakti," literally the energy of Krishna, his female life-force. Accordingly, the river is seen as the goddess.[6] It does

---

[6] Rarely is a male deity considered a complete manifestation of the Godhead. Krishna is worshiped with Radha, Rama with Sita, Shiva with Parvati, Narayan with Lakshmi, etc. The term *goddess* or *mother goddess* also applies in some instances to a female aspect of the deity seen as the supreme divinity. Durga or Kali represents such formulations. When the Jumna is called a

not simply symbolize the goddess, but is actually she, and this active energy cannot be altered by man. A bath in the river, then, is one of those direct contacts with the supernatural that is easily and readily available; it requires no priestly mediation or invocation for the divinity to be present because the river is the divinity.

Jumna Devi, as the pilgrims addressed the river, is approached slowly and with great respect. First, a few drops are sprinkled upon the head, then gradually the pilgrim enters the water. Handfuls are ladled and returned to the current, then poured over the body. Finally, the body is repeatedly immersed until the worshiper feels satisfied. As the men were donning the dhotis which they had removed for their bath, and as the women were replacing their wet saris with identical dry ones, they began to discuss some of their Vrindaban experiences. Among other things, they talked about their experience at the Krishna-Balaram temple. They had been impressed with its beauty, filled with devotion to Krishna, and impressed with the foreign priests.

Yet, there was some apprehension. Surely they made good priests, but priests themselves were not always deserving of the respect they demanded. After all, Indian priests are sometimes incompetent and lazy, performing their role only for its financial benefits. What do these foreigners really feel for Krishna, for Vrindaban, for the Jumna? ''They will not drink or wash in the sacred waters,'' one man suggested. ''It is dirty to them, so they avoid it fearing disease. That is the difference. To die from drinking this water is *mukti* (liberation), for them it is hell.'' The pilgrims will return several times to the river, insuring their utensils, amulets, jewelry, and clothing are properly purified by its water; and they will collect some to take home.

As they secured their belongings and prepared to move on, an ISK-CON teacher and his students from the gurukula—walked past the pilgrims and stopped at the landing some twenty feet way. The pilgrims watched as the devotee spoke for several minutes to the students, then saw the group remove their clothing except for loincloths, and enter the river. The four villagers looked at each other, the men giving the pervasive left-right nod of the head that indicates approval. ''So they are after liberation, too,'' he said, ''more Indian than *videshi* (foreigner).'' One of the boys waved as the pilgrims walked by, and his greeting was

goddess, therefore, there is this dual implication: It is simultaneously an ''incarnation'' of Radha and the mother goddess.

returned with the traditional salutation, palms pressed together and raised to the forehead.

This was not a staged encounter by the devotees in the same sense that the temple performances are staged, yet there was preparation for it. Both written and oral instructions are given to all ISKCON members who come to Vrindaban concerning behavior and demeanor in public. It is stressed that they are "on stage" whenever they leave the temple precincts and devotees are thoroughly schooled concerning interaction with "outsiders." Some of these instructions are printed in a pamphlet written by temple authorities and distributed to all devotees:

> Always endeavor to give a good impression of ISKCON; Maintain a reserved demeanor in public; Do not wear shoes on parikramas; Married ladies should wear kum kum [the red powder applied to the hair's part indicating marriage]; Ladies' heads should always be covered; Never eat with the left hand; Do not purchase prepared food from outside shops; Indicate respect to everyone you meet in Vrindaban, regardless of station. Do not socialize with rickshaw drivers, bhangis [sweepers] and other lower class people; Do not argue with rickshaw drivers or merchants; Always wear bead bag and chant in public; Show full respect to Yamuna River. Take ritual bath, but do not swim for fun or engage in horseplay at public ghats. (ISKCON Vrindaban 1983: 11)

These instructions clearly illustrate ISKCON's concern with the devotees' presentation of self in public, even when this may conflict with ideology. While they should "indicate respect" to everyone in Vrindaban, they should nevertheless avoid socializing with people from "lower" classes. If devotees are to "socialize" with any local residents, Gaudiya Vaishnava ideology would suggest that "caste" or class should not be one of the criteria considered in the formation of relationships. However, since Indian Brahmans do not socialize with the "lower castes," then neither should devotees. Apparently a concern for appearing Brahman-like practically overrides the egalitarian aspects of their religious philosophy.

For devotees who are themselves pilgrims to Vrindaban, these instructions are helpful for protecting the reputation of ISKCON as a whole. For those who live there, these are points of cultural etiquette that everyone is expected to follow. So although the ISKCON devotees did not go to the river on this occasion to impress anyone specifically, the likelihood of such an encounter was virtually guaranteed, and they were well prepared for it. They are instructed to avoid at all costs any incident that will present ISKCON in a bad light or where they will be required to explain why they acted in a disreputable manner.

Negative situations occur, however, and when they do, the devotee is put on the spot to save face and the image of ISKCON in general. There are several "famous" incidents that have required delicate handling, but less publicized ones happen often. One occurred later in the day as the four pilgrims from Pallia were returning to the dharmshala for an afternoon meal and nap, and it required considerable remedial work from the devotee concerned.

There is only one temple in Vrindaban that excludes foreigners, and devotees are strongly cautioned to respect this rule and not to try to force the issue. The temple of Ranganath, usually called Rangji, is a branch of the South Indian Shri Vaishnava sect, and has very strict standards of entrance. An attempt is even made to exclude Indians wearing Western rather than traditional clothing, although this restriction is not uniformly enforced. One of the most elaborate and dominant structures in town, this temple has several large festivals every year, and one was in progress during the visit of the Pallia villagers.

Approaching Rangji, which the pilgrims passed as they walked from central Vrindaban back to Mizrapur dharmshala, they noticed a large crowd gathered around several people who were shouting at each other. An ISKCON devotee had managed to enter the temple undetected by draping a cloth over his head as some sadhus do, and sneaking in with the crowd. As he exited, however, he was spotted by one of the priest-guards who loudly and quickly summoned reinforcements to evict him. He was roughly escorted out as the priests announced to everyone within hearing range that a videshi had trespassed onto the sacred grounds, polluting the ritual, and spoiling the day for everyone in attendance. The devotee, known around Vrindaban for his outspoken opposition to Rangji's policy, yelled back just as loudly that he was a Brahman whose presence was auspicious, not polluting. The interchange was heated with neither side willing to give any ground, and others quickly became involved.

Many Vrindaban residents consider Rangji's attitude outdated. In fact, at one time this temple allowed ISKCON devotees to enter, but the policy was discontinued when the priests decided it was too difficult to discern which foreigners were devotees and which were "hippies." Since that time the position that all foreigners were polluting had re-emerged. As the scuffle reached the temple gates, a large crowd of Vrindaban residents and pilgrims gathered to listen and participate, and sides were generally taken along sectarian lines. Those considering themselves members of the Shri Vaishnava sampradaya took the priests' point of view; other Vrindaban residents supported the devotee. Most pilgrims observed from the sidelines, talking among themselves.

Evidently the incident had sparked old sectarian rivalries and the ISK-CON devotee, realizing that he had been caught in the act, ultimately wished to extricate himself as honorably as possible by acting with contrived humility. One priest shouted to the devotee, "You are a despicable troublemaker!" to which the foreigner replied in broken Hindi and English, "I am indeed a Brahman, but one that is not worth the horsedung in the street. You are all my gurus, and I was here only to learn how to properly worship God."

A merchant from Loi Bazaar shouted to the priest, "You are the foreigner here (the sect being a South Indian one). He is more Brajbasi than you. What do you know of Krishna? (Rangji is a temple to Rama.) Krishna accepts the videshi's devotion but I wonder if he accepts yours."

The devotee forced himself to be heard over the crowd and claimed ignorance of the rule, although most residents knew that this was not the case: "I am a fallen and ignorant soul. Accept my apologies and my obeisances. Krishna is not so biased, so I will only go to his temples from now on. He is my only lord."

The priests retreated to their temple with some in the crowd cheering, others jeering them. A few pilgrims broke ranks to acknowledge the devotee with a softly spoken "*sadhu, sadhu,*" while others simply stared. He walked away from the scene with several of his Loi Bazaar acquaintances who scolded and praised him at the same time. The devotee had made the best of a difficult situation.

The villagers were only peripheral to this situation, but as they walked back to the dharmshala the interactions they had observed became the topic of conversation. The men argued among themselves about Rangji's policy of excluding foreigners and other "untouchables." One felt that it was both reprehensible and illegal, the other rationalized that the priests were just upholding tradition and should not be criticized so severely.

One of the women interjected that since the devotee knew the rules, he was therefore a troublemaker and got what he deserved. Her husband responded that Gandhi was also a troublemaker and sometimes the troublemaker was right. He added that he felt the devotee was correct in his actions and that Krishna-Balaram was a superior temple because all people were welcomed there. He explained that all people were the same in the eyes of Krishna and Rama, and asked why men should discriminate when the gods did not, concluding that the priests of Rangji were "hateful" men.

The second woman sadly reflected upon the incident. She asked why this was happening in such a sacred place. The priests did not behave as she thought Brahmans should. "Where are the real Brahmans today?" she lamented.

The sadhu jokingly queried, "At the Angrezi Mandir?" One of the men nodded and laughingly said, "And that is the state of our civilization. No more Brahmans, so we must recruit from America." His friend, also laughing, added, "It's a good joke, but one that has some truth."

For the four villagers at least, the devotee apparently succeeded in making the best of the situation. Not only was he able to salvage his own reputation, but the pilgrims furthermore concluded that it was the Indian priests at Rangji who were in error. The Krishna-Balaram temple, in the final analysis, was evaluated to be more consistent with their own cultural expectations than the Indian temple of Ranganath.

The pilgrims from Pallia continued their visit to the main sites in Vrindaban during the afternoon of their third day in town, and that evening they returned to Krishna-Balaram for a final darshan. The women also wanted to speak with the girl they had encountered there earlier to find out why she was wearing the dress of a widow, since each had her own opinion.

They found this American girl at the visitors' desk in Bhaktivedanta's room, now preserved as a museum, and were surprised that she spoke fluent Hindi. As they discovered, the reason for her austere dress was neither widowhood nor her husband's renunciation. She was indeed married, but by her own decision (agreed to by her husband) had taken vows of celibacy and austerity. There is no formal institution of sannyas for women in Indian society or in ISKCON, but informally, a number of Hare Krishna women have taken this step. The village women found this action extreme, agreeing that it was "not natural"; still they respected her for it. The devotee gave them some Hindi ISKCON literature, and talked to them about the supremacy of Krishna and about her guru. Soon the women rejoined their husbands and concluded their Vrindaban pilgrimage with another round of the main temples and a visit to Loi Bazaar.

Quite by accident, I had the opportunity to visit these pilgrims in their home village later during my stay in India. In Delhi I had met the parents of an Indian friend, a lawyer educated at Oxford. His father was a prosperous Sikh landowner and farmer, his mother an English lady who had met her husband in London. They lived near Bareilly, not far from Pallia, and invited me to spend a few days at their farm. While there, I visited the four Vrindaban pilgrims, and was greeted hospitably. We reminisced about Vrindaban, and one of the women told me that the Angrezi Mandir had been the high point of their pilgrimage. "It is the number one temple there," her husband added.

In one corner of the tidy but sparse house, constructed of mud and cow dung, was a family altar that included a number of brass images and lithographs of several deities and holy men. It was an eclectic assemblage, but one that was worshiped daily and regularly. The husband pointed out two small images of Radha and Krishna that his wife had purchased for four rupees on their last night in Vrindaban. "After talking with the videshi woman, she wanted to purchase some murtis. We had a big argument, but she bought them anyway. Now Krishna is here with us; we have brought him back from Vrindaban."

A Family from Kota, Rajasthan

Four generations of the Maheshwari family from the town of Kota in Rajasthan came to Vrindaban for five days during the month of Shravan in 1982 and stayed at Kishor Ban, the pilgrims' hostel where I was living. The ten relatives, ranging in age from five to seventy-eight, had wanted more space, but since it was one of the most crowded times of the year, centered upon the festival of Jhulan, they had to settle for two single rooms that were separated by a third. In that room lived an English ISKCON devotee, a resident of Kishor Ban for several years.

The Maheshwaris are an extended patrilineal vaishya family that share a large house in their home town. The family includes the patriarch, Satya Narain, his son and wife, two grandsons and their wives, and three great grandchildren, all boys. I first became aware of this group of pilgrims around four o'clock the morning after they arrived, when gathered in one room they all began singing *bhajans* (sacred songs), accompanied by two drums. Unnoticed, I observed them through a window as everyone joined in the singing. The next morning the same thing happened, but this time the ISKCON devotee sat among them, drum in lap, leading the singing.

This family's first encounter with ISKCON was not at the Krishna-Balaram temple, but a personal contact with Prahlad, the devotee at

Kishor Ban. Soon after their late afternoon arrival, the men had met
Prahlad in the office of Kishor Ban's Brahman proprietor, Govinda
Kishor Goswami, where he and the devotee often sat and talked. After
introductions, the Maheshwaris invited Prahlad to visit them for tea,
and he accepted the invitation for the following afternoon. Prahlad explained that he did not drink tea, but would be happy to visit with the
family if he was allowed to bring a sweet rice pudding called *khir*.

Evidently the visit had been a success since Prahlad joined the family
for early morning devotions on their second day in town. After the
bhajans, Prahlad went back to his room, and the men sat talking on
Kishor Ban's rooftop while the women prepared breakfast. Satya Narain reminisced about his first visit to Vrindaban in 1928 and how
things have changed since then. He explained to his sons and grandsons:

> This was a quieter place in those days; it was little more than a village. Loi
> Bazaar was a small dirt road and Kishor Ban was just like a jungle. No
> electricity, of course, and fewer people were coming for pilgrimage. Who
> knew exactly where Vrindaban was? We were devotees of Shri Krishna, so
> my mother insisted to my father that we must come on pilgrimage as she
> was getting old. I knew of Vrindaban by name, but where it was, that was
> a mystery. Now, who in India does not know where is Vrindaban? Who in
> the whole world does not know?[7]

His son and grandsons listened attentively as the old man spoke, one
of the younger men finally breaking into the soliloquy with, "And what
about these videshis, what about this Prahlad?" Satya Narain replied,
"He is a Krishna bhakta, of that I am now convinced. He knows more
bhajans than you do, and he plays pakhawaj much better."

"I think he is a strange one, a misfit in his own country," the other
grandson added. Satya Narain was pensive for a few seconds and then
said, "Who are you to say? This man is a sadhu. He is living here in
Vrindaban for so many years in poverty and thinking only of Krishna.
Sanatan dharma[8] is his life, so how can he be a misfit? I think now as
an old man about these things, but if I had been a wiser young man, I
would be better off now."

"Babaji, do you mean that you should have become a sadhu as a

---

[7] All quotations from Satya Narain and his family translated from Hindi.

[8] *Sanatan dharma* literally means "eternal religion," or perhaps more accurately, the eternal,
"natural" duties and responsibilities of man. Since "Hindu" is not an indigenous word, many
Indians prefer this term to label their religion, which they see as a general way of life.

young man instead of having a family and being well-off? Are you regretting your successful family now gathered around you?''

''Sadhu or householder is not the point. I am saying that I pushed Krishna to the back, being only concerned with money and luxuries. Now I see this Prahlad which Govinda Kishor explains comes from the best English family, and I see how he has chosen to live for a better purpose. We should learn from this example.''

Satya Narai's son then inquired, ''But father, how do you explain these Western devotees? Always sanatan dharma has been the property of Indians alone. Why do we see American Hindus now? What do you think?''

The old man's reply was based upon his own cultural knowledge. ''These people come here to Vrindaban due to samsaras, their karma. Now, due to the modern world, a person born in America comes to India for his spiritual benefit while in the past they would have to wait for the next birth. There is really nothing new, it is just faster. Due to the good fortune of American birth, the facilities are there to benefit from karma without first death and rebirth in India. So I think there is no difference. Coming to Vrindaban by jet plane or by transmigration of the soul, the process is the same. It is always resulting from karma, so there is really no difference.''

''You have become philosophical in your old age, Baba,'' replied one of his grandsons. ''It is a very thoughtful explanation.''

One of the wives called the men in for breakfast, and the conversation ended. They would visit the ghats and sacred sites around town during the day and were looking forward to the Jhulan festival at Banke-Bihari temple in the evening, the single most attended temple ceremony of the year. The following day the family would visit Krishna-Balaram, although it had not been high on their agenda. They would go out of politeness to Prahad who had personally invited them. Later that night after the Banke-Bihari swing festival, the entire family sat in a Loi Bazaar cloth shop with Govinda Kishor Goswami, and as the women inspected saris and shawls, the men talked about the day's events.

Next morning the entire family attended mangal-arati at Radha-Raman and several other temples, bathed at Keshi Ghat, and circumambulated the town. After resting, they all walked with Govinda Kishor and Prahlad to the ''Glass Temple'' which was managed by Govinda's father and brothers, and then went to Krishna-Balaram by rickshaw.

Prahlad, a teacher at the gurukula, left the party to attend to some business, and after an hour, they returned to Kishor Ban.

The morning of their departure, the men again sat with Govinda Kishor in his office, and the goswami questioned them about their visit. Satya Narain said it was the best pilgrimage he had been on, and that he would return the next year if he were still living. His son and grandsons, who had expressed reservations about ISKCON and the legitimacy of foreign devotees at the beginning of their stay, were now lavish in their praise:

Son: "Krishna-Balaram is now Vrindaban's finest temple, I think. The others are wonderful also, but it is the best."

Grandson 1: "I have to agree. They have built a fine temple with the highest standards. I believe Vrindaban is now centered on the Angrezi Mandir."

Grandson 2: "It has the richest and finest worship I have seen. My sons laughed at the goswamis in Bihariji, but they stood with their mouths open at Balaram temple. My wife purchased a Krishna coloring book for them; such things cannot be found elsewhere. One has asked me if he could be allowed to join them and if they would take him to America. That would be better than some other nonsense things he might do."

Govinda Kishor: "My oldest son goes there often and has enquired also. But he plays cricket very well, and I may see to his education as a professional player. If that doesn't happen, he must remain here. He must be prepared to take over my responsibilities here someday. I asked him what would happen if all the Vrindaban boys joined ISKCON. Vrindaban would turn into ISKCON city (everyone laughs). Anyway, ISKCON will continue here—it is a benefit—but Vrindaban will also continue undisturbed. Vrindaban is eternally the same and cannot be really changed."

Satya Narain: "It is India's best place. Krishna is still alive and well here."[9]

The experiences of the Maheshwari family in Vrindaban introduced them to ISKCON primarily through interactions with a single devotee. Some members of the family were initially reluctant to take the foreign devotees seriously, but by the end of their stay they evaluated the devotee they had met as a sadhu, and saw the ISKCON temple as the best in town. They had come on pilgrimage as a devout Hindu family, and in

[9] Translated from a conversation in Hindi and English.

Vrindaban had expanded their conception of Hinduism to include ISK-CON. The next case, however, shows how a Westernized pilgrim, generally cynical about her traditional belief system, experienced a revival of her religious beliefs largely due to her experiences with ISKCON devotees.

The Westernized Pilgrim

Striking examples of meaning transformations during pilgrimage occur among highly educated, Westernized Indians who, prior to their Vrindaban experiences, are content to put aside Hinduism in favor of a scientific world view. But since the force of Hinduism is so pervasive in Indian society, a psychological tension often exists, and the superficial knowledge of the existence of American and European Hindus only serves to complicate the contradictions they perceive. They often come on pilgrimage as cynics, classifying their visit as a vacation or educational trip. Still, as Turnbull (1981: 76) has pointed out in an article comparing the similarities between the pilgrimage journey in India and other places and the "vacation trip," the same conditions of liminality exist, and the potential for transformations is still there. For an understanding of the processes of learning and meaning change which occur in this environment for the urban pilgrim, it is again best to consider a concrete example. The case of Marathi, an English-educated travel agent from New Delhi, will serve as a clear illustration.

Nominally classifying herself as an *advaitin*,[10] Marathi also claimed agnosticism during our first meeting in New Delhi. "Agnosticism is the only intelligent philosophical alternative." At this time she was planning a cultural tour of Agra and vicinity for a group of Belgian students and scholars, and I suggested that she might add Vrindaban to her itinerary. Agreeing that this would be a novel diversion from her regular schedule, several months later I was invited to join the tour for three days around Agra and a day and night in Vrindaban, with accommodations there at the Krishna-Balaram guest house.

With an art degree from London University, Marathi was well qualified to discuss the fine points of Mughal architecture at Fatepur Sikri and the proportional perfection of Agra's Taj Mahal. As we entered Vrindaban, however, her enthusiasm faded, suggesting to us that the

---

[10] *Advaita* is the impersonal, nondualistic interpretation of the *Upanishads* and *Vedanta-sutra*, especially the nontheistic system presented by Shankara. The Vaishnavas of Vrindaban are united in their distaste for advaita since it precludes the dualistic conception of Krishna as supreme god and man as his devotee.

old temples there were only the crude medieval attempts of unskilled artisans. Perhaps she had failed to study the texts that discussed the architectural significance of the Govindadev temple, or the relevance of Madan-Mohan's spire in the evolution of Hindu domes and Buddhist stupas.[11] Navigating the narrow streets of Vrindaban in our air-conditioned bus, she also revealed her distaste for and apprehension of ISK-CON: "These people are here for some ulterior purpose; we should be watchful of them." Arriving at Krishna-Balaram temple, however, her mood momentarily changed as she viewed the complex for the first time. Its style reminded her of the Lake Palace at Udaipur, a structure she admired. But as we were immersed in the circular flow of pilgrims inside the temple courtyard, her distaste returned. Pointing to an elderly man prostrating himself before an image of Bhaktivedanta, she loudly asked, "How can we win the battle over superstition when the Americans themselves are putting on this display?"

But over the course of the next three days, Marathi was involved in a series of interactions that resulted in a transformation of her attitude toward ISKCON and of her own religious identity. A number of important situations occurred where either new information was presented which she would ultimately evaluate as positive, or in which she would experience an emotional state prompting a reevaluation of her religious outlook.

Awaiting room assignments at the ISKCON guest house, Marathi was approached by a Dutch devotee conversant in both Hindi and Flemish. Identifying himself as our guide, Radha-Govinda offered to conduct us around the grounds before we settled in. He first took the group to a well-appointed room containing a scale model of the temple planned for Mayapur in Bengal. When completed, he explained, this would be the tallest building in India with a dome larger than St. Peter's in Rome. Marathi refused to comment about the structure, asking instead, "Is it your organization's intention to prevent India from becoming a modern country? These traditions have held us back for centuries, and now you are pushing us further back." Radha-Govinda countered, "Try to understand us without animosity, otherwise we will remain enemies. This can never lead to good. Consider that perhaps your traditions provide everything necessary for progress. Prabhupad taught us

[11] For a discussion of these points concerning the architectural significance of Vrindaban temples, see Growse 1979: 241–57.

that modern technology can be used in the service of Krishna. If Krishna is pleased with India, then India will achieve greatness.''

The group was next led to ISKCON's school where an English class was in session. Radha-Govinda explained that several of the male students from Uttar Pradesh villages were studying on scholarships. ''Perhaps they are doing some good after all if literacy is being increased,'' Marathi concluded. ''Certainly education is the first step, and discipline is needed also. God knows there is discipline here!''

Finally, we were escorted to a visitors' lounge where a film concerning the life of Swami Bhaktivedanta was shown. At its conclusion Marathi thanked our guide and revealed that some of her initial assumptions concerning ISKCON were in the process of revision. ''Your guru was certainly an amazing man, and some of what I see here also amazes me. This is a slick film. Who produced it for you?'' Radha-Govinda responded, ''ISKCON. Written, filmed, edited, and produced by devotees. In our society is the ability for every kind of project no matter how difficult. If we don't know, Krishna provides the training.''

Returning to the guest house Marathi remarked, ''These people are more complex than I thought. They are no dummies, I can see. With their money and dedication I'm not sure whether to be very impressed or very worried.''

The events that transpired during the first afternoon in Vrindaban had served to give Marathi new information about ISKCON. After an hour's rest, the group boarded rickshaws for a tour of the town's temples; the upcoming evening's events, with ISKCON fresh on her mind, would provide Marathi with an emotional experience which she was initially determined to avoid.

For two hours we were in and out of temples for their evening darshans. The final stop was at the temple of Radha-Raman, the traditional seat of Gaudiya Vaishnavism in Vrindaban, and in a large hall near there one of the temple priests had arranged for a concert of Drupad music,[12] followed by a talk and discussion. It became apparent that Marathi had been moved by the temple darshans and the mass experience that bhakti Hinduism provides in the temple setting. She commented that inexplicably she was feeling a freshness that had escaped

---

[12] Drupad is a musical style that, according to tradition, was sung at Krishna's circle dance with the gopis. Literally meaning ''fixed verse,'' the style was especially associated with courtly traditions of the sixteenth century. Drupad is seeing a revival in Vrindaban, with incorporation into the contemporary ras-lila dramas, representing one of the surviving forms of medieval Indian culture.

her since childhood. This was, according to the priest, a direct result
of the transcendental quality of Vrindaban, something that was impossible to escape.

Being especially affected by the temple of Radha-Raman, she asked
the priest if she might stay overnight there in order to attend the 4:00
A.M. darshan the next day. He complied, and several others remained
there as well, continuing the discussion before retiring. The conversation centered around Krishna, Vrindaban, and ISKCON's history in the
town. Responding to Marathi's final question about devotees, the priest
said, "They are continuing the tradition of Lord Chaitanya; we accept
them as part of the sampradaya. It has been good for our tradition.
Before Prabhupad went West, we knew him here—one sadhu among
many. But when he left for America, he became empowered by
Krishna. There is no other explanation; so we are happy about foreign
Vaishnavas." Marathi whispered to me as she went to her room, "This
is hard to believe, isn't it?"

After the first darshan the next morning at Radha-Raman, Marathi
trekked with other pilgrims to Keshi Ghat for a ritual bath in the Jumna.
With hair still wet, she laughed and said, "I may never leave Vrindaban. There is a peace here that I do not have in Delhi." We walked the
two kilometers back to the ISKCON complex, stopping in the bazaar
along the way, chatting with shopkeepers, pilgrims, and sadhus.

At the Krishna-Balaram restaurant for lunch, Marathi met the temple
secretary, a thirty-two-year-old American girl from the Midwest. They
talked privately most of the afternoon. Marathi later confided to me that
she felt she had made a new friend.

An affective bond had been established that would tie Marathi to
ISKCON through regular correspondence. Such personal relationships
represent one of the primary means for recruiting members and attract-
ing supporters to ISKCON and other similar movements. For Marathi,
the beginning of a friendship with the temple secretary proved to be a
key factor in changing her attitude about the Hare Krishna movement.

On their final day in Vrindaban, the group had lunch at Vraja Academy, an institution founded by a well-known sadhu whose stated mission is the preservation and dissemination of Vrindaban culture. Also
in attendance were dignitaries including the district magistrate from
Mathura, the former Maharaja of Kashmir, and several professors from
Agra University. The sadhu lectured in fluent but sometimes confusing
English, yet his message was pointedly clear: the religious, artistic, and
social significance of Vrindaban is central to pan-Indian consciousness.

"It is the centrum of Indian culture," he explained. Due to this speech, Marathi was certain that the sadhu had gained psychic insight into her state of mind at the beginning of her Vrindaban visit, feeling that his words were specifically directed at her. As the group started to board buses back to ISKCON for a rest before departing for Delhi, she gathered them together and said, "I apologize to you for my negative attitude when we first arrived here. I did not know better, but these days have been an important education for me. My life has been changed, and that is not easy to admit."

With the Belgian group waiting in the bus, Marathi finally emerged from the temple office, smiling and carrying several books. Since I was remaining in Vrindaban, I said farewell and Marathi took my hand, leading me behind the bus. Opening her handbag, she showed me two shiny images of Radha and Krishna which she had purchased in the bazaar. "They will not go in my display case," she whispered, "They will be properly worshiped every day so that I can always remember Vrindaban." Finally, she disclosed that she had become a life member of ISKCON by donating 3333 rupees (about 300 dollars), and planned to become involved in its Delhi activities.

Several months later I visited Marathi and her husband at their New Delhi apartment, and the Radha-Krishna deities were dressed in blue silk, garlanded with marigold and jasmine flowers. "You know," she said to me, "I'm not fully a devotee of Krishna, but it took Westerners to teach me about my own culture, to make me unashamed of it. Someday I may even take sannyas. I can live at ISKCON temples anywhere as a life member. Who knows?" Marathi continues to guide Indian and foreign tourists to destinations throughout India, and her "Agra Package" now includes Vrindaban. My last meeting with her was in Vrindaban, where she was guiding a German group through the streets of the town which she now knows well. She was wearing the *tilak* (forehead marking) of the Gaudiya Vaishnavas.

CONCLUSION

Just as Marathi has communicated her experiences in Vrindaban to people in her own social networks, other pilgrims from all parts of India return with accounts of their journeys, all but a small percentage having visited the Krishna-Balaram temple during their stay.[13] The

---

[13] Survey data indicate that 98 percent of one-day pilgrims to Vrindaban visit the ISKCON com-

flow of information inherent to the pilgrimage journey, therefore, has an effect upon the conceptual, symbolic, and social systems in places far from Vrindaban, and the extended impact of pilgrimage there warrants further study.

The institution of pilgrimage in India incorporates all social groups (including "untouchable" ones) and economic classes, and any understanding of social and cultural processes in India must therefore take pilgrimage into consideration. While there is no information that systematically analyzes pilgrimage distribution according to caste or economic criteria, my observations suggest that Indian society is reflected in microcosm in most pilgrimage populations.

Poverty is apparently no obstacle for the pilgrim. Even the poorest villagers manage to travel to far-flung sacred places today, following the Hindu injunction to wander the length and breadth of India for spiritual benefits, primary among them being a better birth in the next life. Some informants insist that pilgrimage has even healed them of incurable disease and rejuvenated them in old age.

Only in Vrindaban (and perhaps in Mayapur,[14] which seems to be increasing in popularity as a pilgrimage destination), however, do pilgrims encounter the Western devotees of ISKCON. The situations presented in this chapter, and other situations similar to them, indicate that several types of encounters occur there that are leading to a broad integration of Western bhaktas into the framework of modern Hinduism. The most pervasive situations are the ones that take place in the Krishna-Balaram temple, and few pilgrims leave Vrindaban without participating. Even if this includes only a brief stop for darshan, sup-

---

plex. For pilgrims staying two or more days, only 6 percent fail to go there. It may seem logical that pilgrims staying for a longer period in Vrindaban would be more likely to visit the Krishna-Balaram temple, but this is empirically not the case. Short-term pilgrims prioritize the sites they intend to visit, and ISKCON is usually high on their list. If traveling by bus, the Krishna-Balaram temple is likely the first place they will stop. Those pilgrims that stay longer often have sectarian affiliations that determine their activities which may revolve around only a few temples and sacred sites. Although most express the intention of seeing the ISKCON temple, they sometimes never get around to it.

[14] Mayapur, the birthplace of Chaitanya, is not as significant a place of pilgrimage to India as a whole as Vrindaban is. Its history as a popular pilgrimage site only dates back to its "rediscovery" and development by Bhaktivinod Thakur in the early part of this century (see chapter 4). Yet, for ISKCON, Mayapur is just as important as Vrindaban, and their establishment of a temple and ashram there has attracted pilgrims, especially Bengalis, in large numbers. Because of heightened Hindu-Muslim tensions in Bengal, and the popularity of the communist party there, ISKCON tends to be more intimately involved in political affairs in Mayapur than in Vrindaban. Research at this site would yield important additional information concerning the overall picture of ISKCON's situation in India.

portive interchanges occur that at least inform the pilgrim of the existence and legitimacy of foreign priests.

For many visitors to Vrindaban, there are also personal encounters with Western devotees that have consequences when they are evaluated by the pilgrims. ISKCON members are agressively engaged in positive impression management, and this includes avoidance of situations where negative impressions may be formulated. When these do occur, the devotee is concerned to minimize the damage through remedial behavior, and this too may reinforce legitimacy in the pilgrims' eyes.

Furthermore, for Westernized Indians, their experiences in Vrindaban may act to resolve psychological tension caused by a perception of dichotomies between East and West, traditional and modern. The number of life members recruited by ISKCON from affluent pilgrims to Vrindaban indicates that individuals from this segment of Indian society are among the most affected by their encounters.

Temple performances provide an important foundation for ISKCON's Indian strategy; yet, situations of personal interaction, especially those that establish affective bonds between Indian and Westerner, have the highest transforming potential. Their importance can be seen in the situations discussed above.

ISKCON's strategy of impression management with pilgrims is amazingly effective. This is largely due, to the liminality of the pilgrimage experience and the limited number of interactions most pilgrims have with devotees during a short stay. Success with permanent Vrindaban residents, however, is dependent upon creating positive impressions and sustaining them over a long period. In situations of interaction between ISKCON devotees and Vrindaban residents, the transforming power of personal relationships can be most clearly seen.

Symbolic Interactions in Vrindaban Town: Making Sense of a New Reality

SYMBOLS do not simply stand for other things; they bring things into meaning. During situations of interaction or sequences of situations, people attempt to work an unfamiliar reality into forms they can understand. In the everyday life of Vrindaban, Indian residents are faced with making sense of the reality of foreign devotees in terms of their own cultural system; as people who live there repeatedly say, "Vrindaban never changes."

The symbols used in interactions between ISKCON devotees and Vrindaban residents are common to both parties, but since meaning is not simply "stored" in the symbols, there is no guarantee that ISKCON and Indian actors will evaluate and use these symbols in the same way. Even within the same culture, common symbols can have different meanings for different people; when individuals from "outside" the culture who are attempting to become part of it use the same symbols as people within it, differences in meaning should especially be expected. Coming to terms with the meaning of these symbols is therefore a crucial part of everyday life in contemporary Vrindaban.

Culture does not bestow meaning, people do. In Vrindaban, actors from both sides are trying to make sense of common symbols, and there is an effort to determine what the symbols "really" mean; how they should be properly used. The common symbols, the objects they refer to, and the meanings actors attribute to them must be brought into new relationships. In this sense, Vrindaban culture is being reorganized as a result of Indian-ISKCON interactions, though most residents will still say that it has not really changed.

Although the situations of face-to-face interaction between ISKCON devotees and Indian residents of Vrindaban have appeared to some observers to be isolated episodes outside the bounds of normative Indian society (Hawley 1981; Burr 1984: 231–38), this is not the case today. Normative principles that regulate Indian social organization apply to these interactions as well; moreover, many of the sociocultural norms of Indian society are reinforced by these interactions. Ultimately, it can be seen from the interactions described in this chapter that both ISKCON and Indian actors are striving for short-term, practical agreement, as well as long-range, cultural resolution of divergent symbol meanings. It is a fact that ISKCON is in Vrindaban, by all indications, to stay, and foreign devotees and Indian residents have no choice but to deal with this reality. This is being done not by mutual isolation and an emphasis on contradictions, but by incorporation and resolution through interaction. It is a process that Indian informants themselves describe as an attempt to understand the meaning of ISKCON in Vrindaban. This method of coping is not so much a conscious decision on the part of Vrindaban residents, as it is the natural consequence of the town's core values of tolerance of diversity and respect for individuals who conform to norms of behavior and belief, and the firm conviction that all events that happen in Vrindaban are part of Krishna's lila.

As a result, everyday life is able to continue in much the same way as it always has, with ISKCON devotees trying to conform to the local ideals, and residents accepting them as long as they do generally conform. The sociocultural system that is created in the process is a new one because it incorporates the Westerners who have traditionally been excluded; the concept of ISKCON (and more generally, foreign) Brahman, or at least ISKCON and foreign Vaishnava, is being created. At the same time the system is still conceived as traditional because it makes sense in terms of and is continuous with the preexisting one.

In this chapter I will demonstrate the transformative dynamics of this cross-cultural conjuncture by describing situations that involve ISKCON devotees in three interactive domains: with merchants in Loi Bazaar, with temple Brahmans, and with the youth of the town.

LOI BAZAAR

There are five principal bazaars in Vrindaban whose shops sell diverse types of merchandise. Before ISKCON's arrival in Vrindaban, Gopinath, Purana, Pratap, Retiya, and Loi Bazaars were perceived as being about equal in importance to the town's economy. Today, however, Loi Bazaar is referred to as "the best bazaar," or "the expensive bazaar," and far exceeds the others in economic productivity.[1]

---

[1] The average reported income per business in Loi Bazaar is 630 rupees per month (about $63).

A merchant who sells beads in Purana Bazaar commented on the present state of affairs: "There is no reason why Loi Bazaar should be most important. When I was growing up, everyone earned about the same, according to his efforts. Today, if you wish to be wealthy, Loi Bazaar is the place to be. ISKCON has made this situation. I am not bitter because devotees still buy from me because I have superior quality merchandise, but they put most of their money in Loi Bazaar."

Loi Bazaar derives its name from a type of blanket made from recycled cloth. Formerly, this was the primary merchandise sold in the bazaar, and other markets were similarly specialized according to products. One sold mainly beads for necklaces and rosaries, one had shops that manufactured and sold gold and silver jewelry; one bazaar dealt principally in staples and spices, another in vegetables and milk products. Informants suggest that diversification of the bazaars was gradual, but by the early 1950s, their makeup had become basically the same as it is today.

Table 3 shows the present diversity of Loi Bazaar shops according to type of merchandise sold or services rendered.

In the bazaar today are ninety-nine operating merchant businesses, seven darmshalas, four warehouses, two temples, and four private residences. Twenty-seven shops sell cloth and clothing in some form, composing about 30 percent of total businesses in the bazaar. Fourteen deal in spices and/or staple food items (rice, flour, ghee, potatoes, tea), and ten market fresh milk and milk sweets (sweet merchants are called *halwai*). There are six general merchants; seven sell betelnut products (*pan*) and tobacco; five shops sell pots and utensils; and four market fruit and/or vegetables. There are five *kantiwalas*, individuals who make and sell neckbeads and rosaries, primarily from tulsi wood. Four shops sell metal images and religious paraphernalia;[2] there are four electric shops; and three shops manufacture and sell gold and silver

---

The lowest monthly income reported for Loi Bazaar was 250 rupees (a sweet shop), the highest was 3000 rupees (a cloth store). Average monthly incomes (in rupees) for the other bazaars are as follows: Purana—350, Gopinath—300, Pratap—270, Retiya—175. The highest reported monthly income in these bazaars was 450 rupees. As noted in chapter 5, accurate information concerning income was the most difficult to obtain. This is especially the case in Loi Bazaar, where merchants are reluctant to admit their full income since much of it is unreported to the government; the Loi Bazaar figures may therefore reflect lower than actual incomes. In other bazaars, however, few merchants have this motivation to lie about their income, primarily because they do little or no business with ISKCON devotees. Cross-checking opinions of various Vrindaban residents over the course of the study indicates these figures are reliable.

[2] *Wala* is a suffix roughly meaning "person"; murtis are images and their makers and sellers are *murtiwalas*; *mukuts* are crowns for the deities and those who make and distribute these and other ritual supplies are *mukutwalas*.

Table 3. Loi Bazaar Businesses

TYPE	NUMBER
Books	1
Tailor	1
Shoe	1
Paint	1
Health	2
Chapatis	2
Tea Stand	2
Jewelry	3
Electric	4
Fruit / Veg	4
Religious	4
Beads	5
Pots	5
General	6
Betel	7
Sweets	10
Spice	14
Cloth	27
Total	**99**

jewelry. There are two tea stands; two shops that sell cooked chapatis; and two health-related businesses (one pharmacy, one clinic). There is one paint store, one shoe store, one tailor, and one store that rents books. Three positions in the bazaar are occupied by people who distribute free cool water (*pyao*).[3] There is one post office and one research institute affiliated with Agra University. The Vrindaban Research Institute, however, has recently broken ground for a new building in Raman Reti, near ISKCON.

The two temples in Loi Bazaar are small, but unique. One has the largest *shalagram* in Vrindaban, some say in all the world. (The shalagram is a rounded stone that contains a fossilized spiral cone shell which bears a resemblance to Vishnu's discus like weapon, the *chakra*, and is therefore worshiped as a Vishnu or Krishna deity. They are found only in one location in north-central Nepal.[4]) The other temple is notable because it shelters stray cows. Every evening, cows from all over Vrindaban find their way back to this temple, climb the stairs, are fed, and sleep inside the temple itself.

A casual stroll through the bazaar reveals that some of the shops are

---

[3] Free water is distributed by residents of Vrindaban who are self-supporting or have some other institutional support (such as widows who live at charitable institutions). They perform this activity as a community service and to gain spiritual merit.

[4] See Shapiro 1979 for a discussion of the shalagram and its importance in Vrindaban.

doing much better than others. Some have wooden floors and are minimally furnished with wooden shelves; others have marble floors, comfortable cushions for patrons, and glass display shelves. The businesses in the latter category either now have or have previously had an active economic relationship with ISKCON. Most of these have enjoyed continuous, long-term patronage from the devotees, while several others have recently been "blacklisted" by temple authorities.

During temple meetings and on bulletin boards around Krishna-Balaram temple, devotees are informed about which Vrindaban businesses temple authorities suggest they should favor, and most of these are in Loi Bazaar. With shops situated on either side of a quarter-mile street, Loi Bazaar is not only the principal market area today, but is a prime location for casual conversation, gossip, circulation of rumors, and the dissemination of all types of information as well. Much of the gossip and information, and many of the rumors concern ISKCON.

The Mahesh Kumar Cloth Shop Incident

Those merchants who respect members of ISKCON as Vaishnavas and do large-scale business with them often must walk a fine line between the practical demands of business and their devotional sentiments. The ones who have been successful in this attempt have profited the most. ISKCON tends to favor those merchants who are Gaudiya Vaishnavas, see Bhaktivedanta Swami as a jagadguru, and openly support ISKCON as part of the Chaitanya religion. The shopkeepers who have become the most affluent were among the early moral and financial supporters of the foreign devotees in Vrindaban. Many became life members of ISKCON when the devotees first came to Vrindaban, requiring a sizable initial donation (around five thousand rupees for businesses), and have responded with financial support periodically throughout the organization's tenure in the town. ISKCON reciprocates this support by promoting these merchants to devotees who come on pilgrimage, and buying supplies for the local temple operation from them.

One of the first supporters of ISKCON was Krishna Ballabh Kumar, a Gaudiya Vaishnava who heads one of the most successful businesses in Loi Bazaar. His three sons participate in the business, each nominally owning his own shop as part of the integrated family enterprise. Mahesh, the oldest son, became friends with some of the senior devotees when they first came to Vrindaban, and these relationships served to establish him as one of the devotees' favorite cloth merchants. For many years ISKCON recommended that its members purchase cloth items from Mahesh's shop, and when the temple administration decided to lease shops to Indian merchants at their complex, Mahesh was one of the first to be invited. Not only did ISKCON devotees do business at the shop he opened there, but Mahesh also profited from a brisk pilgrim trade.

Mahesh made periodic donations and invested heavily in a stock of items that appealed to a mainly ISKCON market. These specialized items included the saffron dhotis and *kurtas* (shirts) worn by all celibate ISKCON males, as well as kurtas and *chadars* (shawls) imprinted with the Hare Krishna mantra. These Hari Nam chadars have since become very popular with pilgrims.

From 1978 to 1981, Mahesh spent much of his time and energy establishing and expanding his business at the ISKCON complex, to the exclusion of his operation in Loi Bazaar which was maintained by his father and brothers. Although he was required to become a life member of ISKCON, gave additional monthly donations to the temple, paid rent on his shop space, and extended credit to many devotees, his profits were still large. In 1981, however, a new ISKCON administration decided to end the policy of allowing Indian businesses to operate on temple grounds.

Mahesh, along with four other merchants with shops there, was shocked and angered to learn they were being evicted, and decided that they would do everything they could to stay. Their shops were just too successful to give up without protest, and they felt that this new policy was being pushed by a few uninformed individuals; that most devotees wanted them to remain there. In July 1982, one devotee expressed this opinion concerning the situation:

> There is a "cold war" now going on between the ISKCON administration and the Kumar family. Devotees owe Mahesh about 10,000 rupees for things bought on credit, and some of this will be difficult to collect because they are no longer here. Mahesh is legally right, I think, so there is really no chance of this going to court. It will probably continue at a stalemate for a time, and then the conflict will be forgotten. The temple will rethink its position, and then Mahesh and the others will remain out here. Seems to me there is just too much benefit for us to go through with this eviction.

Temple authorities, however, remained adamant although they did not want the negative publicity that a forced eviction would create. Instead, they blocked access between the temple proper and the shop area, forcing would-be shoppers to walk completely around the complex to another, almost hidden entrance. According to Mahesh, this virtually eliminated the heavy daily pedestrian traffic by the shops and decreased monthly income by more than half.

This "cold war" continued for about a year. The temple opened its own "boutique" which stocked many of the same items sold in the shops, and tried to persuade devotees that they should avoid the Indian businesses out of loyalty to ISKCON. Signs around the devotee ashram were posted reading "Keep Lakshmi devi in ISKCON," "Lakshmi" being the goddess of fortune and a synonym for money. Mahesh tried to rally his ISKCON support on several fronts. He encouraged devotees to purchase cloth from him in Loi Bazaar, and asked his long-term ISKCON friends to intercede with the temple hierarchy. He also had one of his assistants solicit business among the pilgrim crowds at Krishna-Balaram.

The temple administration neither changed nor reconsidered its position, and in February 1982 filed a suit against the shopkeepers who still refused to leave. In April, Mahesh's father made an appointment to present his case before the ISKCON governing board chairman who oversees the administrative area in which Vrindaban is located. He was never granted an audience with this official, being interviewed instead by his secretary. Both Mahesh and his father were willing to negotiate to avoid going to court, but they were never given the chance. They wanted above all else to keep the shop and were willing to pay an increased rent, make more donations to the temple, and forget the debts owed by devotees. If this was not agreeable, they would leave peacefully if two conditions were met—payment of debts owed to them, and reimbursement of money they had personally spent making improvements on the shop. The Kumars never received a reply.

According to Mahesh, a suit in India usually takes about seven years before it is heard in court. He thinks that the decision should be made in his favor, but believes that ISKCON will probably use its political and financial resources to influence the case somehow. He would try to influence the court himself, but feels impotent in the face of ISKCON's institutional power. The shopkeepers have now all left their temple shops, ISKCON has proceeded with new construction that eliminates any commercial space within the temple compound, and at the most Mahesh thinks he may eventually receive a token monetary compensation as a result of the case. His thoughts concerning these events reflect an attempt to make sense out of ISKCON on two separate levels:

I have some bad feelings with ISKCON because of this. Not only have I lost so much money, but I have also lost time, and that is even more dear. Three hard years I put into building up my ISKCON store that could have been spent building up a business elsewhere. But I do not hate ISKCON. There are some devotees that I love dearly, many are trying very hard, just like me, to be good bhaktas. It is not so easy. Some will always buy from me no matter what the temple president says. . . . ISKCON is Vaishnava and I am also Vaishnava. Prabhupad was a great saint, so these are really small things. But I don't like the way they do business. Some of them are too ruthless, not gentlemen. So I still love ISKCON devotees, but not as businessmen. What is the choice?

Even in the face of being cheated out of money and time, Mahesh and his family do not have a completely negative view of ISKCON. He considers devotees as generally sincere in their religious endeavors, and a few he even describes as holy men. This incident, however, has made Mahesh more aware of variation within the local ISKCON population. "Brahman or *bhangi* (sweeper), people are people. Some you can trust, some you cannot," he rationalizes. His present attitude is to treat devotees on an individual basis and to get on with his life and business. Mahesh has subsequently directed money that in the past would have been donated to ISKCON into other religious endeavors. Presently, he is coordinating an effort, along with several ISKCON and ex-ISKCON devotees, to renovate the "tooth samadhi" of Gadadhar Pandit, an associate of Chaitanya.[5]

The big winner in this dispute has been another cloth shop, run by the family of Ganga Prasad on the other end of Loi Bazaar. Before this incident there was roughly an even distribution of ISKCON cloth purchases between Ganga Prasad and the Kumar family business. Now most go to Ganga Prasad, who has the reputation of being the wealthiest of all Loi Bazaar merchants. The Prasad family, also Gaudiya

---

[5] Gadadhar Pandit Goswami is one of the Pancha Tattva (literally, five elements or realities). Although Chaitanya is considered Krishna, the full incarnation of Krishna's energy includes four of his associates as well. Besides Chaitanya, in Bengal Vaishnava theology the Pancha Tattva includes Nityananda, Advaita, Gadadhar, and Shrivas. Gadadhar is therefore considered a divine incarnation. In a flier distributed to residents of Vrindaban, Mahesh Kumar wrote:

Śrī Śrī Gadādhara Paṇḍita Gosvāmī, associate of Śrīman Caitanya Mahāpraphu, is amongst the Panca-tattva and is Śrīmatī Rādhārāṇī amongst the associates of Śrī Krṛṣṇa. . . . This Samāja (samādhi) is now crumbling like so many other monuments of devotion. Are you going to be a silent spectator or are you going to get out of your selfish stupor and take this opportunity to do your duty to help preserve our heritage? You can help NOW!

Vaishnavas, are probably the most ostentatious in their show of support for ISKCON, and often defend devotees when criticism arises from pilgrims and other merchants. Ganga Prasad himself, nearly eighty years old, bases his position on a high regard for Bhaktivedanta whom he knew well as a resident of Vrindaban. Sitting beneath a large portrait of Bhaktivedanta in his shop, he responded angrily to a pilgrim from Bombay who voiced criticism of the swami and his disciples:

> What do you know of gurus? There are so many gurus in this town, so many who have traveled outside India, but absolutely none of Prabhupad's caliber. Of course some devotees are still not very realized, but give them time. They are at least making a good effort. What is your effort? Citizens of Vrindaban should give support and respect for these devotees out of duty because they are part of Prabhupad's energy. They should make us ashamed of our own devotion. They are a sign from Krishna that even in this dark age of kali yuga the world is not completely doomed.

Mahesh Kumar, despite his bitter business-related feelings, is still a valuable asset for ISKCON, especially in controlling the spread of rumors that often sweep through the bazaar. The number of rumors, many fantastic in content, indicate, if nothing else, the high degree of interest the population of Vrindaban has concerning ISKCON activities. The most potentially explosive rumor that occurred during my stay in the town took place in early May 1982, at the height of tension between ISKCON and the shopkeepers they were trying to evict. This rumor had spread so widely that residents of surrounding villages and pilgrims from Delhi were inquiring about it.

Regularly, stories are told about ISKCON's being an arm of the CIA, that in their temple are sophisticated intelligence acquisition devices, that devotees are stockpiling weapons to stage an overthrow of the Indian government; and detractors often use these unfounded rumors to augment their criticism of the foreigners. But these rumors rarely inspire any overt reaction from residents.

Early one morning, however, a small crowd that had gathered in front of Mahesh's shop was engaged in a heated argument. Two shopkeepers, who are among ISKCON's severest critics, had rallied supporters and were demanding that everyone in the bazaar march to ISKCON and "force" the devotees to leave Vrindaban. The rumor was circulating that the temple had been closed by the army because a member of India's parliament had been murdered in the guest house. The politician was supposedly there to establish and publicly disclose that weapons, including an "atom bomb" were indeed being stored at Krishna-Balaram.

Since he had just returned from the ISKCON complex, Mahesh knew that the Krishna-Balaram temple was not closed, and that these rumors were false. He implored those who were causing the disturbance, therefore, to go with him to the temple and see for themselves.

The merchants and their supporters refused to accompany Mahesh to the ISKCON temple. Instead, they dispatched a "servant" to investigate who returned with a report that basically verified Mahesh's account. By the next day the rumor had subsided, replaced with speculation about why the president of India was coming to Vrindaban, and why he was staying at ISKCON. This single incident served to dissipate a building anti-ISKCON sentiment in the bazaar. Not only did Mahesh gain supporters for ISKCON by his firm stance, but he also won considerable political clout in the bazaar, and was selected as the informal "president" of the Loi Bazaar merchants' association.

After this incident, vocal animosity toward ISKCON largely subsided, and three shopkeepers who had never been to the Krishna-Balaram temple accompanied Mahesh there for the first time. The experience transformed their rumor-based negative opinions, and drew them over to Mahesh's side. Even after his "betrayal," and in the face of a prolonged legal battle with ISKCON, Mahesh is still instrumental in the transformative process that is changing how Vrindaban residents perceive the foreign devotees. Rumors still fly, but few people take them very seriously anymore.

An Explainable Beating

The interpretation that Vrindaban is actually Krishna's supernatural habitat and that events there must be seen as part of his often incomprehensible play, works time and again in ISKCON's favor. This goes beyond simply accepting devotees as part of a common religious system; residents seem compelled to explain even the most negative episodes involving ISKCON devotees by employing a supernaturally based interpretive framework. The following incident demonstrates how strong this tendency is.

A poor but educated Brahman, Brij Bihari, was employed by Gopaldas, a British devotee and seven-year resident of Vrindaban, as a secretarial assistant and interpreter. During the course of their association, Gopaldas became increasingly dissatisfied with Brij's work and personal habits, culminating in a scene where he struck the assistant solidly with a staff. The young Brahman ran away angrily and in tears to the Loi Bazaar shop of a friend, one of the less affluent cloth merchants.

The shopkeeper's initial response was sympathy for Brij and animosity toward Gopaldas and ISKCON, but this emotional reaction was simultaneously tempered by his admission to friends that Brij was indeed lazy and prone to bad habits. After a few days' reflection on this event by the merchants in Loi Bazaar, an interpretation developed that contrasted considerably with the initial one. The merchant, who is not one of ISKCON's enthusiastic supporters, incorporated this situation into a broader cosmological framework, as part of Krishna's Vrindaban lila: "Some problems are there . . . but all are part of Krishna's Vrindaban. We cannot understand. Gopaldas is crazy, Gopaldas is demon—these things are heard. But he is really *avadhut* (a holy man not bound by rules of society). Who are we to say? We cannot understand. This is the Vrindaban; this is Krishna's lila always. Gopaldas is part. Briju is part.''

Vrindaban residents do interpret situations according to norms of right and wrong, good and evil. However, they still remind each other that ideally things must not be seen so simply; that there is hidden meaning in events that superficially seem to violate normative rules of behavior. Such potentially negative events as the one just described initially create animosity toward ISKCON, but later are often interpreted by an invocation of broader cosmological resources. Certainly there is a tension between these two interpretive compulsions, and there are logical limits beyond which a supernatural framework would probably not be utilized. No murders, rapes, thefts, or other felonious crimes were committed by any ISKCON devotee during my stay, so I cannot say how such events would be handled by the population. Such an incident would certainly pose severe problems for ISKCON. But after appropriate punishment of the offender, ISKCON would survive, at least in part, because of the invocation of a supernatural frame.

The Tailor's New Son

In a few cases the religious context of ISKCON interaction with the merchant community has served to integrate devotees deeper into the local culture, though sometimes they are reluctant participants. The following case demonstrates how such interaction may serve to alter social and cultural precedent.

Prahlad, the English devotee living at Kishore Ban just off Loi Bazaar, is well known to the people there. In the bazaar Prahlad purchases fine silks and cottons and has a favorite tailor whom he regularly contracts to make kurtas and other garments. While his penchant for fine clothes might appear to conflict with his devotee status, Prahlad explains that he does not claim to be a sadhu who has taken vows of poverty; yet, he is still respected as a "first-class" devotee by many Vrindabanbasis. People in the bazaar observe his early morning baths in the Jumna, his making the temple rounds, his constant chanting; and Prahlad's goswami landlord often has gossip to pass on concerning the devotee's renunciation and observance of religious ritual.

Shortly before the incidents that I am about to describe occurred, the goswami passed on to the regulars in the bazaar two bits of information which served to immediately frame the events that would transpire: Prahlad had joined ISKCON in London at age thirteen and from that time had maintained celibacy, a period of twelve years. This was important information since celibacy is seen as a primary technique for increasing the efficacy of spiritual practice and individual power. Furthermore, this served to impress upon the merchants that devotees—and Prahlad in particular—did not fit the popular stereotype that all Westerners were incorrigibly promiscuous.

Secondly, Prahlad had recounted to the goswami that during a recent visit to Delhi he was invited to dine with some peripheral ISKCON supporters who served a mutton curry. Upon discovering what would be served, he immediately left the house, proclaiming that he would fast to the death before eating meat. This strong reaffirmation of his vegetarianism was another point in Prahlad's favor, for although most Vrindabanbasis are themselves lifelong vegetarians and would never prepare or eat meat, especially within the precincts of Vrindaban, a few did admit that on occasions away from the town they had in fact tasted mutton, chicken, and eggs. Prahlad made it clear that under no circumstances would he be so enticed. These facts, among others, helped to create a positive image of Prahlad among the merchants, and set the stage for his being drawn deeper into Vrindaban's cultural system.

During the research period, the wife of Prahlad's tailor became pregnant for the first time. Since his marriage of ten years had been a barren one, the tailor was understandably overjoyed, and saw this as an answer to daily prayers to Krishna and various other gods and goddesses. Since Prahlad was such an important economic resource for the tailor's family, and because he was considered a friend, he was invited to eat at the tailor's home in celebration of the expected birth, still some months away.

The next day Prahlad's visit was a subject of discussion in Loi Bazaar, especially because of an event that happened as he was leaving the tailor's house. Upon his departure, the tailor's wife bent down to touch the devotee's feet out of respect. As is the custom, Prahlad quickly made a show of trying to prevent this ritual, gently pulling her up by the arms as she bent over, yet allowing the act to be completed. After she was standing again, Prahlad spontaneously placed his hands upon her stomach and said, "I know Krishna will bless you with a son."

Relating this interaction, Prahlad was concerned about the story now circulating in the Bazaar, thinking that his reputation might be affected due to his touching the woman, although no sexual connotation was intended. "I did it without thinking. I was just inspired to do it. It just happened," he said.

Nothing more was said about this incident until months later when the tailor's wife delivered a healthy son, and along with this news, the people of Loi Bazaar learned that the tailor was giving Prahlad credit for the boy's birth. Prahlad congratulated the tailor but at the same time admonished him : "Stop this business of saying my blessing gave you a son. It was Krishna; only Krishna provides. Celebrate a healthy son but give only Krishna the credit."

The tailor, Daoji, responded: "You gave the blessing. My family has daughters only. All my brothers only daughters, and now this son. It is Krishna's grace, but your blessing also. You must give the name-giving ceremony." Prahlad was quick to reject this new request. Most families are in a *jajmani* (patron-client) relationship with a Brahman pandit who conducts the life-cycle rituals, including the ceremony that names a newborn child. Not only was Prahlad unfamiliar with the ritual, he was also aware that negative repercussions would result, especially in the Brahman community, if he usurped the pandit's authority. The tailor's response to Prahlad's objections was uncompromising: "*Panditji* is not so good at rituals. Always he consults the book; always he is arguing with other pandits. He mainly wants the money, and I will give it. You are also Brahman; you wear the sacred thread, and you are a great devotee of Shri Radha."

Surprisingly, there was a strong sentiment in the bazaar supporting the tailor's request, with much discussion going on considering whether or not there were any absolute prohibitions against Prahlad's conducting the ritual. The general consensus was that there were not.

Moreover, the merchants reasoned that if the pandits felt threatened by foreign devotees, perhaps they would improve their services. Prahlad ultimately refused to escalate the drama by conducting the ceremony, and it was performed by the family priest. However, he was again invited to the tailor's home the day prior to the ritual in order to give another blessing, this time for the child. Daoji requested that Prahlad decide what the child should be called, and Prahlad complied with this request. The tailor's son was named Anupam.

This is but one instance where ISKCON devotees have assumed roles from which they would be logically excluded according to common cultural rules. Other Vrindaban residents have openly accepted ISKCON members as gurus, attested to by pictures on private altars.[6] Not infrequently, devotees are also guests in Brajbasi homes where they deliver discourses and discussions (*katha*) about Krishna, conduct pujas, and lead kirtan. These examples indicate an acceptance of ISKCON devotees as religious specialists by many Vrindaban residents, roles usually monopolized by Brahmans. Since the foreign devotees claim Brahman status, one of the most pertinent questions, then, is whether or not they are achieving it.

THE BRAHMAN PROBLEM

When Bhaktivedanta first came to America, his intention was not to just make Vaishnavas of his disciples, but to make them all Brahman. Although no one had attempted to do this in America, it was not Bhaktivedanta's innovation, for his own guru, Bhaktisiddhanta Saraswati, had begun giving Brahman initiation to Indians regardless of caste shortly after instituting the Gaudiya Math in 1918 (see chapter 4).

In Vrindaban there are basically three positions regarding the question of who is legitimately a Brahman, a question that practically asks who can act as priest, guru, or other type of religious specialist. The first position is a conservative interpretation based primarily on the texts such as *Manu Smriti* (a textual codification of Hindu laws). Those Vrindabanbasis who hold this position insist that Brahman status is al-

---

[6] Kirtanananda Swami, who heads New Vrindaban community in West Virginia, is especially popular. Pictures of Siddha Swarupananda, formerly an ISKCON devotee who now has his own following, are also found on several private altars in Vrindaban. None of the people who are paying ritual homage to Siddha are aware that he no longer has ties with ISKCON. One of the Indian ISKCON gurus, Gopal Krishna Swami, is also claimed as guru by several Vrindaban residents.

ways ascribed; to be a Brahman you must be born a Brahman.[7] The second attitude is associated with many Vaishnava sects, including the Bengal Vaishnavas. Those adhering to this position generally feel that caste affiliations are irrelevant if you are a Vaishnava; that the Vaishnava designation supercedes caste categories. When questioned concerning their jati identity, people adhering to this position respond with ''Vaishnava'' or a sect name instead of their birth jati. The third position is associated mainly with the Gaudiya Math subdivision of the Bengal Vaishnavas and sects and gurus who have taken a similar position. This attitude goes beyond the idea that caste is irrelevant and suggests that non-Brahmans can be turned into true Brahmans provided they possess the specific knowledge and behavioral attributes and go through proper ritual initiations.[8] This last attitude toward Brahmanhood is the one taken by ISKCON, and the position that Bhaktivedanta and his own guru put forth.

There is also a more analytical approach taken by a few Vrindaban intellectuals which states that there are two complementary systems in effect: a social system and a religious system. In purely social terms a person's caste cannot be ignored or changed, and rules concerning interaction between castes must always be observed. On the other hand, when the context is purely religious, it is allowable to judge people according to their Vaishnava or devotee status. This position is held by a few educated Brahman priests who have evolved it in order to simultaneously maintain their superiority while acknowledging the egalitarian ideals of their religious system. Depending on the situation, then, those who hold this attitude may take either of the other positions. Prac-

---

[7] Even the *Manu Smriti*, however, details some rare situations where Brahman status may be achieved rather than ascribed. The well-known process of Sanskritization, described along with other processes of mobility within the caste system by Srinivas (1966), shows how lower jatis in the most traditional context may improve their collective status, even up to Brahmanhood, over the period of several generations. This entails a ''revelation'' that the low-status classification is somehow incorrect, followed by a concerted behavioral effort to act like Brahmans, i.e., assume Brahman dress, renounce alcohol consumption, forbid widow remarriage, and eat only vegetarian food.

[8] In a Gaudiya Math publication on the history of that institution, the author writes:

Another aim of Srila Saraswati Thākur was to free the Vaishnava followers from the caste prejudices. The Vaishnava writers untiringly rebuke those who regard a Vaishnava as one belonging to a caste in which a Vaishnava happens to take birth. He traced the origin and object of the Varnāshrama system and proved that it was not the accidental circumstances that should be the true criterion to decide whether one is a Brāhman, a Kshatriya, a Vaishya or a Sudra. . . . Srila Saraswati Thākur emphasized the necessity of introducing Diksā to confer Brahmanhood. . . . Initiation is not a mere social or family affair—it is a divine enlightenment conferred by the Guru on his disciple. . . . Srila Saraswati Thākur fought against the evil and practice of accepting herditary Gurus. (Yati 1978: 78–79)

tically, this leaves them vulnerable to ISKCON arguments that in effect posit that the religious and social spheres are inseparable. Few others in Vrindaban, however, make such distinctions.

Table 4 portrays the distribution of attitudes in Vrindaban concerning the acquisition of Brahman status. It is based on an interview sample that specifically questioned whether or not a person could become a Brahman if he was not born into a Brahman jati. The percentages correspond with general observations and informal interviews.

What is again apparent from these figures is the flexibility of Vrindaban society. Only 20 percent of the total sample population was adamant that Brahman status is purely ascriptive. If the Brahman component of the sample is ignored, then only 13 percent rule out the possibility of non-Brahmans becoming Brahman. Furthermore, it suggests that for ISKCON devotees to win legitimacy as Brahmans in Vrindaban, the primary obstacle to their acceptance is the Brahman population of the town, especially those in control of the main temples. To evaluate ISKCON's overall success, therefore, it is essential to investigate whether or not ISKCON interactions with hereditary priests demonstrate the same transformative characteristics as interactions with pilgrims and other segments of the Vrindaban community. The cases that follow show that even with the most conservative Brahmans—the caste goswamis—there are significant changes in attitude taking place.

Marriage and Commensality

Soon after I arrived in Vrindaban, a priest at one of the main temples explained that although ISKCON Vaishnavas may exhibit the qualities

Table 4. Vrindaban Attitudes Concerning Achievement of Brahman Status

	Yes	No	Irrel	Dual	Totals
Priests	9	12	2	4	27
	33%	44%	7%	15%	
Merchants	12	8	12		32
	36%	25%	38%		
Service	21	4	10		35
	60%	11%	29%		
Mendicants	21	2	14		37
	57%	5%	38%		
Totals	63	26	38	4	131
	48%	20%	29%	3%	

and qualifications of the Brahman ideal, in reality they could never be accepted as true Brahmans: "There is no doubt by becoming a Hare Krishna devotee you become Brahman on the true spiritual level, but my question is whether or not a Brahman in Vrindaban will offer you his daughter in marriage and whether or not he will eat freely with you. The reality is that caste is a social institution and the answer is no to both."[9]

This priest on a number of occasions had invited ISKCON devotees to dine in his home, which seemed to contradict his opinion that commensality was forbidden. He pointed out, however, that "they ate at a table reserved for outside guests and I joined them only in conversation. I can be a gracious host without violating purity rules."

About one year later, an uncle of this same priest invited several ISKCON members to the marriage of the sixth of his seven daughters. Represented at the wedding were Brahman lineages from other temples in the town, as marriages often take place between these lineages although they may be of different sectarian affiliation. During the evening the bride's father was lamenting the cost of marrying seven daughters and the problem of finding suitable husbands for them all. His seventh daughter was also of marriageable age, and during a conversation with friends that included other priests, he disclosed that he was considering an ISKCON devotee as a potential husband for her. Queried about the seriousness of this proposal by the others, he said, "I am very serious. This boy ranks high on my list and may be the very best choice." I am not aware whether the marriage took place or not, but what is significant is that he was considering it at all, and that some other Brahmans in the crowd agreed that it was a possibility.

Several days after the wedding I returned to the priest's home to find two ISKCON men enjoying a meal, one of them being the devotee his uncle was considering as a future son-in-law. They were not at the "guest table," but in the family quarters, and the priest was eating with them. Later I questioned him about the contradiction between this behavior and the notions expressed at our previous meeting. "If these men are eating freely with you, and your uncle is willing to marry his daughter with one, then they must be Brahmans in the social as well as the spiritual sense," I commented. "In this case," was his reply.

The Brahman explained that certain situations had caused him to broaden his interpretation of the caste-based rules concerning marriage

---

[9] Quotation in English.

and commensality. He explained: "We must question ISKCON as a whole. Each devotee is different—different motives, different qualifications. From my own experience I think there must be only five or six out of all of them that are truly bhaktas that I could accept as Brahman, but because of their spiritual force the whole movement is going on."

"Then there exists the possibility of foreigners becoming Brahman in the social sense too, and by extension the possibility of lower-caste Indians becoming Brahman," I stated. After a long pause he replied, "It seems that must be admitted too, theoretically."

For temple Brahmans in Vrindaban, this is not a new dilemma; they have been confronted with the same challenge by the Gaudiya Math since the 1920s. Although many temples came under the same sectarian umbrella as Bhaktisiddhanta and his men, most priests rebuked this fledgling monastic arm of the tradition because it threatened their superior position which had, up until that time, gone unchallenged. Not all Vrindaban goswamis at that time, however, rejected the Gaudiya Math argument that Brahman status was determined by qualification instead of birth. The same is true today. At a number of temples, ISKCON priests are being instructed by some of the Indian goswamis who are concerned with transmitting the esoteric details of ritual Krishna worship to them. Some have accepted ISKCON since its arrival because their fathers agreed with the Gaudiya Math position. Others have formulated the attitude as a result of interaction with ISKCON devotees.[10]

Learning the Details

Within ISKCON there are two often conflicting attitudes concerning devotees' knowledge of ritual temple worship. The conservative position is that Bhaktivedanta taught everything essential for successful image worship and that seeking additional information is unnecessary or even heretical. The opposing viewpoint is that while their guru did transmit the basic essentials, an attempt to increase that knowledge from other acceptable sources should be ongoing. The devotees who espouse this latter position argue that if ISKCON priests and gurus are to increase their acceptance in India, acquisition of the more esoteric details is essential.

---

[10] Whether or not an ISKCON devotee can speak Hindi, Bengali, or some other Indian language does not directly enter into a determination of whether he possesses "Brahman knowledge." There is a diversity of languages spoken in Vrindaban, including English, although most people do speak Hindi in day-to-day conversation. Ability to read, understand, and use Sanskrit is necessary for Brahman ritual activity, however, and this is a criterion. All ISKCON devotees study Sanskrit in temple classes and privately, with proficiency varying from person to person.

Occasionally devotees have therefore sought additional instruction from some of Bhaktivedanta's Gaudiya Math contemporaries and have arranged internships at some of the most renowned temples. At the South Indian temple of Venkateshwara in Tirupati, Andhra Pradesh, considered by many Indians to be the highest Vishnu temple in the country, several ISKCON members have studied, including the French devotee who is head priest at Vrindaban's Krishna-Balaram temple. One of the chief priests at Tirupati has also given additional instruction to ISKCON pujaris while visiting temples in the United States. In Vrindaban the Gaudiya Vaishnava temple of Radha-Raman is considered to have the most authoritative ritual since the goswamis there trace their ancestry back to Gopal Bhatt, the disciple of Chaitanya who is credited with writing the ritual codes of the sect. His treatise on ritual, *Hari-bhakti-vilasa*, is strictly followed by the priests there.

One Radha-Raman priest, Premanand Goswami, has been open to ISKCON devotees since they arrived in Vrindaban. He is cautious, however, in imparting esoteric knowledge, agreeing to teach only those he considers qualified. While many have approached him, few have received the teaching. One devotee, Murti Das, convinced Premanand that he was worthy of studentship only after a six-month period that tested his perseverance.

When Murti first arrived in Vrindaban he possessed a Govardhan Shila (stone from the sacred Govardhan Hill) which he worshiped daily. His purpose for coming to the town was specifically to learn more about proper worship of the sacred stone which is considered a form of Krishna, and because of Premanand's reputation, this goswami was the first person Murti approached.

Premanand received Murti cordially and listened politely to the devotee's request for instruction. After their first meeting, however, the goswami patiently told Murti that he would not give instruction on Govardhan Shila worship because the stone had been improperly obtained. Moreover, he explained that if the devotee did not return the stone to Govardhan immediately, he would suffer severe consequences. Murti agreed to return it, but that was not all Premanand wanted. If Murti was serious about studying with the priest, he had to obtain a shalagram stone which is found only in Nepal. Murti agreed, and set out on what would be a three-month journey to fulfill the goswami's requests.

He returned to Vrindaban from Nepal with a shalagram, but when the devotee presented it for Premanand's approval, the goswami pronounced it too small. Murti relates:

> It made sense for him to send me after a shalagram since Radha-Raman (the temple image) is actually formed from a shalagram. It was a difficult journey, and the *shila* (stone) I selected seemed to be the best one available. I could have bought a larger one, but I wanted to find it myself. I wanted Krishna to lead me to it. Now Radha-Raman was originally a very large and rare kind of shalagram, but I didn't think Premanandji was concerned with size. The whole trip was a test; I knew that. But I also thought he would instruct me with the shalagram I found. At the same time, I knew at this point I'd do whatever he wanted, so I wasn't too disappointed.

Premanand Goswami told Murti Das that the shalagram was a good one and that he would place it on an altar where it would receive proper worship, but he refused to instruct the devotee with it. Rather, if Murti was still interested, he should acquire an image similar to the temple deity. The goswami explained that it was best for a true bhakta to worship an image of Krishna playing his flute. The image did not have to be carved from a shalagram as Radha-Raman had been, but it should be as close in size and form to the original image as possible. Premanand suggested that Murti might find a suitable image somewhere in Rajasthan since there were still some good stone carvers in that state, and bid farewell to the devotee until he returned with the proper statue.

Two months later Murti returned to Vrindaban from Jaipur in Rajasthan with an image that was a faithful replica of Radha-Raman in all respects except for the eyes. The temple image has conch-shaped eyes which are rarely seen on other images, so Murti's statue also had to have them. The devotee found a craftsman in Delhi who made the proper eyes and mounted them onto the image, and after another month's delay finally returned to Vrindaban with a deity that Premanand judged adequate. For the next several months Murti was instructed by Premanand Goswami concerning the worship of Radha-Raman. The goswami later commented on his relationship with this ISKCON devotee: "Prabhupad did not teach any of the *tantra*, especially the *mudras* (hand positions) that are absolutely required, so that is the main thing I can teach. I have learned there are a few of them that are pure enough—not all, but a few; and now and then some will come. But this is not for just anyone. These ISKCON boys I teach will also teach their disciples, and the knowledge will continue like that after I am gone. That is my concern, that it continues with the best of them. That is my duty also.''[11]

Not all of Premanand's relatives who serve as priests in the temple of Radha-Raman agree that he should be teaching ISKCON devotees, but the goswami is undeterred in his efforts. When challenged, he quietly states that only qualified Brahmans are being taught. Asked about those who challenge him, Premanand replied, "I am concerned with the proper transmission. No one can criticize me for that. If they do, I ignore them. They will not keep it up because I am the most expert and the most renounced, and the oldest. If I say it is proper, then no more discussion.''

Maintaining the Standards

Temples like Radha-Raman are financially sound and conduct elaborate deity worship which is expensive to support. Other temples, traditionally just as important, have lost their economic resources over the years and struggle to continue the costly routine of regular deity worship. There may be many reasons for this: loss of village land that once provided rental income; theft or sales of jewelry and ritual items made from silver or gold; a decrease of wealthy patrons; or priests ignoring their traditional pursuits to find work or amusement elsewhere. Bhaktivedanta and his ISKCON successors, therefore, have undertaken a program to identify the traditional temples that are in need and provide various types of assistance. The aid is usually welcome, although the proud goswamis who manage some of the temples resent the need for ISKCON's help. More than that, some Brahman priests in these temples find it degrading to play a subservient role to the foreigners who have only so recently learned anything about temple worship. Indeed, in these situations the roles are practically reversed, with ISKCON devotees monitoring and criticizing the behavior of Indian priests, presuming to teach them the proper standards for worship of Krishna.

Assistance to Indian temples usually takes the form of gifts of ritual paraphernalia and clothing for the images. In image worship, the ritual is expected to be as elaborate as possible, and ISKCON spends a significant percentage of its operating budget on new clothes and crowns for the deities, and floral and food offerings that are made throughout the day.[12] The lavishness of deity worship at Krishna-Balaram temple is

[11] Quotation translated from Hindi.

[12] About one-fourth of Krishna-Balaram's monthly income is allotted for expenses related to deity worship. General ISKCON policy demands that at least this amount be spent, and some tem-

one of the things that attracts Indian worshipers, and twenty-five local craftsmen are employed full-time there for producing items like crowns, necklaces, and embroidered clothing which are used to clothe the temple deities. These products are also sold to other ISKCON temples around the world, and some are sold or donated to Vrindaban temples.[13] The head priest, French devotee Omkara Das explained ISKCON's attitude concerning gifts to local temples:

> Krishna-Balaram sets the standard for temple worship in Vrindaban, and we see it as our mission to help increase the standards of other temples when they are found lacking. We cannot finance every temple, but we can help by gifting them the best crowns, clothing, and so forth. Some very important temples are struggling, and their deities used to be dressed in rags; now they are beautiful. Krishna must be worshiped in opulence and we find it a pleasant duty to make gifts to Their Lordships Shri Shri Radha and Krishna when the temples cannot adequately provide.

One temple that has been of particular concern to ISKCON since devotees came to Vrindaban is Radha-Damodar. At this temple are the tombs of Rup and Jiv Goswami, Krishnadas Kaviraj who wrote *Chaitanya-charitamrita*, and other Bengal Vaishnava saints. This is also the place where Bhaktivedanta Swami lived before coming to the West and where the first Indian headquarters for ISKCON was located. For many devotees, Radha-Damodar is the first Indian temple they worship in, and ISKCON has had a vested interest in it from the beginning. As early as 1967, clothing for this temple's deities was donated by devotees living there, and since 1971 there has been an arrangement for ISKCON to indefinitely lease Bhaktivedanta's old rooms in exchange for a "considerable stipend" to the goswamis in charge.

These rooms have now been renovated and decorated by ISKCON to serve as a worthy memorial to their guru, and they present a striking contrast with the rest of the temple. Several times daily there are offerings to Bhaktivedanta in these rooms, and the temple is usually one of the first sacred sites that ISKCON pilgrims visit upon arriving in Vrin-

---

ples budget up to half their income. The ideological rationale behind this policy is that whatever is given to Krishna will be returned many times over. Devotees sometimes point to "opulent" deity worship as the direct cause for ISKCON's financial successes.

[13] Adjacent to the altars at Krishna-Balaram temple is a large room where the deities' garments are carefully stored and maintained. The appropriate color and type of clothing is specified according to season and the ritual calendar, and some ensembles are used repeatedly according to the yearly cycle. However, new garments are always "given" to the deities on major festival days.

daban. Today, however, the ISKCON hierarchy is not satisfied with the lease arrangement, the physical condition of the temple, or the quality of deity worship there, and is involved in a prolonged attempt to gain more control of Radha-Damodar's management. This idea has been around since devotees first came to Vrindaban, for when Bhaktivedanta was looking for a suitable temple site there, he proposed to the goswamis at Radha-Damodar that the temple be handed over to him and his foreign disciples: "We shall prepare the whole temple nicely . . . and shall make a silver throne for the Deity. Fifty to one hundred men will take prasādam here. It will be unique. If you want to, we can do it. Otherwise we start our own temple somewhere. We are prepared to spend money. If you give us a chance we will spend it here. We want to make this a great festival in Vṛndāvana, because it is Jīva Gosvāmī's place" (Goswami, Satsvarupa 1983a: 26).

There have been several meetings between ISKCON officials and the hierarchy of Radha-Damodar temple which have focused upon increased ISKCON participation in temple affairs. For most of ISKCON's tenure in Vrindaban, the chief priest at Radha-Damodar was Gauratam Goswami, a contemporary and friend of Bhaktivedanta. While these two men were alive, negotiations were conducted informally between them, and there was a tacit understanding that ISKCON would eventually subsidize the temple operation, even if this was not publicly admitted. As Bhaktivedanta's death drew near and Gauratam Goswami's health also weakened, Bhaktivedanta repeatedly encouraged devotees to negotiate a formal agreement with Radha-Damodar; he eventually wanted a total takeover—regardless of cost. The ISKCON devotee presently involved with negotiating a solution presents an apparently intransigent position: "Radha-Damodar is the most important temple in India for the sampradaya. But for ISKCON it is more than this—it is our heritage, our history, our origin, our future. Even if it is done underhandedly, we must get that temple away from the lazy goswamis in charge now. The worship of Krishna in that temple is a disgrace—[it] must not and will not continue."

In practice, however, ISKCON is willing to accept, at least for now, a compromise arrangement. After the death of Bhaktivedanta and Gauratam Goswami's demise several months later, the management of Radha-Damodar passed to a trust headed by Pancham Goswami, who inherited the position of head priest. According to ISKCON the standards have deteriorated steadily since Pancham Goswami took over. Just prior to the 1983 Gaura Purnima festival which celebrates the birth of

Chaitanya, a meeting was held between the Radha-Damodar trust and ISKCON officials. Ostensibly the meeting's purpose was to coordinate activities for the festival which would bring many pilgrims into town, including about five hundred ISKCON devotees from around the world; however, it was also an opportunity for ISKCON to increase its involvement at Radha-Damodar.

It was agreed that ISKCON would arrange and pay for repairing and painting the main temple structure, but the devotees were more concerned that punctual and elaborate deity worship be conducted during the festival. The chief ISKCON spokesman chided the temple management for laxness in ritual and suggested that for the festival period ISKCON priests should be in charge of deity worship. ISKCON's chief spokesman argued that "this is the only way we can assure it is being done properly."

Pancham Goswami was outraged and proceeded to defend himself, protesting the slanderous accusations against his management. Another spokesman for the temple, however, an older relative from Bengal, agreed that the ritual standards were poor, and insisted they be improved. "Without help we cannot give *thakurjis* (the images) very nice food and clothes, but we can make sure they are fed on time. Only laziness would prevent that," he said.

The ISKCON representative explained to the assembly that for several years he had observed a haphazard temple operation and had no hopes for its improvement. He implored the goswamis: "Just for this important period turn over the worship to us and you will see how wonderful the temple becomes. If the Deities are pleased, then automatically everything else will improve. Just make an experiment, and you will quickly see that it is all for your benefit. After the festival things can return to normal if that is your wish."

The majority of Radha-Damodar's management was willing to accept the ISKCON proposal, but Pancham Goswami and two other allies were adamant in their refusal. After a prolonged and boisterous private conference among the goswamis, a compromise was presented which ISKCON accepted. A staff of ISKCON priests could reside in the temple during the festival and insure that each offering was conducted on time. ISKCON would provide new clothing and ornaments for the deities, but the local goswamis insisted on dressing them. No ISKCON priest would be allowed to conduct pujas at the main altar, but they would assist and could offer suggestions. ISKCON could arrange and conduct other activities elsewhere within the temple without interference.

The Gaura Purnima festival took place without major incident and was judged a success, mainly because participants from both sides had been instructed to show deference and respect to their counterparts. Temple goswamis were pleased that they were able to conduct more elaborate worship, but generally were relieved when the devotees left. One commented that "these videshi priests work too much. They never relax and always worry about the thakurji. We are not used to such anxiety." ISKCON authorities were pleased with the festival agreement and felt that it was a step toward more total control of the temple. A precedent had been set for ISKCON intervention and demonstrated the possibility for some sort of negotiated long-term arrangement.

Full ownership of Radha-Damodar for ISKCON is at best a future possibility. If the situation involved only ISKCON and the temple authorities, then some arrangement would probably be worked out eventually, but it has developed into a volatile political issue in Vrindaban with other temples becoming involved. Members of the Brahman community will not allow a traditional temple of such historical importance to come under ISKCON control if they can prevent it. Although most have no vested interest in Radha-Damodar, symbolically their superiority would be considerably diminished. Perhaps in time ISKCON will acquire the political and social assets to take over the temple with the Brahman community's blessing, but this is only conjecture. It is clear, however, that the roles established through the negotiations that have already taken place are still important indicators of ISKCON acceptance by Brahmans, at least those at Radha-Damodar.

The future developments at this temple will be important for ISKCON's standing in the general Vrindaban Brahman community, and the ISKCON hierarchy is aware that the situation must be resolved delicately and over a long period. However, the transitional importance of events to date are significant. Already, Indian Brahmans at Radha-Damodar have accepted ISKCON advice concerning standards of worship, they have allowed priests to assist in temple rituals, and some are willing to consider the possibility of full ISKCON management of their temple. ISKCON has its foot in the door at Radha-Damodar, and the same could be said about another of Vrindaban's historic temples.

Transition at Radha-Gokulananda

Radha-Gokulananda is one of the seven original Gaudiya Vaishnava temples of Vrindaban, the others being Madan-Mohan, Gopinath, Radha-Shyamsundar, Govindadev, Gopinath, and Radha-Damodar.

All of these temples are traditionally owned and managed by descendants of Chaitanya's immediate Vrindaban disciples, but Radha-Gokulananda's goswami lineage ended about eighty years ago when the last of the line died without male progeny. The only daughter of the last goswami sold the temple to the Maharaja of Jaipur, and today the government of Rajasthan is theoretically responsible for its support and maintenance. Until recently, however, this temple has been without a full-time priest, and for a long period was closed to the public. When this situation came to the attention of a devout daughter of the woman who sold the temple to the Maharaja, she tried to buy it back in order to restore the worship there and reestablish Radha-Gokulananda as family property. But the Rajasthan government refused.

In the meantime, an official in the Rajasthan government learned of the temple's condition and persuaded the head priest at nearby Radha-Raman temple to assume responsibility until the case is decided. So until the issue of ownership is settled in Indian courts, Radha-Gokulananda will be under the supervision of Radha-Raman temple, specifically, under the authority of its head priest and his family. Once this responsibility was accepted, the head priest at Radha-Raman was faced with the problem of hiring a full-time pujari. He eventually selected an Indian Brahman for the job, but many people in Vrindaban were surprised to learn that this man had no traditional training for the priesthood. Rather, his knowledge of temple management and deity worship comes entirely from training within ISKCON.

Raghavananda is forty years old. From his teenage years he was involved with his family's import-export business, being stationed first in Calcutta, then San Francisco and Chicago. A lifelong vegetarian, Raghavananda often found it difficult to maintain his strict diet in the United States, but discovered in Chicago he could find ''pure'' vegetarian food at the Hare Krishna temple which was located near his office. Eventually he became interested in ISKCON, primarily because his own family followed the Bengal Vaishnava tradition, and because Bhaktivedanta Swami had been a friend of his grandfather in Calcutta.

Shortly before he was scheduled to be dispatched back to India, the head of ISKCON's Chicago temple asked Raghavananda to become his secretary. This Indian Brahman has been affiliated in one way or another with the organization ever since, working at various ISKCON centers in India and eventually coming to Krishna-Balaram in Vrindaban. His appointment at Radha-Gokulananda is probably not a permanent one, but it has caused residents of Vrindaban to consider transmission of Brahmanical knowledge through ISKCON as sufficient for employment in traditional temples. A Brahman is not eligible for the priesthood without specific training, so although Raghavananda's status was acquired by birth, he could never have served in a temple without the knowledge ISKCON provided him. The situation, therefore, is a transitional one for ISKCON acceptance since it legitimates ISKCON's transmission of traditional Brahmanical knowledge.

Traditionally, Brahman status and Brahmanical training are acquired through direct patrilineal descent. If the professional knowledge required of religious specialists is not taught directly by an individual's father or close male relative, a discipleship with some respected guru will be arranged by them. The ISKCON (and Gaudiya Math) position is that both Brahman status and Brahman training can be conferred by a qualified guru regardless of an individual's birth-status. The situation at Radha-Gokulananda is transitional because although the priest is Brahman by birth, his training was provided by ISKCON. The full acceptance of ISKCON's position will be unequivocally achieved if a non-Indian ISKCON Brahman is ever selected to serve as priest in one of the Indian temples, giving social acceptance to ISKCON Brahmanhood as well as ISKCON-transmitted knowledge.

When I first met Raghavananda, he was busily dressing the deities at Radha-Gokulananda, lamenting the inadequate paraphernalia that the temple now possessed. He explained:

> Today I am very distressed. Srimati Radharani (one of the images) has been upset because she doesn't like her sari. I have changed her clothing and ornaments three times today, and still she is not satisfied. Radha-Raman [temple] has not supplied me with the things I need for the best *seva* (worship); they only give me sixty-five rupees plus ten kilos of wheat for a full month. It is not possible to run a temple with this only. Tomorrow some pujaris from Krishna-Balaram are coming with some new garments and crowns, and then I hope Radha will be happy. It is going on like this. In so many temples the priests are not concerned or don't have the money. So ISKCON has to make sure these important deities are cared for.[14]

---

[14] This quotation demonstrates the ideal state of mind for a temple priest, as exemplified by Rhagavananda. The priest should be constantly alert to "please" the deity through lavish clothing and jewelry, rich food, and proper ritual. Although there was nothing to indicate to the outside observer that Radha was not satisfied with her sari, most Radha-Krishna devotees would see nothing extraordinary in such a statement from a priest. Devotees expect there to be a subtle communication beween the deity and the priest who has intimate daily "interaction" with the image.

Asked why he was selected for the post at Radha-Gokulananda, Raghavanda responded that:

> Actually I am a very, very, fallen man . . . but I met Shri Bhaktivedanta Swami Prabhupad in America. . . . What ISKCON has done nobody else can do, and this is recognized. Even in other [Indian] sampradayas the babajis do all sorts of bad things, whereas in ISKCON they are following the rules very, very strictly. . . . So ISKCON people are much better than the sampradaya people. . . . The Indians also know this and that is my main qualification. Not only I am Brahman but also trained up in ISKCON. . . . ISKCON is both wealthy and Vaishnava. That is the proof of Krishna's mercy, I think. Without money, no worship can go on. Who is a little wise can see ISKCON Vaishnavas are the best. . . . My selection is the beginning of a trend. In the future, many temples will want ISKCON pujaris. Indian or not is no matter. You will see this in time.[15]

Raghavananda's explanation should be carefully considered because he is one of an increasing number of traditionally minded Indians who have had intimate contact with ISKCON and have evaluated Hare Krishna devotees as most important for the continuation of Vaishnava tradition. Raghavananda, however, did not arrive at this conclusion blindly. Rather, he has seriously considered most of the criticisms voiced by Indians against ISKCON. For a two-year period he officially left that organization to study under another Gaudiya Vaishnava guru whom he felt at the time was more legitimately part of the sampradaya. He eventually, however, reestablished his ISKCON affiliation because he felt, as the above remarks reflect, that the Hare Krishna movement's practice of Vaishnava ideals was more traditionally correct than other Indian sampradayas. A Brahman servant to one of the goswami families at Radha-Raman had this to say about Raghavananda's selection to be temple priest:

> Observe the actions of the goswamijis. The way they act is more important than what they will tell to your face about ISKCON. Their experience with foreign devotees shows them they are important in this kali yuga. They are giving new life to the sampradaya and this is very needed. At the present moment for the reason of politics, they must keep some distance, but Raghavananda's selection is a selection of ISKCON also. In some years you may see other ISKCON men in some temples, and all may not be Indian.[16]

---

[15] Quotation in English.
[16] Quotation translated from Hindi.

Other Indians, Brahman and otherwise, who have had close association with ISKCON, in some cases becoming devotees themselves, are young members of the Vrindaban community. Attitudes developing among these Vrindabanbasis of the next generation are of great importance for ISKCON's future success in the town.

ISKCON AND THE YOUTH OF VRINDABAN

One evening around six, Loi Bazaar was crowded with shoppers. Cows and rickshaws were plowing their way through the packed street with difficulty when suddenly a wide path opened, forcing some of the people against shops and into the gutter. Through the opening came a large cart pulled by a large black Brahma bull draped with a red brocaded blanket, horns glistening with gold leaf; atop the cart stood a muscular, blond ISKCON devotee, reins in hand, with freshly shaved head and a prominent sacred thread falling across his bare torso. Normally such an inconvenience would be met with curses, but now shoppers and merchants alike waved and shouted, "Hare Krishna," and the devotee returned the same salutation. One pilgrim shouted "Just see, this is surely Arjun giving us his darshan."[17]

The cart was loaded with cisterns of cow's milk, and the devotee was distributing it to shopkeepers and anyone else who had a container, a common practice whenever there is a surplus at the ISKCON goshala. Also on the cart was another ISKCON devotee, similarly dressed and in the prime of health, and a twelve-year-old Indian boy named Baburam.

Baburam was born in a nearby village, but for several years had lived at Vraja Academy where his Brahman father was employed as a cook.[18] He attended a public school and did well in his studies, but would often skip classes out of boredom, and this earned him the reputation of being a discipline problem. Sometimes he would disappear for several days, explaining on his return that he had been "on yatra" in the Braj countryside. At other times he would be found at the ISKCON goshala or at the Krishna-Balaram temple, where he would attend public lectures and visit devotees.

Young boys from Vrindaban and surrounding areas would often come to the ISKCON temple, and devotees had mixed feelings about

---

[17] Arjun was Krishna's charioteer on the battlefield of Kurukshetra when Krishna spoke the words of the *Bhagavad-Gita*.

[18] The sadhu who runs the academy accepts students regardless of social status, but employs Brahman cooks so that even the most orthodox Brahman visitors can eat comfortably there.

their being there. Many viewed ISKCON as an opportunity for improving their life—better food, a nice place to live, and a perceived increase in status due to their association with foreigners. The ISKCON hierarchy wanted to encourage this interest, but at the same time discouraged the ones who wanted to become part of the organization for only material gain. On the other hand, boys like Baburam who apparently had a keen intellect and expressed a genuine desire for religious studies were welcomed and in some cases actively recruited.

Baburam liked Vraja Academy, but knew the small institution had problems. His father would often complain that there was not enough food for the many guests the sadhu would invite there, and when this happened the staff and their families would have to go without meals. Baburam accepted this because he could always find a meal in Vrindaban at a temple or one of the many institutions that supports the large mendicant population, and since the devotees at ISKCON liked him, he could eat there whenever he wanted to as well.

Eventually Baburam was noticed by the English headmaster of the ISKCON gurukula, who began to discuss with him the possibility of enrolling as a full-time boarding student at the school. At first Baburam was not sure if this was a good idea. Certainly people at Vraja Academy would be against this, and he was not sure how his father would react. Baburam's concern for his father (whom the boy described as a devout, hardworking Vaishnava) and his promise as a bright student and potential devotee, prompted the headmaster, however, to present the situation to the temple's president and the ISKCON guru for the area; this resulted in his father's employment as a guard at the temple and Baburam's enrollment at the gurukula on a full scholarship, all against the wishes of the sadhu at Vraja Academy.

The ISKCON gurukula maintains an austere militarylike regimen for its students. Those who have been initiated by one of ISKCON's gurus wear saffron-colored clothing; others wear bright yellow which indicates their status as celibate students but marks them as different at the same time. There is no requirement for the students to become full members of ISKCON through initiation, but the possibility is always open and they are encouraged to seek initiation if they develop the desire for it. Six months after he began classes, Baburam asked for initiation and the ritual was conducted by the local ISKCON guru, Vishnupad, with the boy's father proudly looking on. Some residents of Vraja Academy also attended and commented on what they saw as a remarkable change in the boy. He now appeared more serious and mature. He now also had a new name—Samukha Das.

Samukha Das eagerly participated in ISKCON activities: sankirtan processions in Vrindaban, a Rath Yatra parade in Delhi, singing and dancing during temple worship. Shortly before my departure from Vrindaban, he was manning a table in the Krishna-Balaram courtyard, handing out Hindi ISKCON literature and talking with pilgrims. In near-perfect English Samukah Das reflected on his experience with ISKCON: "I was lucky to live in Vrindaban because ISKCON has come here. Now I am with ISKCON. This means my life is purified, my mind is only on Krishna. It is a path for me to the modern world; I can stay in holy Vrindaban or maybe I will travel somewhere. I have the best from both worlds and my life is perfect because of my Krishna consciousness. Soon I think my father will also take initiation. Even as an old man with little education ISKCON can perfect his life."

Samukha Das admits that at one time he and his friend taunted Western devotees with off-color remarks. "We used to shout at them 'Hey, red monkeys (*lal bandar*),' and have a good laugh," he explained. But according to this Brahman boy, no prejudice or hatred is intended, as some Western observers have concluded; it is only the playful fun of children. Rather, Samukha Das feels that many of his acquaintances in Vrindaban dream of either being affiliated with ISKCON or "becoming a film personality or cricket star." Practically for the youth of Vrindaban, if Samukha Das is correct, ISKCON represents an opportunity to participate in the "modern world" without having to reject their Vrindaban heritage which is still important to many of them.

Not all of Vrindaban's youth, however, will be accepted by ISKCON even if they want to join. Although ISKCON strives for acceptance among all segments of the Indian community, and attempts to incorporate them formally or informally whenever possible, in the final analysis, if an Indian, regardless of age, cannot demonstrate some potential benefit for ISKCON, his formal membership petition will likely be rejected. As the ISKCON guru for Vrindaban put it, "We are not in the business of parenting every village farmboy who wants to better his position. But I have compassion for them, and if they are serious in their devotion I'll try to arrange for them elsewhere in the community." Most Indian boys enrolled in the ISKCON gurukula either have wealthy or politically influential parents, or exhibit high intelligence and a strong potential for loyalty and dedication to the organization's goals. When Indian children, teenagers, or young adults without such attributes approach ISKCON for membership, their petition will likely be rejected. The case of Jaya Lal demonstrates how such situations are usually handled.

At seventeen, Jaya Lal had already lived at various ashrams and temples around Vrindaban, but for three years he had harbored a strong desire to become an ISKCON devotee. The son of farmers who worked the sandy soil on the outskirts of Vrindaban, Jaya neither enjoyed school nor the hard labor his father expected of him. Instead, from an early age he would run away from home and live with the sadhu community along the banks of the Jumna River. The sadhu life, although it allowed him to pursue full-time religious practices, did not appeal to him either; it was too spartan an existence.

For several months Jaya had been living at a small ashram associated with the temple of Radha-Gopinath, one of the primary Gaudiya Vaishnava temples, and had taken every opportunity to become acquainted with any ISKCON devotee who would visit there or whom he met around town. He would also visit the Krishna-Balaram temple frequently, hoping to find some way to become a devotee himself. Toward this end he began to wear a saffron dhoti as ISKCON members did and made sure his head was freshly shaved except for the shikha in back.

Eventually Jaya Lal met a devotee who lived near Gopinath temple and began a campaign to impress him with his sincerity, devotion, and strong desire to become an Indian member of the organization. The devotee was indeed impressed, and set in motion a process that would take Jaya through the ISKCON chain of command, raising his hopes at each step. First, he met with the temple ''commander'' who agreed to let Jaya Lal live temporarily at the devotee ashram and participate in the daily activities around the temple. Next, he went before the temple president who agreed to let his internship continue, but at the same time cautioned him that permanent membership was not assured. It all depended on the decision by Vishnupad, the initiating guru for Vrindaban, who would make the final decision the next time he came to town.

Several weeks later Vishnupad arrived from Calcutta and was informed about Jaya Lal's case; he firmly rejected the boy's petition for membership and initiation and informed the temple president that he should insure Jaya's return to Gopinath temple as soon as possible. Jaya was emotionally shaken and refused to take no for an answer. In tears, he burst uninvited into the guru's quarters, threw himself at Vishnupad's feet, and implored him. In spite of the boy's insistence that he would commit suicide, Vishnupad would not reconsider and explained to Jaya in an authoritarian manner that he should return to Gopinath temple to continue his spiritual development.

Vishnupad's assistants had to forcefully remove Jaya Lal. He refused to release his grip on the guru's feet, and wailed that his life was finished. Vishnupad instructed one of his men to accompany Jaya Lal back to Gopinath temple and check on him occasionally. Several weeks later Jaya told me that he would obey Vishnupad's orders because he was being tested. He felt that if he could do well at Gopinath, eventually Vishnupad would accept him as a disciple, or perhaps in the future a new ISKCON guru would come and initiate him. In the meantime he would not accept initiation from any other guru.

For other young men of Vrindaban, ISKCON presents an opportunity for employment. Prakash, a twenty-year-old Brahman who was worried about his future, operated a small shop in Pratap Bazaar for years where he sold beads and rosaries along with his two younger brothers. Although he had not learned to write English well, he spoke with competence and dreamed of working in one of the international-class hotels in Delhi. He therefore felt that employment at the ISKCON guest house or restaurant would be good experience for a future job in the city. Prakash is not alone among Vrindaban youths who feel that work at ISKCON could be a stepping-stone to a better job and a better life-style.

After a two-year wait, Prakash finally won a job at the Krishna-Balaram restaurant where he would not only mingle with Western devotees, but also meet Indian politicians and businessmen. After a year's employment at ISKCON he is now planning to move to Delhi, sponsored by the manager of a small hotel there whom he met at the ISKCON complex. Prakash suggests that had ISKCON not come to Vrindaban he would be destined for a "boring" life in Vrindaban, and he sees the foreign presence there as both a spiritual and material asset.

The success of ISKCON's integration into the sociocultural system of Vrindaban ultimately depends on the town's next generation of leaders, a generation which has lived with ISKCON most of their lives. Children of the present merchants in Loi Bazaar already work in their fathers' shops, and someday will run them. Likewise, young goswamis who begin priestly duties in their teenage years will someday be head priests. Generally, Vrindaban youth acknowledge ISKCON as an economic and cultural resource, and promise to support its continued tenure in the town with all the ramifications that this implies.

Ganashyam, the thirteen-year-old son of the Brahman head priest at a small temple wants to attend Benares Hindu University and looks forward to his life in Vrindaban after he obtains a degree. He has known ISKCON devotees all his life and some have lived at his father's guest house for years. When asked if he supported ISKCON's remaining in Vrindaban he looked puzzled and said, "ISKCON is part of Vrindaban now. Why should they want to leave? They are good Vaishnavas and Vrindaban is our Vaishnava holy land. If they leave, so many pilgrims might stay away and pilgrim means money. This will be my temple and I want to make it better. And my father will tell you, this is his opinion also."[19]

SUMMARY

In every segment of the Vrindaban community ISKCON is gaining increased acceptance as a valuable resource. The cases presented in this chapter, although they do not describe every type of interaction with the resident Vrindaban population, are representative. They clearly demonstrate that cultural categories such as Brahman, temple priest, pandit, and guru have been and are continuing to be transformed through interaction. A new social and cultural reality is being constructed that makes sense to Vrindabanbasis because its symbolic framework appears unchanged. As these cases show, however, ISKCON acceptance necessitates a reformulation of meaning for some of the most important traditional symbols.

All situations, of course, are not as productive for ISKCON as the ones cited, but the positive ones are far more numerous than the negative. A short visit to Vrindaban that includes only casual conversations with some of the residents may not demonstrate the full transformative impact of ISKCON-Indian interactions, but situations such as the ones described here occur regularly. One reason some observers have concluded that there is little cultural integration or symbolic change taking place, results from the dual structure of Krishna bhakti itself. Traditionally, there exist two distinct emotional styles of devotion to Krishna which, though actually complementary, may superficially appear to be in direct opposition. Since ISKCON largely appropriates one style and Vrindaban residents another, the differences between foreign and Indian bhaktas may seem unresolvable. The next chapter addresses interactions within this emotional domain of Krishna bhakti, and shows that significant transformations are occurring there as well.

---

[19] Quotation in English.

CHAPTER 7

Cross-Cultural Dynamics of Mystical Emotions in Vrindaban

ALTHOUGH ISKCON devotees are considered legitimate Vaishnavas in the Bengal tradition (see chapter 4), some Vrindaban residents nonetheless perceive that ISKCON Vaishnavism is somehow different from their own. This perception is not a simple recognition of obvious ethnic differences, now largely overcome by ISKCON's behavioral presentation and arguments from traditional texts, but rather an intangible feeling revealed in comments such as "Indeed they are very good Vaishnavas, perhaps the best in Vrindaban, but their mood is different from us"; and "Their understanding is not yet complete—they are only beginning along the path of deep mysteries of Krishna in the *madhurya-ras* of Braj."[1]

In this chapter I explore the dimension of contrast to which these statements allude—the differential selection, interpretation, and use of the various types of emotional experiences considered possible between the devotee and Krishna. By examining the emotional components of Krishna bhakti in the Vrindaban context, two areas are highlighted which aid in the understanding of the emotional aspects of mystical devotion in action: (1) the empirical range of variation existing in the practice of Krishna bhakti by a committed Indian population; and (2) the symbolic importance of mystical emotions in everyday interactions between foreign and Indian bhaktas in Vrindaban.

Devotees of ISKCON and Indian residents of Vrindaban interpret and practice devotional mysticism differently. These distinctions are subtle and complex, yet they can be understood by considering the interrelationships between Bhaktivedanta's transmission of Krishna bhakti ideals to his disciples and the processual dynamics which have taken ISKCON from a liminal phenomenon of revitalization to the highly bureaucratic institution that it is today. This historical context helps to explain why ISKCON has developed emotional attitudes that contrast

---

[1] Direct informant quotations in English.

with the attitudes of the local population—attitudes that ultimately function as contrasting ideologies that help define the separate groups operating within a common cultural domain. At the same time, however, enough symbolic agreement exists for the interactive situations between foreign and Indian actors to be integrative events. Practically, this results in the cultural construction of an essentially new emotional reality in Vrindaban that recognizes and incorporates the differences.

EMOTIONAL COMPONENTS OF KRISHNA BHAKTI: THE IDEAL

Perhaps in no other religious system have human emotional potentials been so considered, categorized, and sacralized than in the codification accomplished by the Bengal Vaishnavas. Although many Vrindaban residents are not Bengal Vaishnavas,[2] this sect has been a dominant force in patterning the town's culture; the vocabulary and attitudes of Bengal Vaishnavism infuse every sphere of Vrindaban's sociocultural environment. This is not surprising since those disciples of Chaitanya who produced the sect's literary classics while living there in the early sixteenth century, also simultaneously and overtly initiated Vrindaban's development from wilderness retreat to pilgrimage town. Moreover, the same pervasive concern for an individual's emotional relationship with Krishna exists in a majority of Vrindaban's other Vaishnava sects, though not in such a systematic, Sanskritized form.

The full content and development of the tradition's "science" of devotional emotion (*bhakti-rasa-shastra*) are beyond the scope of this book,[3] but a simplified depiction of its ideals will serve to frame the situations where mystical emotions are employed in the everyday life of Vrindaban, especially in the interactions between Western devotees of ISKCON and native residents and pilgrims.

The person of Chaitanya Mahaprabhu symbolizes for many devotees of Krishna the perfection of spiritual love. His own followers consider

[2] Other Vaishnava sects in Vrindaban for whom Krishna is considered the supreme God include the Nimbarkis, followers of the saint Nimbarka (*c.* 1200); the Vallabhites, followers of Vallabhacharya (a contemporary of Chaitanya); the Radhavallabhis, followers of Hit Harivamsha (early 1500s); and the followers of Swami Haridas (mid-1500s) whose sect is centered around the temple of Banke-Bihari. Followers of the eleventh-century saint Ramanuja are also represented in Vrindaban, and worship mainly at the temple of Rangji. Ramanuja's sect, the Shri Sampradaya, does not worship Krishna, but other forms of Vishnu such as Narayan and Rama. There are other smaller sects as well, usually centered around contemporary or historical saintly figures.

[3] See De 1961, 1976; Kane 1971; Gerow 1977; Kapoor 1977; and Goswami, Shrivatsa 1982 for a more complete discussion of mystical emotions in Bengal Vaishnava theology.

Chaitanya to be an avatar of Krishna himself, who appeared on earth in order to experience firsthand the perfection of love that a person may have with the deity. While sectarian accounts posit that Chaitanya personally expounded the tradition's complex philosophy and theology, he left little writing.[4] Through his inspiration, instruction, and delegation of responsibilities, however, Chaitanya's immediate disciples produced a monumental literary corpus which is considered by the devout to be revealed scripture.

The specific task of defining and elaborating upon religious emotions was given to Rup Goswami, one of the "Six Goswamis" Chaitanya sent to Vrindaban to codify the religion and establish its organizational headquarters (see chapter 2). In two systematic Sanskrit works, *Bhakti-rasamrita-sindhu* and *Ujjvala-nilamani*, Rup outlines the ideals and potentials concerning man's emotional relationships with the Divine.

The terms most commonly associated with mystical emotion by the Indian laity, *bhav* and *ras*, are often used interchangeably, although Rup explains them in such complex categorical detail that only the adept religious specialist or scholar of Sanskrit poetics can appreciate his precision. As De points out, "the terms Rasa and Bhava are difficult to translate, but they have been rendered respectively by the terms 'sentiment' and 'emotion.' . . . The question whether Bhakti is Rasa or Bhava is more or less academic" (1961: 168 n.). It becomes clear, however, from the works of Rup Goswami and his commentators, that in the religious context *bhav* indicates a predisposing emotion that one has toward Krishna which becomes *ras* only when it is highly refined and integrated into the devotee's entire being through experience.

The term *ras*, which can be glossed as the full appreciation of and involvement in an emotional state, is derived from Sanskrit drama and poetics. In the poetic sense *ras* refers to "the supreme relish of literary enjoyment" (De 1961: 166). It was the combination of Rup's knowledge of rhetoric and his sincere devotion to Krishna that made him uniquely qualified to transform the poetic *ras* into a mystical one.

The *rasas*, elevated for the first time to the realm of sublime mystical sentiments by Rup, are patterned primarily upon the emotions that result from various dyadic relationships common to all humans, and these serve as paradigms for the mystical variety. They are specifically based, however, upon the set of relationships that Krishna had with the

---

[4] Chaitanya is credited with writing only eight verses, called *Shikshastaka*. These can be found in Krishnadas's *Chaitanya-charitamrita* and in Rup Goswami's *Padyavali*.

inhabitants of Vrindaban during his descent to earth, and which are believed to eternally exist in the heavenly Vrindaban.

There are five rasas—*shanta, dasya, sakya, vatsalya,* and *madhurya*—that develop out of corresponding *bhavs* of the same name. These bhavs are dominant feelings or "root emotions" that the bhakta recognizes in his own personality and which propel him toward a particular type of relationship with Krishna.

The rasas can be summarized as follows. Shanta-ras is a quiet, peaceful devotion between man and Krishna who is conceived as an omnipotent, benevolent god. The next, dasya-ras, occurs when Krishna is viewed as master and the devotee his servant. Sakya-ras considerably escalates the bhakta's intimacy with Krishna since it results from treating him as a friend or companion. This is followed by vatsalya-ras, the consequence of adopting a parental affection for him. The highest ras, and the one most elaborated by the Vaishnava writers, is madhurya-ras, the passionate, all-consuming pleasure that comes only when Krishna is taken as one's lover.

Krishna and members of his celestial entourage that incarnated some five thousand years ago, according to his devotees' firm belief, enacted each of these relationships, and each actor in this sacred drama is worshiped as an emanation of Krishna's own shakti. His relationships with the gopis and especially Radha, his eternal consort and the personification of his pleasure-giving energy, or *hladini-shakti*, however, symbolize the religion's summum bonum. In the forests of Vrindaban and nowhere else, the village girls would steal away under the light of the full moon to be with Krishna, their beloved. Disregarding their husbands and familial reponsibilities, they could not resist his powerful charms, and together they took part in the mystical circle dance, ras lila. In this dance, Krishna expanded himself so that each maiden—and there were thousands—experienced Krishna as her own. Still, he was at the center of the circle with Radha as the others danced around him, absorbed in the absolute bliss of divine intimacy.[5]

For the Vrindabanbasis, all other emotions pale in comparison, and they are reminded of this in every aspect of their daily lives. As they greet each other on the street, salutations of "*Jai Sri Radhe,*" "*Radhe*

[5] Most residents of Vrindaban would take exception to my describing the ras-lila in the past tense. Not only does the event continue in the celestial realm, but Vrindabanbasis insist that it still occurs nightly in the Vrindaban forests. Those rare individuals whose vision has been purified by their single-minded devotion, it is believed, can witness Krishna's circle dance with the gopis in Vrindaban today.

Radhe,'' or *''Radhe-Shyam''* are exchanged, each directing the mind to Radha and the ultimate relationship that she shares with Krishna. In shops, tea stalls, and homes, lithographs depicting the circle dance are prominently displayed and attended with devotion. The image of Krishna rarely appears without Radha by his side in the temples of Vrindaban. It is not Krishna who is worshiped, but Radha and Krishna together.

Local residents often say that ''Vrindaban calls''; if a person is in Vrindaban for any reason it is because he or she has heard the music of Krishna's flute, although there may be no conscious awareness of it. Some will say that anyone who walks upon the dust of Vrindaban is an eternal actor in Krishna's cosmic play. But other permanent residents of Vrindaban possess a narrower attitude than this. Although they speak of themselves as bhaktas, they see no need for ritual; they claim to constantly and spontaneously experience the emotion of mystical, passionate love with Krishna, the most sublime emotional state that can be humanly achieved. Some are merchants, some are priests, some mendicant widows, but regardless of social position they see other devotees as inferior. They possess the unique inheritance of Vrindaban's madhurya-ras, and herein lies a principal clue to understanding the difference between the Vaishnavas of Vrindaban and the Vaishnavas of ISKCON.

ISKCON AND *MADHURYA-RAS*

For a full week in March of 1982, loudspeakers atop the temple of Radha-Shyamsundar blared in all directions day and night, broadcasting the ''great chant,'' or mahamantra.[6] The amplified singing, however, did little to suggest what was actually going on in the temple below. Inside, in the large courtyard before the deities' inner sanctum, hundreds of pilgrims and Vrindaban residents sat tightly packed around a square clearing where the performers sang, danced, and played a variety of musical instruments. Over one hundred young men, members of a professional troop from Bengal, alternated in small groups to keep the mantra from dying. Quite apart from their musical abilities, these

---

[6] Chaitanya taught that this chant was especially beneficial for the present epoch, and chanting this mantra forms the core practice for devotees of ISKCON. Its thirty-two syllables are: Hare Krishna, Hare Krishna, Krishna Krishna, Hare Hare; Hare Rama, Hare Rama, Rama Rama, Hare Hare.

men were skilled actors, capable of invoking intense emotions from their audience, and many worshipers wept unashamedly.

During one of the sessions that I attended, two other Westerners were among the worshipers there. One, standing near the entrance barely inside the temple, was recognizably an ISKCON devotee; the other wore clothing that distinguished him from ISKCON,[7] and had slightly different forehead markings (tilak). But the most noticeable thing about this second foreign Vaishnava was that he was the center of attention, rolling on the floor in a tight embrace with one of the performers, tears streaming from his eyes. Members of the crowd jostled to touch his feet and rub onto their foreheads the dust from where he rolled.

The Hare Krishna devotee expressed to me the disgust with which he viewed the entire event: "These are *sahajiyas* (member of a heterodox Chaitanyite sect which uses ritualized sexual intercourse as a primary practice) and Prabhupad warned us that in Vrindaban they are the most dangerous to our spiritual progress. I shouldn't be here at all, even if they are chanting 'Hare Krishna' constantly." Later I spoke with the other Westerner, a thirty-two-year-old Dutchman, and discovered that he had once been in ISKCON himself, having left over a year before to pursue aspects of bhakti which were, according to him, not permissible in ISKCON. He explained: "I came to Vrindaban in ISKCON, and I owe it a lot, but ISKCON cannot give you Vrindaban. In ISKCON, Vrindaban is actually a bother, but now Vrindaban is my salvation. Prabhupad was my diksha guru, but now my shisksha guru is Tripuri Baba. I was filled with desire for the madhurya-ras and now I can practice the proper *sadhana* (spiritual practices). In ISKCON there is no madhurya-ras, no ras at all."

These two individuals personify the struggle that ISKCON has had in understanding and codifying its doctrine concerning the practice of bhakti, especially the dimensions of mystical emotion. The Hare Krishna devotee was expressing his organization's official attitude that for the vast majority of people the proper practice entails disciplined ritual activity, *vaidhi-bhakti*; his former god-brother was happy that he could now indulge in an unrestrained, spontaneous emotional relationship with Krishna, *raganuga-bhakti*. Dimock (1966: 183) notes that "Vaishnavas of all sorts consider that there are two general types of bhakti. The first is an external, ritual activity based on the injunctions

---

[7] He wore a waistcloth, rather than a dhoti as ISKCON members do. The dhoti is a long cloth wrapped around the waist and drawn between the legs, forming a loose pantlike garment.

of the *śāstras* (*vidhi*)[8] and is called vaidhi-bhakti. The second is the internal, passionate relationship of the released jīva [soul] to Kṛṣṇa and is called *rāgānuga-bhakti*. Vaidhi-bhakti is for that great majority of persons who are neither by nature in direct relationship to Kṛṣṇa nor yet released from māyā [illusion] by completion of the disciplines.''

Reflection upon Bhaktivedanta Swami's career and his interactions with American devotees, makes apparent his possession of both a theoretical and practical understanding of the details of bhakti in all its variety. Yet as ISKCON institutionalized, a trend developed toward ritual practice and away from spontaneous emotionalism, especially in the interpretation of passionate love with Krishna.

In his early writings in the United States, Bhaktivedanta Swami shows a professional understanding of the complexities of the emotional theory expounded by Rup Goswami. In the first book published by the International Society for Krishna Consciousness, *Teachings of Lord Chaitanya* (1968), he makes repeated reference to both the title and content of Rup's *Bhakti-rasamrita-sindhu* and *Ujjvala-nilamani*.

The introduction of this book is a transcript of lectures given in New York on April 10–17, 1967, and in it Bhaktivedanta makes reference to all the potential relationships between Krishna and his devotee, concluding that ''above all you can treat Krishna as your lover'' (1968: 6). In the same lecture series, however, he admonishes his disciples that this stage can be obtained only after much study and practice: ''Unfortunately, people of less intelligence turn at once to the pleasure potency sports of Krishna. . . . [This] . . . is not understood by ordinary men, because they do not understand Krishna. . . . These people . . . think that this is a kind of religion where we can indulge in sex and become religionists. This is called *Prakriti Sahajia*—materialistic lust'' (8).

Already at this early stage, Bhaktivedanta has introduced the basic distinction between vaidhi- and raganuga-bhakti, though not by name, and specifically warns about the sahajiya ''heresy.'' In the following chapters, however, he becomes specific and precise, detailing the types of emotions by their Sanskrit nomenclature. He concludes that ''there are sixty-four kinds of devotional service, and by performing these regulative principles one can rise up to the stage of this unconditional devotion of the Gopis. Affection for Krishna exactly on the level of the

---

[8] Indian scriptures are called *shastra*. The specific texts included in the *shastra* category vary from sect to sect. Dimock points out that for the Bengal Vaishnavas ''the term *shastra* means the *Bhāgavata-purāṇa*'' (Dimock 1966: 183). Vaidhi-bhakti is ritual activity based on scriptural injunction.

Gopis is called *Raganuga*, spontaneous love. In the spontaneous loving affair with Krishna, there is no necessity of following the Vedic rules and regulations'' (1968: 279).

One can only wonder what his new disciples were thinking as Bhaktivedanta discoursed upon a strict system of rules they were expected to adopt on the one hand, and the erotically tinged, rule-free model of the advanced bhakta's relationship with God on the other. Many had been recruited from the ''counterculture,'' and their joining with ''swamiji'' was a symbolic rejection of their own culture, complemented by a spontaneous act of spiritual adventurism; few had any idea of the radical transformation that their guru had in mind for them.

But whatever starts out as a revitalization movement must go through processes of routinization and institutionalization if it is to survive the excitement of the formative period, and this was no less the case for the Hare Krishna movement. From devotee accounts, from the thorough biography of Bhaktivedanta Swami by one of his early disciples, Satsvarupa dasa Goswami, and from the writings of Bhaktivedanta after his arrival in the United States, we obtain a picture of the difficulties and conflicts that had to be confronted and resolved in order for the movement to survive. Always in the background was a sense of urgency prompted by the tacit understanding that at anytime the elderly founder-guru could leave the scene. Two cases in particular are revealing. One illustrates how the bureaucratization of ISKCON was initiated; the other provides insight into the institutional emphasis of vaidhi- over raganuga-bhakti.

In the Indian context, the practice of bhakti is highly individualized, structured primarily by an intimate personal relationship between devotee and guru. Subsequently, standardization is minimal; each individual develops his own style of practice over time. As the number of Bhaktivedanta's Western disciples increased, however, he realized that the intimate style of devotee-guru interaction was not practical. Instead, he decided to ''be present'' in his books and in the developing organization. As ISKCON grew, he eventually wearied of the demands of personally managing increasing assets and having to make every decision, no matter how trivial.

This resulted in the formation of the Governing Body Commission (GBC) in 1970 and a decision to allow more disciples to become sannyasis,[9] both critical steps toward the general decentralization of power

---

[9] The word *sannyasi* means renunciate or ascetic, but in ISKCON it takes on added meaning. All

in preparation for his inevitable demise. The first gave decision-making authority to a larger group; the second provided a mechanism for promoting "advanced" devotees to a higher status. The sannyasis in effect became a body of teachers not bound to a single temple, but charged with traveling throughout the ISKCON world to insure standardization of doctrine and practice.

Satsvarupa dasa Goswami (1982: 79–116) details a series of events during the first half of 1970 that Bhaktivedanta perceived as a "threat" to ISKCON, and which culminated in these two decisions. As the guru and his disciples established the new Los Angeles temple, the plan was not only to develop the L.A. center as the movement's world headquarters, but also to turn it into an ISKCON showplace, and Bhaktivedanta took personal supervision over the details. Furthermore, he would stay there and instruct devotees himself in the proprieties of ritual worship and spiritual practice, asking individuals from other centers to visit and observe the standard expected in every temple.

As the center developed, however, Bhaktivedanta became angry over mistakes in ritual practice and a general laxness in the daily practices which he had prescribed, especially in the requirement of chanting sixteen "rounds" of the mantra daily (one round equals a completed rosary of one hundred and eight beads, the mantra said on each bead). He was displeased with the devotees' retention of details from his lectures and their apparent failure to read the books already published. But more than that, he was seriously troubled over incidents that indicated his disciples' misinterpretations and reinterpretations concerning his own status as guru.

Seeing the need to take matters in hand before they got out of control, and before internal politics resulted in competition for power among the managers of various temples, he called a meeting of his senior disciples in order to legally institute the GBC. By doing this he felt that it would free him from management and allow him to personally concentrate on expanding the movement in India. On July 28, 1970, the GBC became a fact, composed of twelve members, each responsible for a different "zone" into which the world had been divided. They would make all decisions except the most major ones, and

---

devotees are required to be renunciates, which implies celibacy if they are not married. However, sannyasi is a higher status than *brahmachari*, the status that most devotees occupy. Only long-term, advanced devotees may become sannyasis through a special initiation from the guru. The sannyasis in ISKCON are all unmarried, are considered enlightened teachers, and are required to not establish any permanent residence, instead traveling from temple to temple.

after Bhaktivedanta's death, as a body, they would be the last word on matters of doctrine and practice.

In effect, formation of the GBC determined the organizational structure of ISKCON for the movement's future. It was an ecumenical body which would share the power of the guru, institutionalizing Bhaktivedanta's unmistakably clear order that no one person should be appointed to a supreme position of power after his death. By forming the GBC, he assured the decentralization of power and the standardization of doctrine and ritual, preventing anyone who maintained allegiance to ISKCON from pursuing a practice of bhakti that deviated from his specifications. And it was clear by this point that the style of bhakti that Bhaktivedanta insisted upon, and the style that ISKCON would institutionalize, was vaidhi, not raganuga. The GBC would have to insure that devotees understood it was their duty to observe the rules and regulations rather than prematurely attempt to imbibe the madhurya-ras.

Those scholars who have studied Rup Goswami's works agree that he elevated madhurya-ras to supreme importance, and that raganuga-bhakti of madhurya-ras was the principal path leading to realization. Madhurya also was a dominant theme for Bhaktivedanta during his early lectures, but as ISKCON developed, it was definitely de-emphasized in favor of the techniques of vaidhi-bhakti.

ISKCON informants who were near Bhaktivedanta during the first five or six years note this shift of emphasis in his lectures and writings. One female disciple still active in the movement offers this explanation:

> At first I think Prabhupad thought the disciples who came to him would be already advanced due to many past lifetimes of devotional service. But then he saw that we were not. . . . I think he had to reevaluate his opinion. Then he knew he had to emphasize the basics, drill us with the regulations, and if ISKCON was to survive, it had to be based on the fundamentals. It became considered a great offense to suggest we had any spontaneous love for Krishna.

Another ISKCON devotee writes in response to my inquiry on the subject:

> Prabhupada . . . frequently warned against what he viewed as the deception of illicitly bypassing the basic rules of purification and putting on pretentious displays of *madhurya*-type sentiment while indulging in sex. It is genuine disgust for this sort of fakery (which apparently is quite widespread), coupled with his realization of the neophyte (and thus vulnerable) status of

his western disciples, that led Prabhupada to strongly emphasize the basics.
The point wasn't to confine his disciples to the lower rungs of the ladder of
bhakti, but to carefully and systematically prepare them for a genuine and
secure ascent. Sahajaya-ism . . . is the result both of impatience and of
pride: an impatience with the usually gradual nature of spiritual progress
(resulting in premature adoption of the external behavioral characterisitics
of advanced bhaktas), and the desire to be regarded and reverenced as a
saint.[10]

If there was any question among devotees concerning the path which
Bhaktivedanta wished them to pursue, it was unequivocally resolved
in 1976. At the Los Angeles temple a group began meeting to specifically research Bhaktivedanta's teachings concerning madhurya-ras.
Known within ISKCON now as the "*gopi-bhav* clique," Bhaktivedanta
became furious when he learned about its activities. As a result, he
directed GBC representatives to send a letter to all temples in an effort
to provide a conclusive statement regarding the matter. An excerpt of
that letter is revealing:[11]

> Srila Prabhupada was disturbed to find that a group of devotees in Iskcon
> were misreading his books, and making a special attempt to fix their minds
> on Krsna's confidential pastimes with the gopis, so that they can be elevated
> to the position of gopis after they quit their present bodies. This unauthor-
> ized hearing attempt greatly angered His Divine Grace. . . . So we feel it
> necessary, in order to please Srila Prabhupada, to make available some of
> Prabhupada's recent statements.

Enclosed in the same letter were questions posed by devotees concerning the "sahajiya tendencies in ISKCON," with Bhaktivedanta's responses. His adamant position that ISKCON devotees were not ready to
participate in the madhurya-ras via raganuga-bhakti had been exhibited
before, and would continue to be until his death in Vrindaban the following year, but these answers left little room for interpretation:

Q: The gopis are pleasing Krsna the most.

A: Gopi is the highest stage, but you are on lowest, beginner, rascal stage,
so how can you understand. Don't become monkeys, jumping over to the

---

[10] Letter from Shubananda das, September 4, 1985. Parentheses appear in the text.
[11] Letter to all ISKCON temples from Hridayananda dasa Gosvami, and Ramesvara dasa Swami,
both GBC representatives, dated June 17, 1976.

gopi's rasa lila. There are already enough monkeys in Vrindaban, we don't need any more.

Q: If this is not to be discussed, why is it in the books, and why are we selling these books?

A: Everything, all subjects, must be in the books. That is another thing. But different sections are meant for different stages. . . . You have introduced some new thing, studying so much about the gopis, without taking permission from your spiritual master—where is the evidence that you have come to the fool stage! Follow Lord Chaitanya's example first—don't jump over like monkeys to rasa lila. Do you think you're better than Lord Chaitanya? . . . Why did Vyasadeva place Krsna's confidential pastimes in the 10th Canto [of *Bhagavata-Purana*]? You must approach Krsna by going through the first nine cantos, step by step.

Q: To develop our ideal spiritual body in the next life, we should have a strong desire for thinking of the gopis.

A: First there must be no lust or sex desire, otherwise you go to hell. To think of Krsna while lusting for sex is sahajiya life. This contamination comes from the babajis in Vrndavana. No devotee should wander around Vrndavana apart from our organized program. If this sahajiya nonsense continues, then all preaching will stop.

MYSTICAL EMOTIONS IN INTERACTION: THE VRINDABAN CONTEXT

When ISKCON devotees come to Vrindaban on pilgrimage, they may try to heed Bhaktivedanta's advice not "to wander around Vrindaban," but to totally isolate themselves from encounters with the Indian population is impossible. Even if a visiting devotee never left the Krishna-Balaram temple, he could not escape interaction, for thousands of Indian pilgrims visit there daily. And for the nucleus of devotees who live in and around the temple, some for as long as nine years, involvement in the community is considerable.

All that I have said in the previous sections of this chapter has been necessary to frame the interactions that I now consider.[12] There are both

[12] Few interactions in Vrindaban between ISKCON devotees and Indian pilgrims and residents lack a concern for the mystical-emotional components of the religious system. A review of the situations discussed in chapters 5 and 6 should further augment this point for the reader. The situations presented in this chapter, as in the other chapters, are representative of many others that are similar and regularly occurring.

similarities and contrasts between the Vaishnavas of Vrindaban and the Vaishnavas of ISKCON. Vrindaban residents see themselves as purer, or more advanced, than their Western counterparts. They either perceive themselves as raganuga-bhaktas, or more ethnocentrically, believe their human bodies are identical with their spiritual bodies (*siddha-deha*), making them transcendental lovers of Krishna by birth. They are always "in the bhav," in a constant state of the mystical emotional rapture of madhurya-ras.

Although ISKCON devotees will admit that this is possible, especially in Vrindaban, they see the vast majority as not true bhaktas at all. Rather, they evaluate many Vrindaban residents as poseurs who present themselves as advanced devotees without the credentials to do so. Furthermore, they interpret those whose claim to the madhurya-ras rests in a sexually oriented ritual practice—justified as an enactment of Krishna's erotic behavior with the gopis—as the most perverted. These, of course, are the sahajiyas, and they represent a threat to all sincere, orthodox bhaktas.

The path of vaidhi-bhakti is visible in the public behavior of all ISKCON members in Vrindaban. Wherever the devotees go, their right hands are constantly fingering beads, and their mantra is constantly being uttered. They initiate and conclude encounters with exclamations of *"Hare Krishna"* rather than *"Radhe-Shyam"* as the local residents and pilgrims most often do. Although Vrindaban is the place of Radha, they generally avoid mention of her name in greeting. Shouts of *"Radhe Radhe"* go on all around them, but few will join in lest they be seen as violating their organization's ritual policy. The ISKCON temple itself symbolizes this contrast, with its central deities of Krishna and his brother Balaram instead of Radha and Krishna whose images occupy a side altar.

This is not the case in most ISKCON temples, for they too are usually Radha-Krishna temples. But as if to say that madhurya-ras is too dangerous in Vrindaban, Bhaktivedanta de-emphasized Radha in the movement's ritual worship there. In the majority of Vrindaban's indigenous temples, Radha and Krishna are central; worship of Krishna without Radha is unthinkable. For ISKCON, worship of Krishna in a manner not prescribed by Bhaktivedanta Swami is unthinkable.

Such symbolic contrasts lead some Vrindaban residents to conclude that the Western devotees are of a different "type," and in these ways they are. Yet each side is justified and sanctioned by different aspects of the same tradition. Through the practical activities that occur in the everyday life of Vrindaban, these differences are confronted, the vocabulary of mystical emotion is used, meanings are altered, and new levels of understanding concerning each side's interpretation and legitimacy are achieved. In short, interaction implies change.

Denzin (1984: 54, 58) writes that "emotionality is a circular process that begins and ends with the transactions and actions of the self in the social situation interacting with self and others." Although Denzin is not speaking of mystical emotions, his analysis still applies; the perception and evaluation of any emotion is ultimately the result of an individual's self-reflection. Whether or not the object of stimulation is real or imagined, human or divine, the emotional experience is similar.

The types of bhakti practiced in Vrindaban are limited only by individual inclination and imagination. One sadhu keeps his image of the infant Krishna (Gopal), in a cage so that he will not crawl away and get into trouble. A teacher worships a similar image with parental affection (*vatsalya-ras*) by bathing and powdering her image before she gently rocks him to sleep with a lullaby. The emotions of friendship (*sakya-ras*) are cultivated by a cloth merchant who imagines both he and Krishna are cowherd boys, and he sometimes accompanies his image into the fields to find fresh pasture for their cows.

But the emotions associated with intimate, conjugal love (madhurya) predominate. In one temple a young priest confided that his guru was teaching him the most esoteric practice, and he reluctantly showed me the sari he would sometimes wear in order to more fully experience the love that Radha has for Krishna. Another ascetic residing along the banks of the Jumna River rarely speaks, but when he does it is with a gentle feminine voice, the result some say of his constantly imagining himself as a gopi sporting with her lover, Krishna. These practices, though not necessarily prescribed by sectarian traditions, are part of Vrindaban's everyday reality.

This reality that highly values raganuga-bhakti confronts devotees of ISKCON full force as they venture into the the social world there; their only alternative is to retreat behind Krishna-Balaram's high walls, a choice that few of them make. The three examples that follow illustrate how their confrontation of this reality ultimately leads to its transformation. In these situations of interaction which focus upon mystical emotions, both Indian and foreign actors alter their conceptions of each other and in the process essentially create a new emotional environment for Vrindaban.

Becoming a Gopi

Ratin, a British devotee, has lived in Vrindaban for nine years. During 1982 he was revising a manuscript about the sacred sites of Vrindaban which he hoped to publish. Some local residents even considered him an authority on the indigenous dance-dramas about Krishna, ras-lila;[13] he knew when and where the most obscure troops would perform, and was often a guest in homes of some of their leaders, the *rasdharis*. Ratin had documented the best-known pilgrimage locations, and was now searching for lesser-known places by spending time with some of the town's sadhus. Throughout his research he strictly followed the rules and regulations prescribed by ISKCON and would regularly participate in the ritual at Krishna-Balaram temple. Other devotees, however, considered some of his activities "unauthorized" and suggested that he was putting himself in spiritual danger.

One hot afternoon Ratin invited me to accompany him and a sadhu he had met to a site called Radharani,[14] and it required a trek of four kilometers across the river in the blazing sun. As we walked, the sadhu explained that the significance of Radharani was in its transformative power. This place was a deep pond surrounded by desert, and many varieties of waterfowl came there from the nearby Bharatpur bird sanctuary. There we would also find, the sadhu informed us, other renunciates who would welcome us. "They are there for one special reason," he said. "A bath in the Radharani *kund* (pond) will give you the body of a gopi so you can love Krishna like Radha. Even Lord Shiva came here so he could take part in ras-lila."[15]

At this point Ratin stopped and announced that he could not go through with the visit to Radharani, feeling that he was in danger of violating ISKCON doctrine. As he put it, his "delicate creeper of bhakti would be wilted by the fire of unauthorized madhurya-ras." The sadhu insisted, nevertheless, that Ratin must go. It was a holy place and very good for *japa* (chanting) even if Ratin did not desire the body of a gopi, and our guide said that he would be personally offended if we turned back now. "Babaji, you are a devotee of Krishna and I cannot commit an offense toward you, so let's continue," was Ratin's reply.

Arriving at Radharani we found an oasis. Palm trees surrounded the large, cool pond and giant cranes walked lazily about. Naked sadhus stood neck deep in the dark green water, motionless, oblivious to our

[13] See Hein 1972 and Hawley 1981 for descriptions of the ras-lila.
[14] This site is also called Mansarovar.
[15] Quotations of the sadhu were translated from a combination of Hindi and English.

arrival. Our guide also walked immediately into the water, but Ratin sat down upon the steps leading into the pond and refused to enter. "What is this?" the ascetic yelled. "You are afraid of seeing Krishna? You are a devotee and will not see Krishna?" For half an hour the taunting continued until Ratin finally relented, but only to please the sadhu. After an hour of listening to the legends about Radharani and songs the mendicant sang about its wonders, we returned to Vrindaban as the sun was beginning to set and the temple bells beckoned the faithful to evening worship.

The next day I met Ratin with a group of ISKCON devotees, headed again for Radharani. Later he told me that he had been overcome with mystical emotion there, and he would not deny the experience. "I cannot tell many people about this or I will be ostracized," he explained, "but I cannot feel threatened by this babaji; I cannot see him as dangerous. I had a true experience of madhurya-ras at Radharani, and this can only help my practice. I can't be obsessed with paranoia about these sacred places around here. I have to take advantage while I have the chance."

The sadhu also experienced a change in attitude about ISKCON: "When the videshi comes with me it is a good thing. Before I thought these videshis were all bad, but not now. Ratin had a hard heart and Radha has softened it. So she can soften all videshi hearts. Ratin is now a Brajbasi because he can feel the ras, so now I know videshis are not all bad."

It may not be surprising for a sadhu to accept the legitimacy of an individual from ISKCON since the sadhu himself makes a statement concerning the importance of his own individuality by virtue of the life he has chosen. A more striking example, however, is the case of a Loi Bazaar merchant, a dealer in general goods who dramatically altered his opinion of ISKCON.

A Merchant's Change of Heart

This merchant had initially told me that foreigners could never become devotees because they felt no ras: "Only Indians can be bhaktas. ISK-CON people are just salesmen. They come to sell cameras and videos to us poor people, and then they buy cloth and silver here and there. It is the decline of Vrindaban. They should all go back."[16] Perhaps these comments reflected to some degree the merchant's anger over his not

---

[16] Quotations of the merchant were translated from a combination of Hindi and English.

sharing in the profits from ISKCON's presence in Vrindaban, while others had obviously become wealthy because of it. A year later, however, this same merchant displayed in his shop photographs of the Krishna-Balaram deities, Bhaktivedanta Swami, and Kirtanananda Swami, one of the present ISKCON gurus who comes to Vrindaban regularly. The merchant's attitude had obviously changed .

I asked the merchant why he displayed these pictures if he felt ISKCON signalled dark days for Vrindaban, as he had said previously. He replied, "No, they are really gopis." Sensing my astonishment, he called me into the shop to discuss his change of mind, or rather, as he put it, his change of heart. Several months before, by the force of karma, he suggested, a new devotee family had moved into town, and they were buying all their supplies from him. Soon other devotees began to patronize his store, improving his financial situation dramatically. "They buy big things: stoves, lanterns, pots, so many things. And every day they come for soap and bisquits." The merchant insisted that his new appreciation for ISKCON was not simply an economic one.

Through a series of encounters, he had begun to notice the sincerity and perseverance of his new ISKCON patrons, especially their perpetual chanting, and moreover, their dedication to Bhaktivedanta, whom he had known slightly as a "sadhu baba" years before his success in the West. "Prabhupad was mahatma, but I felt his disciples were just hippie fools. Now my friends (the devotees) worship him and the new guru, Bhaktipad (Kirtanananda)." The merchant continued to explain that his own guru, an old man he had not seen for many years, was also a mahatma. As his attitude toward the devotees began to change, he learned that Kirtanananda was coming to Vrindaban, and a meeting was arranged.

Kirtanananda finally arrived and spent a full day in the cloth shop across from the merchant's general store, purchasing a year's supply of cloth to outfit the entire population of New Vrindaban, ISKCON's farm community in West Virginia which he heads. The merchant explained:

> He spent *laks* (one lak equals one hundred thousand) of rupees just sitting there, and all the time he spoke only of Krishna. Then he came to my store and told me that my friends were his disciples, and that they gave him a good report about me. He made some small purchases and then asked me about Krishna, and I told him my guru also had instructed me since I was a small boy, and that always I think of Radha. He told me that was very good,

but sometimes I should also chant Hare Ram, Hare Krishna. Then he gave me a tulsi mala, a very old one from Radhakund. Since he was very nice to me, I started to think about my guru who is in Kosi now, and I started to feel that this ISKCON guru has love for Krishna like a Brajbasi. He was so soft in his heart, and then I thought about seeing my own guru maharaj. My guruji read my bad thoughts also about ISKCON people and told me this was not good. He told me they are not demons; they are really gopis reborn as videshis which is why they always chant ''Krishna, Krishna.''

The sadhu, through his experience with Ratin, decided that foreign devotees were capable of experiencing mystical emotions. But more than this, the experience resulted not only in the simple acceptance of some individual ISKCON members, but also a recognition of the type of bhakti that ISKCON as a whole institutionalizes. For the sadhu and others who have had similar interactions with devotees, the ritual approach of vaidhi-bhakti was shown to have validity; to paraphrase the sadhu, the path that ISKCON has taken apparently is sufficient to eventually bring one to the advanced state of being able to experience the madhurya-ras. This is a change not only in attitude toward ISKCON, but also toward the ritual approach in general, which other Indians also utilize. Similarly, the merchant radically altered his opinion of devotees from materialistic ''demons'' to reincarnated gopis, a supernatural explanation which served the same function.

On the ISKCON side, Ratin demonstrates a trend of lessening antagonism toward the local population, especially the ascetics who are often stereotyped as sahajiya. Any acceptance by ISKCON devotees of a display of spontaneous emotionalism represents, at this stage, a significant relaxation of rigid attitudes against sahajiya tendencies. Both cases show that group boundaries created by differences in interpretation of dogma concerned with mystical emotions are weakening.

Another change in ISKCON's attitude is shown by the willingness of devotees to seek information concerning details of ritual from local temple priests, as mentioned in the previous chapter. A particularly revealing case that deals with emotional techniques involves a priest from the temple of Radha-Vallabh whose theology emphasizes the worship of Radha. This priest, recognized as one of his sect's ''experts,'' had always been intrigued by the ISKCON phenomenon, and generally saw it as part of Krishna's plan; he had been anxious to help when some devotees began to inquire about details of deity worship.

Although ISKCON devotees considered the deity worship at Radha-

Vallabh to be of a high standard and were prompted to seek information from the priests there for that reason, they still felt that the sect's emphasis on Radha over Krishna was dangerous and unauthorized, and therefore devotees were warned to avoid being influenced by the priests.

One ISKCON temple priest in charge of deity worship explained that he now considered the movement's official attitude toward Vrindaban priests to be unwarranted, that instead of viewing them with disgust, they should be treated with respect, and he cited a personal example:

> I used to think Jai Goswami represented everything dangerous about service in Vrindaban. He would talk about himself as a gopi and would tell me about the secret meetings he planned with Krishna where Krishna wouldn't show, and how he would hurt so badly about being stood up by Krishna. He did this to feel the love that Radha and the gopis felt for Krishna. I thought he was really crazy at first, but sometimes as he talked about missing Krishna, tears would pour down his face and he couldn't talk, and I would find myself choking up too. I watched *gosvamiji* in the temple also and saw his affection for thakurji, and the painstaking, loving care he would give to Him. . . .[17] He never tried to make me change, but just showed me how to feel the ras by his own example. Maybe Jai Goswami is not typical, but he shows me that ISKCON should take the Brajbasis one by one, not just say they are all dangerous, and be arrogant and aloof with the other people of Braj. We must mature in the way we treat people outside the movement, and especially in Vrindaban cooperate with the Brajbasis to form a solid foundation for the future of Krishna Consciousness in the world.

Beyond Mutual Acceptance

These three representative cases demonstrate the dynamics of mutual accommodation between Vrindaban residents and ISKCON devotees in situations where mystical emotions are either a dominant or peripheral focus. More than this, however, through their dealings with ISKCON in this context, Indians have been forced to bring to consciousness the dual approaches to mystical devotion, and this has had an effect upon the personal knowledge of their own religious system. In some cases this alters their daily routine and subsequently affects relationships with other Indians in the community. Without the stimulus provided by

[17] The Radha-Vallabh sect was founded by Hit Harivamsha, who based its theology on the primary importance of Radha. Although in ritual and spiritual practice Krishna becomes secondary, the Radha-Vallabh temple's main image is Krishna. There is no anthropomorphic image of Radha, but rather a silver tablet with her name inscribed upon it which is placed beside the Krishna image.

daily confrontations with the "opposing" view, the merits of vaidhi-bhakti would not likely have been contemplated.

One of the most noticeable effects of an individual's determining that he should increase his practice of vaidhi techniques is the addition of a bead bag to his everyday dress. The small cloth bag, hung around one's neck with a thin cloth strap or string, protects the sacred rosary and allows the wearer to unobtrusively finger the beads at any time. One tailor commented that in the past few years the sale of bead bags has increased "many fold," not only to ISKCON devotees but also to residents and pilgrims. He also explained that by giving a free bead bag with large purchases, he discovered a useful way to increase sales and win clients from his competition:

When the videshis came here, since they all wore bead bags, sometimes I gave them a free one when they employed my services. It was only good business, and it worked very well. In the beginning no one else would be seen with a bag, except some sadhus maybe. But now I also give bags to Brajbasis also. This used to help my business, but now every tailor does it; it is now an expected gift. Also people will come just to purchase a new bag. This is one change ISKCON has brought: to make the bead bag a stylish item of wardrobe. Who could have imagined it?[18]

One Loi bazaar merchant suggested that the popularizing of the bead bag simply allowed him to wear one without derision from his associates, and he did not feel that it identified him with ISKCON in any way. "After all, they got the idea from us," he explained. Others admitted that it was a new practice for them—that their increased practice of chanting necessitated it—and that without ISKCON's influence they probably would not have thought about their own spiritual deficiencies. A Brahman restaurant owner reflected:

When I saw these videshis were so serious for chanting, they made me a little ashamed. I would boast about how I felt for Krishna—I was a proud Brajbasi, always loving Krishna. Really, it was so much show. So I thought, "Why I should deceive myself?" What I needed was some serious effort to bring me closer to Krishna, so now I am chanting, and doing some better puja in my home and here where I work.[19]

Adoption of more precise ritual practice, however, is not without its effect on day-to-day interaction among Indians in Vrindaban. For some

---

[18] Translation from conversation in Hindi.
[19] Translated from conversation in Hindi and English.

it has altered relationships within families and in public social life. Among sadhus, mendicant widows, and those who "retire" to Vrindaban there is little consequence; but for others, especially merchants and craftsmen, the changes have considerable impact. The wife of one Loi Bazaar merchant commented that her husband's demands for stricter worship of Radha-Krishna in the home had disrupted the family routine:

> Always the "gods' corner" was the household center, but it did not demand time. Anyone could light some incense and place flowers and water there. Now my husband insists we formally offer food to Krishna each meal, and all must attend. Of course this is good practice, but who must prepare the special food? Certainly not the men! And he desires that we all chant with him, and there is no time in a busy household that is properly run. I am not saying that ISKCON has brought about this, but only since they have come has this happened. Every day he is having dealings with so many [ISKCON devotees], so their influence is certainly there. Perhaps it will pass. Or perhaps I will grow accustomed.[20]

In the bazaars those who have in some way increased their practice of vaidhi-bhakti have found that some social relationships have been restructured. This is especially the case in relationships that include persons critical of ISKCON. One perpetual ISKCON critic who would be happy if the devotees left, refuses to talk to a former friend whom he claims (appropriating a Western media stereotype) was "brainwashed":

> We Brajbasis have no use for their mumbo-jumbo superstitions. We are born on an advanced level. Our birthright is eternal relations with our Gopal. This Hare Krishna chanting is kindergarten stuff, that's all. After many thousands of lifetimes these videshis may reach our present stage, but it is degrading to our sensibilities to see good Brajbasis imitate them. I will not visit with him (his former friend) while he keeps this up. We were born in Vrindaban, so what is the need of magic to bring us to the Krishna consciousness. This is automatic to us.[21]

Professional religious specialists have also felt the effect of an increase in personal ritual practice in the general community. This is primarily because, again, some feel their status and power has been threat-

---

[20] Quoted from conversation in English.
[21] Quoted from conversation in English.

ened. One priest angrily explained that ritual order should be maintained only by legitimate Brahman priests. He admonished: "If one is inclined, he should consult a priest and take instruction from him as guru. Sadhana must be tailored to the person, not just on whim start chanting one mantra. The mantra must be tailor-made and secretly given. Actually, our people have the ras by living here only. Let them (ISKCON) do their thing by all means, but let them keep it to themselves without confusing our people's minds."[22]

These examples suggest that interactions concerning mystical emotions are not without tensions, but nevertheless have resulted in more than a general acknowledgment that ISKCON's style of emotional practice is legitimate. Beyond mutual acceptance, residents of Vrindaban have in some cases altered their own conception of how to achieve the goal of an emotional relationship with Krishna, and this has in turn affected relationships between Indians themselves. This, of course, does not always work in ISKCON's favor, alienating even more severely those Vrindaban residents who have always insisted that the foreign devotees were intrusive and disruptive. The situation, however, underscores again the integration that ISKCON is achieving in Vrindaban, an integration that necessitates changes and transformations on numerous levels.

The situational dynamics occurring in Vrindaban are certainly not one-sided, however, and some ISKCON devotees have been affected just as dramatically by their exposure to the spontaneous emotionalism exhibited by Vrindabanbasis. But the "official" ISKCON attitude at this time is intransigent; if a devotee wishes to practice raganuga-bhakti instead of vaidhi-bhakti, he has no choice but to leave the organization. Some ISKCON members, such as the former devotee who participated in the events at Radha-Shyamsundar noted earlier in this chapter, have done just that. This too serves an integrative function in that ISKCON-created foreign Vaishnavas plunge deeper into the indigenous Indian culture, taking their own culture change one step further.

SUMMARY

In this chapter I have discussed the ideals of Krishna bhakti as they relate to the individual's experience and expression of mystical emotions; and as they are embodied in the dual paths of Krishna devotion-

---

[22] Quoted from conversation in English.

alism, represented by the practices of vaidhi-bhakti on the one hand, and raganuga-bhakti on the other. Although these are two complementary components of the same religious system which idealizes the achievement of mystical emotional states, they have practically functioned as divisive ideologies between ISKCON and Indian devotees of Krishna in Vrindaban.

Neither side fully embodies the emotional ideals as explicated in the religion's texts. Vrindabanbasis claim a natural inheritance of spontaneous love for Krishna, and ISKCON officially does not admit to a range of possibilities outside the boundaries of Bhaktivedanta's instructions, which are extensive but by no means exhaustive. However, in the actual situations of interaction between devotees from both groups, an accommodation is being achieved through the processes of conflict resolution and meaning negotiation which occur in the practical enactment of their cultural ideals.

More than simple mutual acceptance, however, these situations result in social transformations. Adoption of ritual techniques espoused by ISKCON in their practice of vaidhi-bhakti affects the quality of established relationships between Indian residents and constrains the type of new relationships which might form. ISKCON devotees who are influenced by the attitude of raganuga-bhakti exhibited by many people in Vrindaban may well decide to leave the structure of their organization and establish new relationships which provide the opportunity to explore dimensions of spontaneous emotionalism which ISKCON frowns upon.

The evaluation of whether these changes are detrimental or beneficial varies from individual to individual, whether they are native residents or members of ISKCON. The cases presented in this chapter, however, point to one conclusion that few would contest: ISKCON's presence in Vrindaban has significantly altered the texture of that aspect of the town's sociocultural system associated with the knowledge, practice, and experience of mystical emotions in everyday life.

CHAPTER 8

Conclusion

IN THIS book I have described aspects of the social reality of Vrindaban at a particular point in time, a description which, I believe, accurately reflects how the inhabitants—Indian residents, pilgrims, and foreign devotees of the International Society of Krishna Consciousness—go about their daily lives. This report is a result of my own attempts to become part of that reality in order to understand the various cultural resources of informants and how they use these resources to make sense of their everyday activities and relationships. In describing the cultural domain of ideas, symbols, and meanings; the social domain of real-life interactions; and the relationships between the two, I have endeavored to be both analytically revealing and, at the same time, faithful to the perceptions of those who allowed me to participate in their world.

It should be remembered that social reality is not a unitary system or "structure" where ideal pictures of society in the minds of informants or heuristic models in the mind of the anthropologist are neatly reproduced in social action. Rather, it is created as real people interacting in specific situations attempt to make sense of their own actions and the actions of others based upon their unique knowledge, which is constantly changing with experience. Social life is a process carried out by real people in their particular physical and social world, and this very process continually creates, recreates, and changes that world.

In this final chapter I will review the processes of social reality in present-day Vrindaban—the dynamics of a conjuncture of ISKCON's and Vrindaban's historical development—that have been discussed in this book. First, I will consider how the continued presence of ISKCON in Vrindaban has affected the sociocultural world of its inhabitants. In doing this, I will make more explicit the reasons for selecting and emphasizing certain sources and types of apparently contradictory data. Secondly, I will consider how the experiences of ISKCON devotees in Vrindaban are affecting the future of their institution. Finally, I will suggest how this study can contribute to a better understanding of Indian social life in general.

199

SOCIAL REALITY IN VRINDABAN: A REVIEW OF THE PROCESSES

In chapter 1 I stated that this study was framed by four interrelated questions: (1) What types of interaction are occurring between ISKCON devotees and Indian pilgrims and residents of Vrindaban? (2) In these situations of interaction, what categories and symbols are designated as significant by the actors; what degree of agreement or disagreement is present concerning the meanings of these categories and symbols; and how (and to what degree) is disagreement resolved? (3) What historical and cultural resources are used by the actors to make sense of the situations? (4) What are the consequences of the interactions; are these interpreted as "change" by the actors; and should they be viewed as change from the observer's perspective? In this section I will answer these questions as succinctly as possible.

ISKCON-Indian Interactions

Interactions between the foreign devotees of ISKCON and Indian pilgrims and residents of Vrindaban occur regularly in a variety of social settings: in temples, bazaars, dharmshalas, private residences, at pilgrimage sites, and places where various cultural peformances are held. While each situation is in some way unique, they can be categorized as belonging to one of two basic types. The first type is where the physical setting is highly organized by one of the actors or group of actors in order to present a particular conception of themselves and their setting, and to convince other actors that desired meanings should be attributed to themselves or other objects. The other type of situation is unscheduled and spontaneous, and therefore less capable of being contrived or manipulated by any of the actors. While actors still try to influence the opinions of others, these interactions demand creative responses to meaning challenges, and for ISKCON participants, leave them more vulnerable to charges of cynicism and ineptitude.

Situations of the first type most commonly occur at ISKCON's Krishna-Balaram temple, where devotees encounter thousands of pilgrims daily along with other individuals who reside permanently in Vrindaban. The temple conveys to the worshiper a feeling of normalcy in that it is similar enough to other Hindu temples to be recognized and accepted as a valid Hindu temple itself. The Indians who visit Krishna-Balaram employ the same type of ritual etiquette as they would at any other Hindu temple, as they are expected to do by other worshipers and the temple's religious specialists. The key difference at ISKCON's tem-

ple, however, is that it is staffed and managed largely by Western devotees, a fact that stimulates contemplation by Indian participants of the
foreigners' legitimacy as occupiers of Indian statuses and evaluation of
their competence in performing the associated roles. Apart from the
formalized interactions between priests and worshipers, interactions
also take place in and around the temple as visitors encounter Western
devotees who live and work there. Some of these interactions are initiated by the foreigners as "preaching" endeavors, others are initiated
by Indians out of curiosity.

Especially for pilgrims who are first-time visitors, these encounters
demand a novel, personal confrontation with elements of their cultural
knowledge, and initiate thought processes which consider if and how
the foreign devotees are what they present themselves to be—legitimate and proficient occupiers of traditional Indian statuses, and if ISK-
CON is what its members claim—an accurate and legitimate form of
traditional Vaishnava Hinduism. In this setting ISKCON is remarkably
successful in achieving its goals. Few pilgrims indicate that they are
not impressed by the temple's physical setting or conclude that the foreign priests do not perform their roles properly. By capitalizing on the
pilgrims' inherent curiosity, and by their strict adherence to behaviorial
norms traditionally associated with Brahman religious specialists, ISK-
CON has created a temple which has become one of the most popular
pilgrimage destinations in Vrindaban.

At other temples, at places where cultural performances (such as the
ras-lila drama) are conducted, and at numerous other sacred sites, interaction between the Indian cultural specialists and the worshipers or
audience is similarly staged by those specialists. For most Indian participants these situations reaffirm and reproduce their sociocultural ideals. ISKCON devotees who involve themselves in worship at traditional
temples or attend indigenous performances also reinforce their Vaishnava cultural identity and ideals, although for them the process of socialization dates only from their entry into ISKCON, rather than birth into
an Indian family. Oftentimes, simply an ISKCON devotee's presence and
apparent appreciation of the performance increases the Indian perception of his cultural competence. In these situations, active participation
without errors in cultural etiquette further enhance the devotee's possibility of gaining cultural acceptance.

The second category of situations, those that are not staged and in
most cases are spontaneous, includes the majority of everyday interactions in Vrindaban. As residents go through their daily routine in

homes, offices, shops, and fields, they meet other people, and situations of interaction are initiated. These encounters typically include less formalized action than the other type, and through them the actors pursue questions of meaning and behavior in more detail. ISKCON devotees are more closely scrutinized by Indians for personal attributes or deficiencies, and Indians are evaluated by devotees for their personal congruence with ISKCON's perception of Vaishnava ideals. In the process, individuals from both sides may change their perceptions of the others and the social groups they represent.

Such spontaneous situations occur most frequently in Vrindaban's bazaars, especially Loi Bazaar, where many ISKCON devotees and Indian pilgrims and residents shop and stroll daily, and where individuals spend hours in conversation with friends and associates. Apart from the fact that bazaars provide a setting where people inevitably meet, they are also frequent locations for significant interactions because they are in a sense "neutral"; it is possible to negotiate controversial topics in a shop as "hidden agendas" while the situation overtly is focused upon negotiating a price for goods. As one merchant put it, "you can be a gentleman here with your arguments and not fight about if a person is [ritually] unclean and you are not."[1]

Not only may both types of situations focus upon the categorization of actors, but they may also be concerned with other related ideological matters such as personal ritual practices, techniques of temple worship, emotional aspects of the religious system, matters of personal character, and the like. Regardless of the situation's goal or project, however, if it includes both foreign and Indian actors, there is likely to be some level of disagreement.

Meaning Conflict, Meaning Negotiation, and Meaning Change

Underlying all interactions in Vrindaban between ISKCON and Indian actors, is the question whether ISKCON devotees legitimately occupy the status categories which they present themselves by, and by extension, whether or not ISKCON is an authentic Indian institution. These are cultural questions which focus upon what significant symbols mean or stand for, symbols whose meanings and referents are not stored once and for all in an ideational system, but which have the capacity for alteration and transformation as their users attempt to work reality into intelligible forms.

---

[1] Quotation in English.

The Vrindaban reality includes foreigners who claim to be Hindus, Brahmans, Vaishnavas, bhaktas, gurus, and priests—all symbolic categories that are normally thought to traditionally exclude non-Indians. Since ISKCON devotees have generally internalized traditional cultural meanings from their guru, Bhaktivedanta Swami, the conflict is not so much over what a Brahman (for example) is, but rather who is a Brahman. ISKCON's strategy is to convince Indian actors that they are legitimate referents for the symbols in question, and this strategy employs two predominant courses of action. One course is to exhibit the behavioral characteristics of these categories to such an acceptable degree— to enact the roles associated with the statuses so proficiently—that no argument can be tendered on the basis of performance; they attempt to look and act as ideal Brahmans should look and act. The second course is to prove through argument and debate, or to simply point out during the course of interactions, that the textual codification of the ideal sociocultural system does not in fact exclude them; that Brahman status is not always ascribed, but may also be achieved.

Since the underlying perspective of symbolic interactionism (and cultural anthropology in general) assumes that symbols inherently have these adaptive and transformative potentials, it is left to determine whether or not the ones used in Vrindaban interactions are in fact changed. My conclusion is that they have been, and continue to be transformed, as the situations described in other chapters demonstrate. In a variety of settings, the observable actions of Indian pilgrims and residents indicate that ISKCON devotees are being treated in many cases as Indian Brahmans. They are eating with Brahmans who refuse to eat with non-Brahmans; Brahman fathers have inquired about the possibility of marriage between their daughters and ISKCON men; Vrindaban residents have accepted ISKCON devotees as gurus; devotees have acted as family priests and are approached for spiritual advice. Regardless of what residents may say about ISKCON to pilgrims, tourists, and other observers, their actions indicate that the symbolic categories which traditionally have excluded foreigners are being altered to include them.

The broader question as to whether ISKCON is accepted as a legitimate branch of the Bengal Vaishnava tradition, a claim upon which their textual arguments are based, is best understood in the context of inter- and intrasectarian rivalries. The Gaudiya Math, to which ISKCON is linked through Bhaktividenta's own guru succession, is considered by some Bengal Vaishnavas, especially the temple goswamis, to be a divisive offshoot of the sect. Controversy among Indians rests upon the

challenge of the Math's founder (and Bhaktivedanta's guru), Bhaktisiddhanta Saraswati, to Brahman superiority, and ISKCON's claim for
the potential Brahmanhood of every devotee rests upon Bhaktisiddhanta's interpretation of traditional texts. This is an old debate, and mainly
concerns the temple Brahmans themselves, who in most cases at least
theoretically concede the validity of Brahmanhood, or a status qualitatively equal, through achievement. Moreover, those Indians who insist
upon discrediting the Gaudiya Math often question Bhaktisiddhanta's
position as a legitimate guru. They suggest that technically he did not
undergo the correct initiation ritual from his own guru which therefore
invalidated his ability to transmit the sect's knowledge authentically.

Interaction between Vrindaban residents who belong to different
Vaishnava sects, however, is generally unaffected by sectarian rivalries; the differences between them are small and of little consequence
to the average person. Interestingly enough, many who do participate
in such rivalries are more than willing to grant ISKCON "Gaudiya
Math" status because they see this as an automatic discreditation of the
foreign devotees by association. But ironically this only assists ISKCON
in accomplishing its goal with the other residents who see the debate a
trivial one that only a few Brahmans are concerned about.

For the majority, the phenomenon of ISKCON seems to verify the vitality of the Bengal Vaishnava tradition of Chaitanya. As Vrindaban
residents accept devotees as Vaishnavas, Brahmans, priests, and gurus
generally, this feeds back positively into their perception of ISKCON's
parent tradition and its guru lineage. This in turn works in ISKCON's
favor vis-à-vis the Bengal sect's Indian members.

In short, ISKCON's presence in Vrindaban has altered the town's cultural system. The meanings of those symbols which are called into
question when Indians have to confront the reality of ISKCON devotees
in the face-to-face situations of interaction in everyday life, are being
altered so that the reality is intelligible. And continued symbolic transformation should be expected as long as ISKCON, or any similar group,[2]
resides there.

The people of Vrindaban have been able to successfully incorporate

---

[2] As ISKCON continues to adapt to the problems created by their guru's death, the organization
is becoming more factionalized. Those devotees who leave the organization do not usually renounce Vaishnava ideology, however, but attempt to practice it on their own. This has resulted in
several offshoots which are now attempting to establish their own temples in Vrindaban and elsewhere. There is little practical difference between these new groups and ISKCON, and the dynamics
between them and Vrindaban residents are similar to the ones occurring between Indians and
devotees who maintain ISKCON allegiance.

the devotees of ISKCON because they possess the cultural resources which have allowed them to make sense of this new aspect of their sociocultural reality; they have been able to justify and explain these changes in terms of their inherent cultural and historical knowledge. Furthermore, the manner in which various residents of Vrindaban have made sense out of the changes heralded by ISKCON has also provided some of the analytical resources necessary to understand how and why this incorporation has occurred.

Historical and Cultural Resources

Vrindaban is a symbolic locus which embodies a complex of historical and cultural resources that pilgrims and residents have availiable for explaining the ISKCON phenomenon and their reaction to it. These same resources are internalized by ISKCON devotees as they undergo their own conversion and culture change. While these cultural resources inherently codify mystical and egalitarian ideals that could naturally lead to ISKCON's acceptance, they are not necessarily invoked in practical action; conflicting values associated with a caste-based hierarchical society where status is purely ascriptive sometimes take precedence even in Vrindaban. The advent of ISKCON especially threatens high-status residents who depend upon acceptance of the latter values for the maintenance of their superiority.

ISKCON's presence has made it necessary for the Indian population to confront these conflicting ideals head-on, and devotees have used the inherent religiosity of the people to their distinct advantage. Because of the devotees' active strategies of behavioral presentation and untiring emphasis on the cultural components that favor ISKCON's incorporation, the Indians of Vrindaban are continually confronted with their own paradoxes. Since most Vrindabanbasis ultimately see themselves as part of Krishna's lilas, they at least intellectually find it difficult not to accept ISKCON's logic. Vrindaban embodies the cultural resources which allow for ISKCON's incorporation. The foreign devotees cause these resources to be brought to consciousness, resulting in the reality created by their presence being made intelligible.

The ideal meaning of Vrindaban has developed and been transmitted through both textual and oral sources. Through the sacred texts and oral religious traditions of Krishna bhakti, the perception that Vrindaban is a celestial rather than material space has become predominant. Because of the locale's mystical importance, its development as a pilgrimage town was initiated in the early sixteenth century predominantly by the followers of Chaitanya. The egalitarian ideals of devotional Hinduism that inspired the town's developers to make Vrindaban's attributes available to the masses, have been augmented by the institution of pilgrimage and the popularity of the town among India's sadhus.

Vrindaban is the name of Krishna's heaven, and when he came to earth his heaven also came with him and stayed. The earthly Vrindaban is therefore considered to be a spiritual anomaly in the otherwise purely material world, and it is not bound by the rules and constraints of normal human society. Rather, it is quite possible to explain occurrences that contradict or violate normative expectations by citing the mysterious incomprehensibleness of Krishna's will. In its most basic manifestation, this attitude concludes that any event taking place in Vrindaban, no matter how disruptive, is part of Krishna's scheme, and any person, no matter how despicable, is in some sort of relationship with him. The fact that Krishna's activities are termed lilas, meaning "sports" or "play," conveys the idea that they can be understood only in a context much different from the context that frames most regular activities. Even in play activities of the "material" world, as Bateson has shown (1956, 1975), some "metamessage" must be communicated in order to understand the meaning of what is going on. Just as people must know or be told that "this is play" ordinarily, Vrindabanbasis know and are constantly reminded by ISKCON devotees that in Vrindaban, "this is Krishna's play."

This mystical meaning which the inhabitants project upon Vrindaban compels many of them to interpret ISKCON in terms of Krishna's "plan" for the world, or to evaluate devotees themselves as part of Krishna's celestial entourage. Subsequently, ISKCON is seen by some as a fulfillment of various textual prophecies, individual devotees are often categorized as gopis, and apparently immoral or illegal acts are sometimes interpreted as tests of true belief in Krishna's omnipotence.

Primary sources for this conception of Vrindaban are the *Bhagavata-Purana*, the most important Vaishnava sacred text which concerns Krishna, and its further elaboration and commentary by the early writers of the Gaudiya sampradaya (Bengal Vaishnava sect), who resided in Vrindaban and developed it into a pilgrimage town. These immediate followers of Chaitanya, the sect's founder, shared their master's conception that the locale was the singularly most sanctified place on the planet; that simply by being there a person was spiritually transformed. Chaitanya himself and others who followed "rediscovered" the original sites of Krishna's earthly activities through psychic intuition. They enshrined each of these sites and built temples to Krishna which together anchor the town's present geography.

The pilgrims that Vrindaban has subsequently attracted provide the town's economic sustenance, and the institution of pilgrimage has further contributed to setting Vrindaban apart from the social mainstream of Indian society. The pilgrim population is composed of all social and economic statuses which freely intermingle in the town's streets, shops, and temples. Pilgrimage adds to the town's inherent social flexibility by reinforcing the religion's egalitarian ideals. The pilgrims see themselves on a journey that removes them from many of the constraints of their everyday lives; they are in what Turner (1974) calls a state of *communitas* which predisposes them to the emergence of new relationships and meanings. This functions to increase the probability that the impression-management techniques of ISKCON devotees will be successful.

Related to Vrindaban's nonphenomenal attribution and its importance as a pan-Indian pilgrimage destination is its large sadhu and "retired" population. Both of these groups represent the enactment by their members of a paradoxical aspect of a general Indian sociocultural ideal. While society is vertically organized by hierarchical stratification, its horizontal (or personal) organization is based upon an orderly transition through the stages of life. The final stage is renunciation, or sannyas, and those that "retire" to Vrindaban at the end of their lives to concentrate on spiritual activities and await death are carrying out the ultimate ideal. Sadhus, however, and there are many, enter the sannyas phase often very early in life, and usually live at places they consider sacred, including Vrindaban. The paradoxical aspect of sannyas is that it abjures the limitations and constraints of the dominant society in favor of the accomplishment of personal goals and an individualistic life-style, but the dominant society nevertheless sanctions this attitude. And wherever there is a large sadhu population, a subsequent force of egalitarianism operates to loosen the rigidity of the broader social structure, especially as it entails a de-emphasis of "caste" consideration in social interaction. In Vrindaban the sannyas ideal is highly valued by most residents, and the cultural attributes associated with it compose an important part of its general symbolic system.

Not only do the people successfully invoke aspects of Vrindaban's cultural and historical meaning to make their situations intelligible, but these same emic components are also essential in any description or analytical interpretation of the events. The concept of Vrindaban as a celestial space, knowledge of the Krishna bhakti ideals promulgated by the Bengal Vaishnava founders of the town, the social and cultural attributes of the institution of pilgrimage, and the egalitarian influence of the sannyas model, all intersect at this point with ISKCON's presence to form a unique conjuncture. These indigenous forms allow the native actors to understand ISKCON as an Indian phenomenon that is part of a continuous tradition functioning within Vrindaban's historically transformative context. The invocation of Vrindaban's cultural and historical meaning permits Indian actors to emphasize the aspects of the town which have not changed rather than the things that have been altered by ISKCON's presence there.

Results of Indian-ISKCON Interactions: Continuity and Change

"People cannot change Vrindaban; Vrindaban changes people," is a phrase often cited by Indian informants and quoted several times in this study. It emphasizes that although residents will admit to the broadening of symbols to encompass the reality of ISKCON, the majority still feel that the essence of their sociocultural system remains unaffected. From the outside observer's perspective, however, significant changes have occurred on many levels. ISKCON has had an economic impact on the town; not only have new social relationships been created between Indians and foreigners, but relationships among Indians themselves have changed; the importance of caste status in interaction has been de-emphasized, and the ideal of status by achievement has increased in acceptance. Underlying these changes, which can be seen as alterations of Vrindaban "society," corresponding and interrelated changes have necessarily occurred in the town's culture; meanings have also been transformed.

Since its inception, Vrindaban has relied on pilgrimage for its economic survival, and it is imposible to ignore the effect that ISKCON's Krishna-Balaram temple has had on the total number of pilgrims who visit Vrindaban yearly. ISKCON's temple was opened in 1975, and a comparison of pilgrim influx during my stay with figures from a 1973 government survey indicates an increase of approximately one-third over that ten-year period (see chapter 6). The Mathura Tourist Bureau as well as Vrindaban residents attribute much of this increase to ISKCON. Moreover, about one-fourth of pilgrims surveyed at various times throughout the year indicate that a primary reason for coming to Vrindaban on pilgrimage was to see the Krishna-Balaram temple. One reason given by wealthy Westernized pilgrims, government officials, and foreign tourists who come to Vrindaban is the "comfort" afforded by guest house facilities available at the ISKCON complex; during the field-work period, Krishna-Balaram was chosen over sites in Delhi or Agra for several "conventions" and group meetings. The increase in numbers of pilgrims means that more money flows into the Vrindaban economy; merchants sell more goods, dharmshalas house more guests, temples receive more and larger donations, and people providing services are more fully employed.

Besides the obvious economic impact of more pilgrims, some segments of the population have directly benefited economically from ISKCON. ISKCON patronage of some shops has made their owners wealthy, and there is constant competition among merchants to increase their ISKCON market. Craftsmen and laborers have been employed in various projects since construction was started on the Krishna-Balaram temple. Besides the temple, a guest house, school, and ashram facilities have been constructed, and presently Bhaktivedanta's tomb and adjoining museum are being completed. Future projects also insure continued employment in this area. The guest house and restaurant employ cooks, waiters, and service personnel, who often see their jobs there as a stepping-stone for better jobs in Delhi or elsewhere.

While ISKCON has no doubt increased the economic vitality of Vrindaban, some members of the community do not see this as an asset, and their perception of ISKCON's impact reinforces the fact that it has been considerable. Organizations who wish to keep Vrindaban a rural retreat see ISKCON in opposition to their goals, and many people complain about the inflation in prices that has occurred since the foreign devotees came to town. The cost of a rickshaw ride across town has tripled, they say, and basic commodities are more expensive.

Changes in Vrindaban's economic structure have also affected social dynamics in the town, especially in the business community. Merchant families which have had friendly relations for generations but which now are economically far apart because of differential ISKCON patronage, rarely speak. Those merchants who have profited from business with devotees have been able to improve their physical facilities, increase their stock, and subsequently attract more business from the pilgrim population as well. In order to attract ISKCON business, merchants increase financial support to that organization, stock items especially attractive to the foreign devotees, overtly display pictures of ISKCON gurus and "Life Membership" certificates, and generally present themselves as supporters of ISKCON in Vrindaban. This has the effect of further alienating those who have benefited from and support ISKCON from those who have not and do not.

Outside or peripheral to the social effect of economic disparities, other traditional relationships between categories of Indians have also been affected. ISKCON devotees acting in the roles of religious specialists have altered some interactions between the non-Brahman population and the Brahman community. By seeking religious advice from devotees, utilizing them as gurus and family priests, and worshiping at the Krishna-Balaram temple, residents decrease the number and types of relationships with traditional religious specialists.

The acceptance of ISKCON devotees as religious specialists, regardless of whether they are categorically considered Brahman by the non-Brahman population, has increased the community's adherence to the Vaishnava ideals of caste-irrelevance and achievement of status by devotional purity. The question of hereditary Brahman superiority is more often questioned and joked about, and an individual's personal spiritual qualifications are increasingly considered in an evaluation of his ritual status. Many residents have become more concerned with their personal spiritual practices, often adopting techniques emphasized and espoused by ISKCON, and have initiated religious projects, such as the preservation of sacred sites, apart from the supervision and control of temples and formal indigenous organizations.

The traditional avenues of ritual status enhancement available through organizations such as the Gaudiya Math have been explored and utilized by some of the Indian inhabitants of Vrindaban, and a few have also chosen to do this through formal association and initiation by ISKCON gurus. Few temple Brahmans can dispute these developments on ideological grounds, but some practically align themselves against ISKCON and that organization's influence on their traditional clients because they see their superior status and power as hereditary Brahmans threatened.

Such changes in the everyday life of Vrindaban directly attributable to ISKCON imply that cultural changes—changes in the knowledge people use to make sense of their experiences and direct their behavior—have also occurred; and these are substantiated by observation, conversation, interviews, surveys, and questionnaires. While on the one hand, available cultural resources have allowed for the interpretation of cultural continuity, on the other hand, it seems clear that the process of ISKCON's incorporation into Vrindaban's social reality has caused significant changes in these resources.

It is not difficult to see why many Vrindaban residents do not interpret their incorporation of ISKCON as cultural change. Their traditional notions are seen as fixed, divinely created and transmitted, and perfect to the degree that any apparent change is really a manifestation of aspects that previously were only implicit and unrecognized. This attitude has assisted ISKCON in their attempts at acceptance because devotees have presented themselves effectively as new manifestations of traditionally implicit notions. In this view, the active meaning-bestowing agent is culture itself. Some social and cultural analysts also adhere to this very same position which posits that symbolic or cultural phenomena have intrinsic meanings quite apart from their actual use by real actors.

This study, however, has been informed by the perspective that symbolic resources can, and usually do, vary in meaning depending on the practical demands of their usage. Cultural phenomena are meaningful not because of their intrinsic nature, but because they are vehicles of meaning for the actors; because people ascribe meaning to them and perceive meaning in them. And new meanings have been ascribed to a variety of cultural categories in Vrindaban as they have been used by Indian and ISKCON actors in the practical situations of everyday life there.

The categories by which ISKCON devotees present themselves, and which have been the focus of most of the situations described in this book, are also among the most important cultural categories traditionally used by pilgrims and residents of Vrindaban. Vaishnava, bhakta, Brahman, goswami, guru, pujari, sadhu, and sannyasi are all terms which Indian informants have been familiar with all their lives. ISKCON has not challenged the basic cultural understanding of these symbols, nor the expected behavior of people who occupy the statuses named by these terms. What ISKCON has challenged and changed, rather, is who may legitimately be a Brahman, or a guru, or a Vaishnava, and this is just as significant a transformation of meaning, perhaps even more so, than if other attributes of meaning had been changed.

The changes that have occurred, and are continuing to be reinforced, allow the foreign devotees of ISKCON to more fully realize their own personal cultural transformation which was initiated when they joined the Hare Krishna movement. Before their arrival in Vrindaban, to be Brahman meant that one was born into a Brahman family; to be a Vaishnava meant that one was born into an Indian family that worshiped Vishnu or chose that deity at some point; to be a guru meant that through the course of one's socialization as a person born in India, through the relationships established throughout that process, one developed the ideal characteristics of personality and behavior that finally revealed to others that he was a spiritually enlightened man of knowledge. At least in Vrindaban, these possibilities are now open to ISKCON devotees. Moreover, as a result of the changes caused by ISKCON, some Indian residents have also been given new opportunities for achieving these statuses that traditionally have been denied them. In a very real sense, the devotees of ISKCON are achieving Bhaktivedanta's goal of reviving what he saw as the system's original "democratic" form, applicable not only to the Indian context, but intended as a universal religion. That is not to say that everyone in Vrindaban accepts, or will ever accept these changes, and this is to be expected. More problematic, however, is the fact that many who through their actions seem to acknowledge and accept the changes, do not verbally admit their acceptance.

Differing Opinions, Conflicting Data

Some examples have shown, especially in chapter 6, that ISKCON has its critics in Vrindaban, and that not everyone is willing to accept ISKCON as a legitimate Vaishnava institution nor its members as legitimate Vaishnavas, bhaktas, or even Hindus. Those who take a firm stance one way or the other, either as supporters or detractors, are relatively easy to identify, and both have provided revealing information about the processes of social change. From ISKCON supporters I have been able to elicit details concerning their perceptions about initial encounters with devotees, initial and subsequent attitudes, and the resources they used to make sense out of what was developing around them. Those who were obviously severe critics of ISKCON when I arrived in Vrindaban were ideologically intransigent and quick to give me their reasons. Some underwent transformations during my stay, providing especially important information for understanding the processes of ISKCON incorporation. Others have staunchly maintained their opposition. There is, however, a more problematical group of informants who appear by their actions to have accepted devotees as part of Vrindaban's present sociocultural system, yet reveal a very strong anti-ISKCON bias when given the opportunity to express themselves privately. This discrepancy was initially revealed during private interviews with two informants, but at the time did not seem to represent a significant contradition. Upon analyzing the questionnaires distributed toward the end of my fieldwork, however, I found that approximately 10 percent of the respondents who I expected to provide supporting comments about their acceptance of ISKCON, answered questions relating to the foreign devotees' legitimacy in strongly negative terms. Others who also responded negatively presented no conflict with their observed behavior, but the responses of this 10 percent were puzzling.[3]

One merchant whom I had observed in an ostentatious presentation of expensive cloth to several devotees, touching their feet with humble respect, responded that ISKCON offered "hypocrisy in the name of religion," and that "because of ISKCON, culture has been lost daily. The dham is in great danger." There was no reason to believe that the observed performance was cynical because the merchant's behavior always seemed congruent with this particular performance.

Another shopkeeper who had repeatedly told me of his love for the devotees and who often entertained them in his shop wrote that "Krishna-Balaram temple has beautiful darshan, but it is made for deception. Foreigners can never be bhaktas. If institutions like ISKCON are allowed, there will be nothing but darkness." Why had these informants not aligned themselves publicly with the opposing camp? Why was there such great discrepancy between their actions and their privately expressed notions? More importantly, what did these responses mean in the context of my research?

Obviously, observations of practical behavior and information obtained from confidential verbal and written inquiries represent two very different types of data. Although they are often treated identically by anthropologists, verbal and written responses refer to ideal, often hypothetical situations, while observable behavior is a result of dealing with actual people in specific situations. When the merchants responded negatively to my questions, they were telling me what they considered was the ideal, expected behavior for them. Regardless of the wording of the questions, they were not telling me what they actually do; to ascertain this, one cannot depend upon being told, but must rely on observations in actual situations of interaction. The questionnaire responses were not equivalent to actions, nor were they predictions of actions that would take place in the future.

There are several possible reasons for the contradictions revealed by the questionnaires. As an overused dictum states, it is easier to change

---

[3] See questionnaire in appendix 4.

a person's behavior than it is to change his attitudes. Some practical behavior, in fact, may appear to the actor to necessitate the violation of his ideals. Certainly, it is practical for merchants who desire to profit from ISKCON's business to appear to support the devotees even if this contradicts their true feelings. Devotees patronize shops where they are welcome, and other merchants will refer business to them if they expect the devotees to be treated politely and given a fair deal. To display behavior that appears to support ISKCON is congruent with the behavior of most other merchants in the bazaar, all of whom want to make as much money as possible.

Just as the interchanges that occur in a bazaar shop take place in a particular context where contradictory behavior may be socially and practically advantageous, it must be remembered that the execution of a questionnaire is also a social act. My questionnaires caused quite a stir in Loi Bazaar, and most were completed only after much consultation with family members. Many of the people who were involved in the discussions did not have the same type of daily contact with the devotees that the merchants themselves did, and may have persuaded the respondents to reflect anti-ISKCON attitudes in their answers. Answering the questions was for most a joint effort, and the dynamics of each particular situation were reflected in the final responses.

A more general consideration of context and meaning also informs the Vrindaban data. As Beitielle (1974: 150) has said, "people see themselves as belonging to units of different orders in different contexts." The Brahman category is a flexible one. It may refer to a specific jati or to the highest varna, but in Vaishnava culture it may also mean "pure devotee." ISKCON efforts of impression management and textually based debate can be seen as attempts to force a change in the context of interpretation. If Brahman is considered a jati status, its counterstatuses are other jatis. If it is evaluated as varna, then the other three varnas are counterstatuses. But if it is used in the sense of "pure devotee," then the counterstatuses are defined in terms of relative devotional sincerity and psychological attachment to Krishna with the direct opposite of pure devotee being nondevotee.

If we ask whether or not ISKCON has become a Brahman jati, then the answer is unequivocally no. But this is not the question since in Vrindaban it is the least likely notion to be considered. Varna categories are often used, and some would grant Brahman varna status to ISKCON devotees in a loose sense. But ISKCON's efforts have had the effect of defining a broader context for meaning interpretation. They have been most fully accepted as Brahman in the sense of devotee. They have shifted, or at least have caused to become dominant, the meaning context in which "Brahman" and "devotee" are practically equivalent terms.

This does not mean that purity and pollution are not concerns, nor does it imply that individuals do not consider the relative "rank" of others. Indeed, purity and pollution are engrossing concerns in a town where Krishna is ritually worshiped in so many temples. An individual's personal substance must be considered pure before he can come in close contact with the deity or the people who ritually serve the deity directly in the temples. But what is clear in Vrindaban is that a person may *achieve* ritual purity. As Marriot and Inden (1977) have shown for other situations, purity enhancement can be a life-long process, and many mechanisms are available. By associating with things that are pure, by eating the proper diet, by behaving in specified ways, by acquiring certain knowledge, people can increase their ritual purity; and this is the path ISKCON has taken. Furthermore, those who are evaluated as having achieved purity by these methods also may be seen as having acquired high ranking when compared with others who do not have it or possess it to a lesser degree. This important component of status, when combined with other significant factors such as displays of religious ecstacy, may override other considerations which would be relevant in other contexts.

The fact that ISKCON insists in being defined in the "devotee" context may pose a conflict for others who choose a different context for meaning evaluation. The fact remains that the context of each situation of interaction serves, in varying degrees, to establish a broader dominant context. Those people who present conflicting behavioral and written (or verbal) data may be caught in between contexts. In public one context may be employed; in private, another may be used.

Regardless of the actual reasons for these apparent conflicts in data, they further indicate the continuing process of sociocultural transformation that is occurring in Vrindaban. Everyone is not able to easily relinquish traditional ideas concerning the participation of foreigners in their social world. Some continue to refuse to have anything to do with ISKCON devotees, while others have practically altered their behavior without a subsequent change in their ideals. The majority of informants, however, have already dealt with this conflict effectively and have used their traditional resources to interpret ISKCON as acceptable. If ISKCON remains in Vrindaban, and situations continue to occur as

they do, the practical behavior produced in actual situations of interaction should continue to affect the cultural domain of normative rules
and meaning.

A FOOTNOTE ABOUT ISKCON'S FUTURE

Social reality is constantly changing and unpredictable, and as ISKCON
continues its own process of development it too will inevitably undergo
changes. Today that organization's form is considerably different than
it was in its early years. It has dealt with Bhaktivedanta's death by
trying to institutionalize his power and authority, something that any
group that starts out as a revitalization movement must attempt to do if
it is to survive. Since it still exists, and since non-Indians from around
the world continue to become Vaishnavas through it, we must conclude
that ISKCON has been practically successful in its attempt to routinize.
It is quite likely that an ISKCON organization of some type will be in
existence for the foreseeable future, but current developments also indicate that its present form is changing.

The main problem that continues to confront ISKCON's governing
body is one that also greatly concerned Bhaktivedanta. Bhakti religions
in India have never been centralized, but have depended instead on
personal relationships between guru and disciple. Few gurus in India,
although exceptions do exist, have developed large followings, being
content instead to pass their knowledge down to a small number of
disciples by personal instruction and frequent contact. This is the accepted ideal among most Vaishnava sects, and it also represents a stated
ISKCON ideal. Every devotee is a potential guru and that status can only
be conferred upon those who wish to be his disciples. Bhaktivedanta
repeatedly stated this as his own position, and ISKCON-Indian interactions in Vrindaban and elsewhere in India have reinforced it.

Upon Bhaktivedanta's death, however, a group of ten senior disciples were revealed to have been appointed by him to assume the mantle
of guru. They alone were given the authority to initiate disciples, and
they demanded and were given authority and power similar to ISKCON's
founder. From the time of this revelation, other devotees (especially
those who were not chosen but felt they should have been) questioned
whether Bhaktivedanta actually appointed these ten since it seemed to
contradict basic ISKCON doctrine. The recorded "appointment tapes"
(conversations made during the last days of Bhaktivedanta's life) were
ambiguous at best, but the interpretation that this indeed was their gu-

ru's wish was accepted by the governing board and was supported by the majority of devotees. At this time some long-term members disassociated themselves from the organization, some taking other Indian gurus, some starting their own smaller groups which maintained the basic beliefs and practices of ISKCON.

Internal dissension continued, however, creating factions within the organization. Each guru had his own committed following which still acknowledged the institutional authority of ISKCON to make major decisions and to conduct the large-scale projects in progress in India and elsewhere. After years of power politics, those factions that disputed the original appointments finally garnered enough power to force an official reinterpretation of the appointment tapes, and this new interpretation was formally accepted at ISKCON's annual meeting at Mayapur in Bengal in 1985. Although the original ten gurus were not stripped of power, guidelines were established that enabled any senior devotee to become an initiating guru unless cause could be found to deny him that status.

While this decision has brought ISKCON's official philosophy closer to the Indian ideal, it has at the same time resulted in a further decentralization of the organization. This may serve to bring some of the "renegade" gurus back into the ISKCON fold, but may also contribute to continued factioning. Some of the original ten gurus who by now have large followings of their own are contemplating establishing their own separate organizations, and some of the new gurus may also follow a similar course if they can develop enough support.

Some observers, both in and out of ISKCON, have analyzed the new policy as being symptomatic of the broad organization's disintegration, and they could be correct. It should be pointed out, however, that very few of those who have left or are leaving ISKCON relinquish their Vaishnava beliefs or behavior, but rather strive to implement them elsewhere. Especially in India, and particularly in Vrindaban, some of the new factions are attempting to buy land and establish temples of their own. From the Indian perspective, however, there is no perceivable difference between the ISKCON foreign Vaishnavas and the non-ISKCON foreign Vaishnavas. If anything, occurrences of interaction between Indians and foreign devotees will probably increase, and the processes which now involve only ISKCON devotees will continue without any significant change. As more foreigners present themselves as gurus in Vrindaban, it is also possible that more Indians will take initiation from them, augmenting and continuing the processes of cultural and social transformation described here.

Some Indians will no doubt staunchly defend the position that no non-Indian can become Hindu, much less Brahman. They will continue to reflect the attitude of one Indian academic who said, ''As far as my knowledge is concerned, no foreigner of the Hare Krishnas can ever be considered equal to Indian Brahmans and Hindus. If we accept them at all they must be relegated to the lower castes; they must be considered shudras at best.''

Others, however, will interact with the foreign devotees and participate in the processes that will inevitably alter their cultural knowledge and social behavior. Perhaps some of the people who fall into this category, as they engage in these interactions, will have thoughts similar to those of a reporter who wrote in the October 10, 1970 edition of the *Times Weekly* in Calcutta: ''Do you realize what is happening? Very soon Hinduism is going to sweep the West. The Hare Krishna movement will compensate for all our loss at the hands of padres through the centuries.''[4]

BEYOND VRINDABAN: GENERAL IMPLICATIONS

Vrindaban is not the only place in India where ISKCON operates. There are also large temple complexes in Bombay and Mayapur, and every major city and many smaller towns have temples with associated enclaves of foreign and Indian ISKCON devotees. ISKCON activities in India and elsewhere receive frequent media coverage and several popular films have dealt with a ''foreign Hindu'' theme.

Whatever else has affected the general public consciousness concerning ISKCON, however, the direct encounters which hundreds of thousands of pilgrims from all over India have had with the foreign devotees in Vrindaban has been a major factor in spreading the concepts of ISKCON Vaishnava and ISKCON Brahman to all corners of the country. This has caused traditional Indians in many places to consider questions similar to those raised by the interactions in Vrindaban when friends and relatives recount their pilgrimage experiences. The cultural resources, then, which the people of Vrindaban have had to call upon in their dealings with ISKCON, have also been necessarily invoked when considering the Vrindaban context in other locations.

[4] Quoted in Goswami, Satsvarupa (1982: 131).

ISKCON now has plans to construct large temples in several other major cities—including Madras, Nagpur, and Calcutta—and is nearing completion of a major temple complex in the industrial town of Baroda. These centers will create new interactional contexts which will also likely affect Indian perceptions of foreign devotees and ultimately other elements of their cultural system.

Western conceptions of Indian reality—focused mainly upon caste—are incomplete; they need to be updated, augmented, and in some cases changed. The Vrindaban material in this book is a small contribution toward this end. Our common ideas of Indian personality, culture, and society have formed around reifications of caste, and the static models of a pan-Indian caste system derived mainly from an interpretation of selected classical texts. These perspectives, accepted by many sociologists and anthropologists, which largely present a modified view of the historical Brahman ideal, are in many ways a distortion. As Srinivas (1966: 5) comments, "the claims which the Brahmins made for themselves and their view of the caste hierarchy are understandable, but not so the fact that many scholars, Indian as well as foreign, have regarded them as representations of the historical reality."

The phenomenon of ISKCON should be seen as one aspect of the complex processes operating in modern India that are functioning to de-emphasize the importance of birth-status in everyday life. ISKCON emphasizes the egalitarian ideals of bhakti Hinduism that have been part of Indian culture since the earliest Vedic times and which were reinforced by the medieval Vaishnava reformers. Avenues of status enhancement for people from a wide cross-section of Indian society have been created and re-created by ISKCON's existence both directly and indirectly. For Westernized Indians it has also helped to resolve tensions created by a perceived conflict between traditional and modern "scientific" world views.

In Vrindaban, ISKCON's continued presence has increased the possibility for any individual to engage in social intercourse and establish relationships with any other, providing the opportunity to establish status based upon qualification and consistent behavior. The Vrindaban situation shows that social boundaries, no matter how inflexibly conceived, are never impenetrable. The traditional Indian concerns for birth-status and for an individual's inherent state of purity or pollution, while not absent, have been considerably de-emphasized. The Vaishnava ideal that a person's status should not be determined by birth, but by qualifications evidenced in daily behavior, is being more closely approached due to the dynamics of interaction between the Western and Indian residents of Vrindaban. In these situations, changes in meaning and attitude are accomplished which in turn alter subsequent social relationships; at the same time other aspects of the traditional system are being reaffirmed.

The Vrindaban situation is part of a broader picture that shows India's ability to deal with change while maintaining its own cultural identity. The democratic ideals embodied in the country's constitution should not be seen solely as an innovative contribution of British rule, but it should also be recognized that similar concepts have always been available as a traditional resource, lying dormant until the need for their invocation arises. What Westerners consider India's march toward modernization should be tempered by the knowledge that many Indians feel this is only the latest example of the country's ability to successfully adapt to changing times while maintaining its unique identity. The micro-example of Vrindaban should inform us about the macro-processes that are currently creating the broader Indian reality.

Rudolph and Rudolph (1967: 5) have similarly pointed out that most studies of Indian social organization have "reified" the Indian caste system, and that these formulations have in fact "masked considerable mobility and social change." More significantly, however, they have suggested that "recessive themes in cultural patterns and psychological makeup that can be mobilized by somewhat changed historical circumstances become grist for the mill of social change" (10–11). I have described one of those historical circumstances where, indeed, "recessive" cultural resources that perhaps had not been needed in the interpretation of daily life before ISKCON, have been mobilized and effectively used to understand and integrate ISKCON in Vrindaban.

Far from being an aberration, the case presented here illuminates the fact that such resources do exist, and that they are capable of being mobilized. It suggests that in order to understand the dynamics of Indian society, we must move beyond the standard conception of a caste-based organization dependent upon ascribed ritual purity and pollution, or wealth and power, and seek a higher-level paradigm that can encompass situations like the one now transpiring in Vrindaban. An apparently "deviant" example of what is normally considered a "structural" rule, may in fact be best understood as a derivative of more general rules, an opportunity to reexamine accepted preconceptions and deepen our understanding of social and cultural reality.

The Vrindaban situation should challenge some of these preconceptions. Two things underscored by the Vrindaban context should especially be considered for their relevance in other situations: (1) the processes available for enhancing individual prestige over and above group-associated prestige, and the impact of these processes on a location's social reality; and (2) the consideration of religious devotion as a criterion for both individual and group prestige apart from, as well as in addition to, any other criteria.

Religious Devotion as an Attribute of Prestige Determination

Rank, or prestige determination, is a complex activity. In some situations, ritual purity is the dominant variable; in others, material wealth is more important. In still other contexts, a person's or a group's "power"—the ability to achieve its desires and goals by force or political advantage—is the dominant concern. Furthermore, the interplay between these three determining elements may vary so greatly that they are not easily accessible to the observer without extended participant observation. Dumont's depiction of ritual hierarchy being always superordinate to "power," therefore, is not empirically verifiable. ISK-CON's integration and rise to high status in Vrindaban could be seen as related to its ability to convincingly portray itself as being rich in material wealth, political "power," and ritual purity.

The possibilities are not exhausted by a consideration of only these three elements, however. Embedded in pan-Indian culture is also the idea that over and above these attributes, a person or group of persons who successfully fulfills certain religious criteria acquires superior prestige, and this is not and historically has not been limited to the "upper" jatis and varnas. The various "paths" or *margs* of yoga[5] have always been seen as processes for personal "perfection," but they have usually been viewed in terms of horizontal stratification where advancement through the various life stages culminates in a "transcendence" of society. What has not been considered in analyses of rank and status is the potential that religious "advancement" in and of itself has for contributing to prestige evaluation.

[5] Many systems of yoga are discussed in various texts, but the primary ones are usually considered to be *karma, jnana,* and *bhakti* yogas. Karma yoga is the path of liberation based upon an individual doing good works during his life, sometimes considered doing good activities without the thought of its material rewards. Jnana yoga is the path of "knowledge" where one strives to gain intellectual understanding of his oneness with the absolute Brahman. Bhakti yoga is the path of salvation which demands total devotion and surrender to a personal deity. Hatha yoga, though not always thought of as a separate system, is primarily concerned with perfection of the physical body through exercise and bodily postures.

In Vrindaban, of course, the path of bhakti is predominant, and the evaluation of devotional purity—which is not necessarily correlated with ritual purity—is of utmost importance. This is underscored by the fact that some criticism of ISKCON is verbalized in just these terms. Informants who are not ready to attribute high ranking to ISKCON as a group evaluate that "they" are still at a relatively low level of spiritual enlightenment. Conversely, many who grant high status to the organization do so because they see it as a collectively "advanced" entity. The majority of Vrindaban residents who evaluate ISKCON highly do so because of their observations of individual devotee behavior that seem to demonstrate a quality of "pure devotion." Public displays of religious ecstacy, for example, confirm an individual's close mystical relationship with Krishna and this can be the overriding factor in the evaluation of his overall personal prestige. So important is this type of variable throughout India, that in many cases an accurate depiction of status determination cannot be gained without considering it. Purely political and economic studies often overlook or de-emphasize the general importance of religious ideology, but even when this is considered, it usually culminates in a determination of importance for varna-based concerns of purity and pollution.

In Vrindaban, a person's devotional sincerity and adeptness may be the dominant variable in prestige evaluation and has a subsequent correlation in any attempt at "ranking." Vrindaban is hardly unique in this regard. Other places which emphasize different techniques of religious knowledge leading to a culturally defined perfection or enlightenment will have their corollaries to devotion. And in many places in both North and South India, the bhakti ideals that infuse Vrindaban reality are similarly prevalent. Religious competence in India is a personal concern for much of the country's population, not just for and toward Brahmans. Those who have it are attributed with high prestige and are sometimes worshiped. It is too important a variable in the social reality of most Indians to be ignored by scholars who are trying to make sense of that reality.

Importance of the Individual

Even if hierarchy is ignored—something that is almost heretical in Indian scholarship—the Vrindaban processes can still be rendered understandable. The fact is that in some Indian contexts hierarchy is not the dominant concern, or even a concern at all. Rather, an ethos of egalitarianism prevails to such a degree that maneuvering for group status evaluation is overshadowed by individual interests. In Vrindaban the individual's concern for spiritual perfection is at least as much a determinant of social reality as his place in a hierarchy. As discussed in previous chapters, many elements—such as the religious traditions of Krishna bhakti, the institution of pilgrimage, and the population of sadhus, mendicant widows, and retirees—contribute to this state of affairs.

This does not obscure the fact that Western devotees attempt to emulate idealized Brahman characteristics, and I would call this "Sanskritization" although it does not conform to the processes usually labelled by the term. For Srinivas (1966), Sanskritization is a process that only functions to raise the status of an entire group and takes several generations to work. Assuming that the "truth" of a status higher than that granted the group by significant others is initially revealed to or desired by only one individual or a small number of individuals, the process of convincing other group members that this is so, and the enforcement of a behavioral uniformity within the group, are considerable feats. The fact is that individuals must engage in convincing self-presentation first, the transformation of group status coming only, and indeterminately, at a later time. What Sanskritization actually consists of is individuals pursuing their own interests and attempting to increase their personal prestige, rather than "castes" trying to better their positions in a status hierarchy. In Vrindaban, Sanskritization is being accomplished on an individual basis and status conferred on individuals regardless of the actions of group cohorts. Numerous informants have emphasized that individual behavior determines prestige in Vrindaban, not membership in a particular jati or other culturally defined grouping. No group, regardless of size, is composed of members that uniformly learn or agree with the group's "culture." It is therefore a gross abstraction to assume that Vrindaban society, or any other society for that matter, is composed simply of interacting, mutually ranked categories of people. That approaches the problem from the wrong direction. Rather, we must observe how individuals mutually construct the setting's reality, and this forces attention upon complex, situated dynamics rather than structural uniformity. As Meillassoux (1973: 89) has argued, what we call the caste system looks so different to individuals within it, that we indeed must ask if there really are "castes" in India.

Components of Indian culture such as the ideal of sannyas, the egalitarian ideals of bhakti Hinduism, the liminal spirit of pilgrimage, the importance of religious "advancement," and the general dynamics of self-presentation in everyday interactions are all integral parts of the Indian system, operative to varying degrees throughout India, and should be considered in any study of the Indian situation. To limit our observations to the dynamics of hierarchy within the ''caste system'' is to gain, at best, only a partial understanding of Indian reality. The simplistic model of India where an individual's personal worth is determined once and for all by birth must be augmented by the knowledge that anyone, even foreigners, may acquire respect and prestige by personal achievements. This is nothing new in India, nor is it a new discovery about Indian reality, but it is something inadequately considered in standard social analysis.

This study of Vrindaban has started and ended with the presumption that reality can best be described and understood by investigating the cultural resources available to the actors, noting which resources are selected as important and why, and observing how they are manipulated and transformed in the course of everyday life. In the final analysis, however, I have only presented a description and interpretation of my participation in the social reality of Vrindaban, Mathura District, Uttar Pradesh, India, as it existed over the course of my stay there in 1982 and 1983; but questions have been raised that are relevant to our understanding of sociocultural life throughout India. What Vrindaban's, and India's, future reality will be cannot be predicted. Only time will tell.

Map of Vrindaban

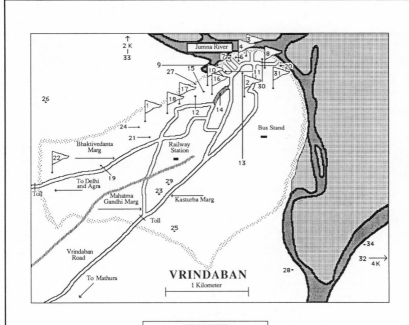

VRINDABAN

1 Kilometer

* 1. Madan-Mohan
  2. Govindadev
  3. Gopinath
* 4. Radha-Raman
* 5. Jai Singh Ghera
* 6. Gokulanand
* 7. Keshi Ghat
  8. Gopishwar
* 9. Chir Ghat
* 10. Radha-Damodar
  11. Shahaji
  12. Seva Kunj
  13. Nidhi Ban
* 14. Loi Bazaar
* 15. Kishor Ban
  16. Shyamsundar
* 17. Radha-Vallabh

LEGEND

⚑ Temple

Railroad Track

Parikrama Marg

Sandbar / alluvial deposits

* 18. Banke-Bihari
  19. Fogal Ashram
  20. Sudama Kuti
  21. Harinikunj
* 22. ISKCON
* 23. Vraja Academy
  24. Bon Maharaj Ashram
  25. Nim Karoli Baba
  26. Pagel Baba
* 27. Imli Tala
  28. Akrur Ghat
  29. Ananda Mai Ma Ashram
  30. Harikhan Baba Ashram
  31. Rangji
  32. Radharani
  33. Bel Ban
  34. Devaraha Baba

* Frequent ISKCON-Indian interaction

Vrindaban Pilgrimage Clusters

Pilgrimage Centers	*Pilgrimage Clusters*
1. *Madan-Mohan temple Sanatan's well New Madan-Mohan temple	Madan-Mohan
2. Govindadev temple Brinda Devi shrine New Govindadev temple	Govindadev
3. Gopinath temple New Gopinath temple	Gopinath
4. *Radha-Raman temple *Gopal Batt samadhi Radha-Raman's appearance place Charbuj temple	Radha-Raman
5. *Sri Chaitanya Prem Sansthan Ras-lila stage Hanuman Shrine	Jai Singh Gera
6. *Radha-Gokulananda temple Lokhanath Goswami samadhi	Gokulananda
7. *Keshi ghat Yamuna Maharani shrine Giriraj shrine Hanuman shrine Shiva/Nandi shrine	Keshi ghat
8. Gopishwar temple Gopinath Bazaar	Gopishwar

Pilgrimage Centers	*Pilgrimage Clusters*
9. Kaliya shrine Chir-lila tree Hanuman shrine	Chir ghat
10. *Radha-Damodar temple *Rup Goswami samadhi *Jiv Goswami samadhi *Krishnadas Kaviraj samadhi Krishna charan shila *Bhaktivedanta swami bhajan kutir	Radha-Damodar
11. Shahaji temple Mira Bai temple	Shahaji
12. Ras mandala Radha-Krishna temple Radha's well *Seva Kunj parikrama	Seva Kunj
13. Swami Haridas samadhi Banke-Bihariji appearance place Nidhi Ban parikrama	Nidhi Ban
14. *Loi Bazaar shops and stalls Go mandir (cow temple) Mahadeva temple Shalagram temple	Loi Bazaar
15. Hari Ram Vyas samadhi Radha-Krishna temple *Ras-lila mandala Ras-lila Kishor Ban parikrama *Kishore Ban dharmshala	Kishor Ban
16. *Radha-Shyamsundar temple Shyamananda Goswami samadhi	Shyamsundar
17. *Radha-Vallabh temple Old Radha-Vallabh temple	Radha-Vallabh

Pilgrimage Centers	*Pilgrimage Clusters*
Radha-Krishna temple *Gonshyamji's deities	
18. *Banke-Bihari temple Bihariji well Sadhu katha platform	Banke-Bihari
19. Ras-lila Sadhu seva	Fogal ashram
20. Ras-lila Ram-lila Rama temple Sadhu seva	Sudama Kuti
21. Ras-lila Sadhu seva	Harinikunj
22. *Krishna-Balaram *Bhaktivedanta Swami samadhi *Goshala	ISKCON
23. *Sripad Baba Jaipur mandir Gopala-Bala shrine Ras-lila	Vraja Academy
24. *Bon Maharaj samadhi Radha-Krishna temple Shiva temple	Bon Maharaj Ashram
25. *Nim Karoli Baba samadhi Hanuman temple	Nim Karoli Ashram
26. Pagel Baba samadhi Pagel Baba temple	Pagela Baba
27. *Imli tala tree *Radha-Krishna temple	Imli tala
28. Akrur ghat	
29. Radha-Krishna temple Ananda Mai Ma shrine	Ananada Mai Ma Ashram

Pilgrimage Centers	*Pilgrimage Clusters*
30. Karikhan Baba shrine	Harikhan Baba Ashram
31. Ranganath temple Brahma kund Rath (charriot) ka Ranganath	Rangji
32. *Radharani kund Shiva temple Chaitanya temple Krishna temple	Radharani (Mansorovar)
33. *Bel Ban forest Lakshmi temple	Bel Ban
34. Devaraha Baba	

* = Sites of frequent ISKCON-Indian interaction

The Situation

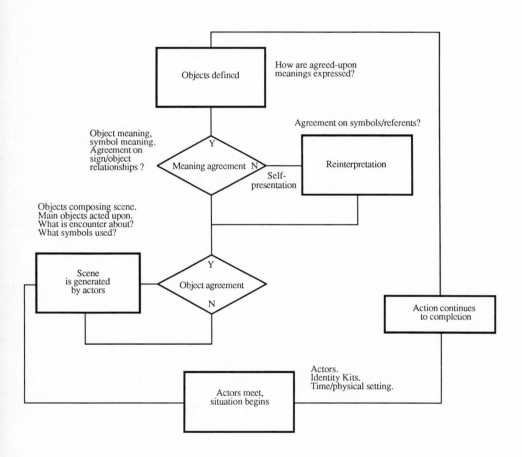

Loi Bazaar Questionnaire

(All questions and answers are confidential)

1. How long has your family lived in Vrindaban?
2. What is your family's occupation?
3. What is your jati?
4. What is your religion (sampradaya)?
5. What other jatis are in Vrindaban?
6. How long has your family been in this business?
7. What is your monthly income?
8. Has your income increased much over the past ten years?
9. Why do you think it has increased?
10. Did the arrival in Vrindaban of ISKCON help to increase your sales?
11. By how much?
12. Are you a life member of ISKCON?
13. Have you seen the Krishna-Balaram temple? What was your impression?
14. Can foreigners be good devotees?
15. What impact has ISKCON had on Vrindaban?
16. How has Vrindaban changed in the last ten years?
17. What do you see for Vrindaban's future?

Methodology

THE DICTUM that method must be related to theory is especially demanded by the interactionist perspective. Symbolic interactionism provides an underlying philosophy about the nature of social reality; it directs the researcher's attention to the specific aspects of a particular social world which should be identified, considered, and interpreted; and it insists on a methodological strategy consistent with its premises and principles. Rather than specific techniques devised prior to fieldwork, a methodology is required that is developmental, open-ended, and capable of capturing the symbolic world of the people under study in the places in which they live.

To do this, the researcher must develop an intimate familiarity with and sensitivity to the social world he intends to describe. It is the method, then, of participant observation that is demanded for a study to be genuinely based upon the theoretical perspective of symbolic interactionism. Research itself must be a process of symbolic interaction, with the observer becoming an actor in the social dramas he studies.

Symbolic interactionism is at base a research tradition. Social reality can never be predetermined; therefore, fieldwork is always an empirical enterprise for the ethnographer. As Favret-Saada has put it: "if nothing in the field corresponds to his expectations, if his hypotheses collapse one after the other in contact with native reality even though he has set up his investigation with great care, these are signs that we are dealing with an empirical science and not a science-fiction" (1980: 13).

In this appendix I will discuss the method of participant observation and the use of other complementary techniques, considering how my fieldwork experience developed in light of this ideal.

PARTICIPANT OBSERVATION

Since symbolic interactionism defines social life as processual, with objects, symbols, strategies, and explanations developing over time in meaningful situations, any methodological technique used to capture

235

this reality must necessarily respond to the developing social world. Data do not factually exist, awaiting discovery by the ethnographer. Rather, the facts of social life are built up through the symbolic work occurring in social situations, and the anthropologist himself must engage in this same work.

Sociological techniques such as unobtrusive observation, formal interviews, random sampling of values, and various quantitative procedures, do not in themselves provide adequate tools, though participant observation does not necessarily exclude them. Active research requires the anthropologist to become part of the symbolic interactions that he intends to describe and interpret. Being part of the interactions, he engages in the process of formation along with the other actors, thereby experiencing firsthand the designation of significant symbols and objects, and the development of their meanings. The observer's own self, in a very real sense, therefore, becomes the principal tool of research.

In other words, the anthropologist must try to achieve competence in the world he studies. While his initial (and probably final) competence will be minimal compared to the other actors, they too are in fact being socialized during the course of each situation. Novel situations especially require even the most experienced actor to reflect, reconsider, redefine, and relearn—procedures that the observer, a cultural novice, must apply consciously and in detail.

Although participant observation is the process of acquiring competence in a new social reality, this does not imply that the researcher will ever become a full, participating member of his informants' world. Rather, he engages in a dialectic that, from the informants' point of view, will likely move him through a series of statuses—from interloper, to novice, to finally (if he is successful) marginal member. The observer sees himself initially as a stranger, and may eventually perceive himself as an "initiate," or fully participating member. But only in the rarest of cases does he actually achieve this level of acceptance from the natives' perspective. Rather than being problematical, however, this condition is a necessary one for the conduct of research. For if full competence and membership are ever achieved, it may become impossible for the researcher to objectify his experiences enough to be analytical.

During the extended period of research, themes emerge and abstractions are inevitably made in order to organize and interpret data, but these themes and abstractions are specifically grounded in meaningful contexts. Since every actor in a particular situation is also going through a similar process, when the ethnographer participates in situations with informants his conceptualizations and interpretations are interrelated with theirs. Although his interpretations may not be identical with others, they will likely be recognized as valid by them. Even if informants deny the perceptions and interpretations of the observer, however, their mutual participation should at least help to ensure mutual respect.

It is impossible to accurately understand any cultural reality by simply describing behavioral, social, economic, or ritual phenomena, whether the approach be quantitative or qualitative. The goal of understanding demands not only an accurate objective presentation of observed material phenomena, but insight into the subjective world of form that exists in the people's minds as well. The research act, therefore, must include three primary phases. First is the actual accomplishment of participation—gaining a place in the world to be studied—and engaging in the process of competence acquisition. The second phase, largely contemporaneous with the first, consists of making detailed observations of interactive experiences, reflecting upon them, and creating written descriptions of the situations in as much detail as possible. The final phase, interpretation of data, develops as the researcher engages in a dialogue with his participatory experiences and his written record of them, along with any taped or photographed documentation he may have.

ACCOMPLISHING PARTICIPATION

Thomas Cottle (1977: 8) has used the term *observant participation* to describe the research strategy primarily employed in this study. Not simply a play on words, this phrase emphasizes that participation in a particular social world is the pivotal requirement for any research directed by symbolic interactionism. Indeed, it is a requirement of any true anthropological research, for without participation a truly emic understanding of categories and processes is practically unachievable.

In order to conduct participant observation, the anthropologist must first locate himself physically in the time and space of the social world he intends to study. Once this physical location is accomplished, the situations of interaction pertinent to his problem or interests must be discovered. Finally, entry into the social world composed of these situations must be gained through the development of an acceptable and convincing role.

Locating myself in Vrindaban was no more difficult than it is for the thousands of pilgrims, both Indian and non-Indian, who daily stream into the town. Though there is no direct train service to Vrindaban proper, Mathura, some six miles south, is on the direct line between Delhi and Agra. From Mathura horse carts, rickshaws, and taxis are available, although many pilgrims, out of devotion, poverty, or both, prefer to walk the distance. There is also a public bus service from Delhi to Vrindaban that runs on an irregular schedule. On different occasions I employed each of these.

When I arrived in Vrindaban, the scene that confronted me at the Krishna-Balaram temple seemed to confirm my assumption that significant interaction between Westerners and Indians would be occurring. It was here, at a temple established and staffed by foreign devotees and priests, that I first experienced the impact of mass devotion and vitality that so defines Indian bhakti in practice. Having seen that interactions were in process in at least one location, I set about the task of becoming part of Vrindaban life myself.

My next step was to locate a local ascetic, for whom I had a letter from an American acquaintance. This sadhu had once been a wandering mendicant, but was now in the process of establishing an institution with the goal of providing an in-depth study of Vrindaban culture and establishing Vrindaban's importance for India in general. It also was hoped that this institution would eventually bring about a moral, religious, and spiritual revival throughout the country. Several Westerners lived at this institution, one of whom (a German girl) presented my letter to the ascetic who, although declining to see me personally at that time, extended his welcome by proxy, offering food and lodging for as long as I wished to help in the "study and preservation of Braj culture." It is at this point that I began the process of achieving participation in the everyday life of Vrindaban.

Although this local institution was not to be my permanent base, I explored the town from there during the first few days, and began to acquire competence in its culture. After a week I had found living arrangements elsewhere, deciding not to stay with this ascetic or at any other location officially connected with a particular sect or personality. To develop a role which would allow me free access into a variety of situations, my relative independence had to be maintained.

My Vrindaban residence was to be located at Kishor Ban, a place neutral in its affiliation where pilgrims from many backgrounds stay during their pilgrimage. The proprietor, Govind Kishor Goswami, holds that the present structure is built beside part of the original Vrindaban forest, and in its gardenlike enclosure is the tomb of a medieval saint of considerable renown. Pilgrims come to circumambulate the grounds, worship the saint's tomb, and receive the darshan of the deities in the small temple there. Kishor Ban is situated beside the garden called Seva Kunj, one of the principal pilgrimage destinations, and from my rooftop rooms I could witness the steady flow of devotees through the garden from dawn to dusk, view the ras-lila performances in the public courtyard below, and participate in other cultural performances that are part of the regular round of activities there.

Kishor Ban is strategically located at the end of an alleyway just off Loi Bazaar, the town's principal market area. Along with temples and other sacred sites, Loi Bazaar is a primary setting for interaction, and passing time in its shops and tea stalls provided a constant flow of information. It would have been difficult to find a place more central to the town's activities. Moreover, through Govind Kishor Goswami, his wife, and their four children, I gained familiarity with the functioning of a traditional Indian family whose occupational duty it is to maintain a pilgrimage site and provide for the pilgrims who stay there. Through the goswami I widened my circle of contacts in Vrindaban and gained insight into the town's history and contemporary culture.

Due to Kishor Ban's ideal location and the people I met there, not only was I able to internalize elements of the culture's symbolic system, but I also came to evaluate my experiences there as personally beneficial, sometimes inspiring. There was no deception on my part, therefore, when I explained to the curious that my presence there was for personal development, a motive that both residents and pilgrims accepted as valid. I would further explain to some that I was a "research scholar," certified by the government of India to study the town's culture and history, and this too was acceptable. The residents of Vrindaban were familiar enough with Westerners seeking some kind of personal "advancement," and I was to discover that others had also considered Vrindaban an important focus of academic study as well.

The details of my role would continue to develop during the course of research, but from the start my presence was never seriously problematical. When problems did arise, they usually stemmed from the use of an interpreter or assistant needed for a specific situation. As Berreman reported in his account of fieldwork impression management in the Himalayan village of Sirkandar (1972), the status of an assistant can hamper or facilitate acceptance in social situations. Consequently, I used interpreters only when unavoidable, and employed assistants only for the backstage organization of data, translation of tape recordings, the administration of the one questionnaire I employed, and the enhancement of my own language competence.

Participation in the symbolic system under study is the main requirement of research directed by symbolic interactionism, and it was my intention to do this as effectively as possible in Vrindaban. My transition from stranger to member through the positive evaluation of my social performances, was facilitated by my own adoption of an appropriate "identity kit." Moreover, my presentation of self had to convey simultaneously an identification with certain aspects of Vrindaban culture, and a separation from those organizations whose memberships included Westerners pursuing their own processes of competence acquisition in a sectarian manner.

Therefore, I wore a tulsi mala, as do all bhaktas in Vrindaban, foreign and Indian; but one that was recognizably different from those worn by ISKCON devotees. My clothing was largely of white khadi worn by most men there, but again I avoided the particular styles that had been adopted by sectarian groups such as ISKCON.

In a pilgrimage town like Vrindaban where there is a large sadhu population, considerable flexibility in standards of dress and behavior exists, the force of individualism being stronger than in other areas. Therefore, any idiosyncracies in my presentation were either ignored or accepted to be within tolerable limits. This allowed me to more effectively alter elements of my persona from situation to situation, if needed, without serious perceptions of discontinuity by informants. Ultimately, the determinant of acceptance rested, as it did for other Westerners in the town, upon my respect for the culture and sincerity in attempts to gain competence in it.

GATHERING AND RECORDING DATA

The implementation of participant observation as a research strategy does not necessarily exclude other complementary techniques. In this section I will discuss the methods used to record situations in which I participated, plus outline other techniques used to amplify and augment the descriptive record. These include interviews, most being informal and opportunistic; the solicitation of life histories; the conduct of random surveys; the use of one written questionnaire; and the utilization of photographic techniques.

Once entry was gained into significant situations and I began participating in them, the problem of recording them became a chief concern. From my first day in India, I had recorded experiences and impressions in a daily journal. Yet, once in the research setting, I was aware that the interactive situations—which I had identified as the basic unit of research—had to be recorded with increased detail and consistency.

Initially I took no care to conceal a small notebook that was always at hand, and felt no compulsion to be unobtrusive in note taking since I had perceived my role as "research scholar" to be consistent with such behavior. This attitude was considerably modified, however, when a crucial key informant said to me, "When you are ready to learn, come back without your notebook." After this incident, in most situations I made a conscious effort to be more natural, refraining from note taking until after an encounter's termination, usually not recording the event until evening.

To record the situations, I developed a flow chart (appendix 3) that not only attempts to account for setting and action, but also considers the objects and symbols being used in communication, the dialectical character of the interactions occurring, and especially the creative role of the actors. The flow chart, apart from aiding in recalling the important details of the situation, allows for the incorporation of data from other sources as well, such as subsequent interviews and life histories, and serves as a basis for the development of an interpretation for each encounter. Similarly, as the recorded situations accumulated, the charts helped to identify the dominant themes as they emerged.

The chart indicates that a situation begins whenever actors meet. At that point, their "scene"—the context of the situation—is generated by each of the actors. Here there may be negotiation concerning the objects which compose the actors' scenes, including the situation's goal or focus. Once enough agreement concerning the specific objects themselves is achieved for the situation to continue, there may also be negotiation concerning divergent meanings of these objects. Although object and meaning negotiation may in fact occur simultaneously, for the purpose of description and analysis it is useful to treat each separately. These negotiations are the primary content of the situation, and through them reaffirmation or transformation is achieved. Once there is mutual agreement, or an agreement to disagree, action continues until all parties are aware that the situation is concluded.

This chart proved to be a successful aid not because it lent any objectivity to the research task, but rather because it provided a minimal structure upon which detailed qualitative descriptions could be built, descriptions which represent an attempt to approximate the subjective interpretations of the actors. It serves as a framework for reconstructing situations recorded in detail with it, and it has also proved effective for reconstructing situations which were not recorded in such detail in the field, such as unstructured journal entries or shorthand notes on the charts themselves. This book is based largely upon situations recorded in this format, plus other less formal notations concerning situations which also have had an influence upon the themes and interpretations that finally emerged.

As all-important as participant observation is, the initially incompetent observer must also employ other methods to increase his cultural competence. Interviewing is one of the principal means for acquiring new information and checking that gained through observation.

Oftentimes, naturally occurring situations provided a setting for informal interviews. In effect, these were also situations of interaction, but instigated in order to explore a particular object and its meaning. Especially when a situation of interest was in some way problematical, informal interviews immediately following allowed for testing observations and interpretations in context. Following Blumer's suggestion whenever possible, I would conduct those interviews with groups of informants rather than single individuals. This approach, either in the natural setting or elsewhere, is often more productive than interviewing persons alone: "Such a group, discussing collectively their sphere of life . . . will do more to lift the veils covering the sphere of life than any other device" (Blumer 1969: 41).

Individual interviews were, of course, also collected; private opinions expressed without social pressures often yield information that would otherwise not be revealed. Furthermore, it was not always possible to arrange a group session. Individual interviews were usually of a more formal nature in both setting and strategy than those that were group-oriented. This was especially so with key informants from whom I wished to elicit specific information such as life histories. Conducted in my "office," the informant's home, or some agreed-upon location, they were overtly taped and organized around a set of predetermined questions. Even these more formal interviews, however, were open-ended, allowing the conversations to develop on their own, with the questions serving mainly to focus the discussion and prod the informant if dialogue lulled.

Especially for those key informants with whom I developed a special rapport, I strove to construct life histories, primarily from oral resources such as interviews, informal discussions, and other situations that we were both party to. Such histories are useful in more closely approximating the subjective understanding of the actors, especially those who were frequent participants in situations of interaction. Insight into their biographical history gives further information about the explanatory resources from which they are able to draw. Twenty-two such histories were collected in varying degrees of detail, and serve to further contextualize the interactions.

I also conducted random verbal surveys to sample attitudes and opinions, and to determine the composition of community and pilgrim groups. These surveys were conducted periodically to provide basic checks on observational findings, as well as to discover information that normally did not surface during everyday activities. The surveys I conducted centered upon three basic problem areas, each of which could be approached by asking simple questions, requiring short answers. The type and frequency of the surveys conducted are as follows:

1. *Indian opinion of* ISKCON *and other Western devotees.* Four formal surveys of this type were conducted during the eighteen months, spaced at regular intervals. During each survey, samples were taken during times of peak participation at Krishna-Balaram temple, Banke-Bihari temple, Kishor Ban, Loi Bazaar, and Sri Chaitanya Prem Sansthan (Jai Singh Gera).

2. Jati *and regional composition of pilgrimage groups.* These surveys were conducted in the same manner as above at Krishna-Balaram temple, Banke-Bihari temple, Radha-Raman temple, Sri Chaitanya Prem Sansthan, Kishor Ban, Seva Kunj, and Keshi Ghat.

3. Jati *and* sampradaya *affiliation of Vrindaban residents.* This survey extended over the duration of my stay in Vrindaban and was part of an attempt to establish more accurate census data than was available from official documents. Information was collected in residential areas, temples, and bazaars.

Each survey aimed at obtaining information from the maximum number of individuals present at each location and ranged in sample size from 75 (the first pilgrim survey) to 530 (the number of Vrindaban residents polled concerning affiliations).

It was also my initial intention to generate questionnaires during the research to provide additional checks on data from other sources. Questions did emerge that lent themselves to this type of instrument, and their amplification could have periodically added to my understanding of the social reality. By the second month, however, I was convinced that the use of any written instrument would be counterproductive. Apart from the fact that distribution and collection of questionnaires do not easily fit into the natural routine of life in Vrindaban, there were two other factors that constrained my use of this technique.

The first was a general suspicion that Americans in India for an extended period are agents of the CIA. It was of crucial importance, therefore, that I did nothing that might be interpreted as a confirmation of this suspicion. An official-looking, probing questionnaire could have been viewed as evidence for such an interpretation.

Moreover, some individuals in Vrindaban profit financially from their association with Westerners, generating from them an income not always reported for taxation. A questionnaire including items concerning economic status could have suggested that I was inquiring about finances on behalf of the Indian government. Key informants admonished me on numerous occasions concerning these two possibilities and provided strong constraints against my using such a written device.

Nonetheless, I felt toward the end of my stay that there were ambiguous issues that could be best resolved by a written questionnaire. I was especially interested in testing opinions by an instrument that could be completed in detail and in privacy to discover if there existed any discrepancies between repressed notions and manifest behavior. During my last two weeks in Vrindaban, therefore, I administered a questionnaire to the merchants of Loi Bazaar, written in Hindi with the help of an Indian assistant, who also assisted in its distribution and collection (see appendix 4).

Due to the intimate relationships established with many of the respondents, there was some awkwardness in the administration of these forms. Although I emphasized that names were not to be included on the questionnaire, many rightly concluded that I could nevertheless infer their identities.

My decision to delay the questionnaire was apparently a good one considering the disruption it caused in the normal life of the bazaar. Family councils were held, elders in other towns were consulted to discuss my intent and their response, and rumors began to circulate about my "real" reasons for being in Vrindaban for so long. Had I done this earlier, further research would likely have been jeopardized;

as it was, the negative impact was minimized. Ultimately, most informants concluded my intent was honorable and consistent, and though some expressed severe reservations about it, sixty-six out of seventy-five forms were returned.

Lastly, I wish to comment on my use of photography in the field. Obviously, a camera can be counterproductive in gaining access to situations naturally. However, the equipment I took with me proved worthwhile. It provided a useful tool for the collection of some types of data; and more importantly perhaps, it gave me a way of repaying informants for their time and hospitality.

The visually stimulating environment of Vrindaban provided a motivation to practice a photographic avocation, and prompted me to integrate photography with other methods of data collection. While there, I developed three visual projects which were beneficial to the overall study.

The first project was to document the physical aspects of Vrindaban's sacred complex, especially the temples and other pilgrimage destinations. Many of the sites, especially the series of four temples built under the guidance of the original "Six Gowamis," are architecturally significant but deteriorating. Over my sixteen months there, considerable physical change in two of the temples was obvious, and although there is much discussion about preservation, little is actually being done. My photographic record not only serves as a visual record of these temples in the "ethnographic present," but may also be useful for those trying to convince the Archaeological Survey of India and private organizations to aid in preservation and restoration.

The second project was to photographically document the people of Vrindaban. Under the general categories of Brahman, merchants, service castes, sadhus, and foreigners, I photographed individuals, families, and groups in association with their temples, shrines, shops, homes, work sites, or other meaningful settings, emphasizing distinctive dress and markings that denote jati, sampradaya, or other status. The Vrindaban Research Institute, loosely affiliated with Agra University, had begun a project to identify and record the various tilaks worn in Vrindaban, but this was not complete. Some of my photographs added to the existing collection, plus they provide a visual record of "identity kits" employed by informants.

Thirdly, I attempted to photograph situational settings either during the interaction or immediately afterwards, including the same actors if possible. When this was not possible, I tried to capture the setting with performances or encounters similar to the ones recorded as data. These have been helpful in reconstructing the situations for analysis and have aided in a more subjective interpretation.

Beyond these systematic projects, there were occasions that allowed me to reciprocate informants. A Polaroid camera was especially useful for this, providing instant gifts if needed. Moreover, the novelty of on-the-spot pictures often helped in gaining access to restricted areas. Thirty-five millimeter film could easily be developed in Delhi, and I used this medium when requested to serve as photographer for specific reasons. I was called upon, for example, to photograph one family's marriageable daughter so that the families of prospective husbands could get an idea of her qualifications. When local institutions received important visitors, I was sometimes asked to record their activities which, needless to say, only augmented my own efforts to be included in them.

Every method of data collection was considered only after being evaluated for its complementarity with participant observation. Always in mind was the question of whether or not it would jeopardize my natural inclusion in the situations I wished to study, and whether or not it would compromise my identity in the minds of informants. The methods just described were successful because they could be employed in conjunction with or in addition to the primary technique of participant observation.

advaita—Nondual. The impersonal, nondualistic interpretation of the *Upanishads* and *Vedanta Sutra*, especially the nontheistic system expounded by Shankara. The Vaishnavas of Vrindaban are united in their distaste for advaita since it precludes the dualistic conception of Krishna as supreme god and man as his devotee.

advaitin—A follower of advaita teaching.

ahimsa (ahiṃsā) — Nonviolence.

amavasya (amāvasyā) — The day of the new moon.

angrezi—English. The term is extended in Vrindaban to mean "foreigner"; hence, the Krishna-Balaram temple is sometimes called the Angrezi Mandir.

arati (āratī) — A ritual performed during temple worship, before ras-lila performances and other sacred occasions, which entails waving lamps and incense in a prescribed pattern before the deity or sacred object.

ashram (āśrama) — 1. One of the four traditional Hindu stages of life: student, householder, retired, and renounced life. 2. The residence or retreat of a spiritual preceptor and his disciples.

avadhut (avadhūta) — A person, usually a mendicant, not bound by the rules of society.

avatar (avatāra) — A "descent" or incarnation of a god, usually Vishnu.

baba, babaji (bābā, bābājī) — Literally, father. A respectful title for a sadhu. Also, within Vaishnavism, a status acquired through initiation similar to sannyasi. *Jī* is the general honorific suffix.

Balaram (Balarāma) — Krishna's older brother, also considered an incarnation of Vishnu.

bhajan (bhajana) — A hymn or chant sung to a deity, usually by a group.

bhakta—A devotee or worshiper of a deity.

bhakti—Love or devotion. The path of salvation through loving devotion to a personal god.

bhang (bhāṅga) — Any of a number of preparations made with marijuana. In Braj it is usually taken as a peppery paste rolled into balls, or in a sweet milk drink with nuts, honey, and rose water.

bhav (bhāva) — Emotional feeling.

bhog (bhoga) — Food that has not been offered to Krishna or some other deity. In Vrindaban, informants say that all food is prasad, not bhog. In other words, it is always offered.

brahmachari (brahmacārī) — Celibate status. The first ashram.

brahman (brāhmaṇa) — The highest varna; one who belongs to this varna.

Braj (Vraja) — The linguistic and cultural area around Mathura which includes Vrindaban. Literally, "cow encampment."

Braj Mandal (Vraja-maṇḍala) — The circular area which encompasses Braj and designated by the pilgrimage path through the area's sacred sites, each a scene of one of Krishna's exploits.

Brajbasi (Vrajavāsī) — Native of Braj.

Braj Bhasha (Vraja-bhāṣā) — Dialect of Hindi spoken in Braj. One of the most popular idioms for Hindi poetry, especially during the medieval period.

chakra (cakra) — A circular form, especially the discus-shaped weapon carried by Vishnu. One of the primary symbols for Vishnu/Krishna.

chapati (capātī) — Round, flat, unleavened wheat cake.

choti (coṭī) — A tuft of hair worn at the back of the head by men of the Braj area and by male devotees of ISKCON. Same as shikha.

danda (daṇḍa) — A staff or stick, especially one carried by a sannyasi.

darshan (darśana) — Direct visual contemplation of a deity or some revered personality.

dham (dhāma) — Holy land. Krishna's eternal residence which includes every object, animate and inanimate, associated with him.

dharmshala (dharamaśālā) — An inexpensive or free lodging house for pilgrims, usually built by a charitable donor or religious institution.

dhoti (dhotī)—The lower garment worn by Hindu men in northern India composed of a long strip of cloth wound about the waist and pulled between the legs.

diksha (dīkṣā) — Ritual initiation where the guru imparts a mantra to the disciple.

Dhrupad (Dhrupada) — A musical style that means "fixed verse." Said to have been the style sung by Krishna and the gopis at their circle dance, it became popular in the courtly traditions of the sixteenth century. Dhrupad is seeing a revival in Vrindaban today through its use in the ras-lila dramas and through a resurgence in the formal teaching of this style.

Gaudiya Math (Gauḍīya-maṭha) — The monastic institution of Bengal Vaishnavism founded around 1915 by Bhatisiddhanta Saraswati, guru of ISKCON's founder, A. C. Bhaktivedanta Swami.

Gaudiya Vaishnava Sampradaya (Gauḍīya-Vaiṣṇava-Sampradāya) — The Bengal Vaishnava sect founded by Chaitanya in the late fifteenth century. Chaitanya's immediate disciples, the Six Goswamis, initiated the development of Vrindaban into a pilgrimage town.

ghat (ghāṭa) — A place for bathing along a riverbank, often with steps leading into the water.

Golok (Goloka) — The highest heavenly realm where Krishna resides, usually equated with Vrindaban. Sometime the phrase *Golok-Vrindaban* is used. Literally, "heaven of cows."

gopa—A cowherding man or boy of Braj, especially one of Krishna's cowherd friends.

gopi (gopī) — A cowherding woman or girl of Braj, especially one of Krishna's intimate female associates, the primary one being Radha.

goshala (gośāla) — Dairy and place for the protection of cows.

goswami (gosvāmī) — A title meaning "master of the senses." It is the name taken by the priestly families of Vrindaban's main temples, and also a title taken by sanyasis of the Gaidiya Math.

Govardhan (Govardhana) — The sacred mountain of Braj and the name of the town located at its saddle. The "mountain" is some five miles long and not more than a hundred feet high. One of the earliest myths associated with Krishna depicts him raising the mountain above his head to protect the animals and residents of Braj from a deluge sent by the angry god Indra.

guru—A spiritual preceptor who initiates disciples into the symbols, rituals, and teachings of his religious tradition.

guru-bhai—An individual who shares the same guru with another. Literally, "god-brother."

gurukula—School established by a guru.

Hare Krishna (Hare Kṛṣṇa) — An invocation to Krishna (also called Hari) sometimes used as a salutation in Vrindaban. The first two words of the mahamantra.

hladini-shakti (hlādinī-śakti) — Krishna's blissful, pleasure-giving energy which is considered to be personified by Radha.

Holi (Holī) — A major Hindu holiday celebrated on the last day of the bright fortnight of the month of Phalgun (February–March). This festival is said to be one of Krishna's favorites and provides opportunities for role-reversal behavior. The most pervasive activity is the throwing of colored water and powder by participants on each other.

ishta-devata (iṣṭa-devatā) — The personal god selected by an individual for worship, without denying the existence or significance of other deities.

jajmani (jajmāni) — system of patron-client relationships.

jagadguru—Guru of the world.

Janmashtami (Janmāṣṭamī) — The celebration of Krishna's birth on the last day of the waning half of the month of Bhadrapad (August–September).

japa—Measured chanting of a mantra, usually counting the number of repetitions on a mala.

jati (jāti) — An inclusive, self-classificatory grouping of people, usually associated with family, region, language, or religious affiliation. Literally meaning "species" or "kind," it roughly denotes what Westerners refer to as "caste."

Jhulan (Jhūlana) — The "swing" festival beginning on the third day of the month of Shravan (July–August) and lasting for a fortnight. Swings are hung in trees throughout Braj, and in temples swings of gold and silver are brought out upon which the deities are swung.

Kali-yuga—In Hindu cosmology, the fourth and worst age (yuga) of the world which is currently in progress. It will end with the destruction of the present creation.

karma—The force generated whenever an act is performed which ultimately brings upon the actor an appropriate award or punishment.

kartals (karatālas) — Hand cymbals.

katha (kathā) — stories and discussions on religious themes, especially from the *Puranas*.

khadi (khādi) — Homespun cotton cloth.

khir (khīra) — A sweet pudding made from rice and milk.

kirtan (kīrtana) — Glorification of a deity, usually by congregational responsive singing.

kurta (kurtā) — Long, loose shirt worn by Indian men.

lila (līlā) — Literally "sport" or "play," any deed or activity of Krishna, or its portrayal in a dramatic performance.

madhurya-ras (mādhurya-rasa) — The passionate, adoring mood of a lover toward the beloved. In Bengal Vaishnavism, the highest emotional state that results when the devotee treats Krishna as his/her lover.

mahamantra (mahāmantra) — The "great chant" containing three names of Vishnu/Krishna (Hari, Krishna, Rama). Chaitanya taught that the chanting of this mantra was the best means for acquiring salvation in this age. Chanting of this mantra is the core practice among ISKCON devotees, and is pervasive throughout the Braj area. The chant is: Hare Krishna, Hare Krishna, Krishna Krishna, Hare Hare; Hare Rama, Hare Rama, Rama Rama, Hare Hare.

mahapuri (mahāpurī) — One of the "great cities" in India where residence is considered to be liberating. The seven mahapuris are Mathura, Ayodhya, Hardwar, Varanasi, Kanchi, Ujjain, and Dwarka.

mahatma (mahātmā) — "Great soul"; a saint.

mala (malā) — A rosary used for counting the number of mantras chanted. Among worshipers of Krishna, the mala contains 108 beads made of tulsi wood.

mandir (mandira) — A temple.

mantra—A word or group of words with mystical power.

mela (melā) — A fair usually associated with a religious festival.

mlecha (mleccha) — An untouchable, especially a meat-eater.

moksha (mokṣa) — Liberation from things of the material world; salvation.

mokshada (mokṣada) — Liberating. Vrindaban is considered to be mokshada since residence there is a guarantee of moksha.

mridanga (mṛdanga) — An elongated, two-headed drum used in bhajan and kirtan.

mukti—Liberation, salvation. Same as moksha.

mukut (mukuṭa) — A crown or tiara worn by a deity.

murti (mūrti) — A cast or sculpted image of a deity.

naga (nāga) — 1. A serpent. 2. A mythical being which has serpentlike features and behavior.

nagar-kirtan (nagara-kīrtana) — A term not often used today, referring to kirtan conducted publicly which enlists the participation of most of the inhabitants of a city (*nagar*).

pakhawaj (pakhāvaja) — Elongated two-headed drum. Same as mridanga.

panda (paṇḍā) — A Brahman who guides pilgrims to sacred sites and assists them in performing local rituals.

pandit (paṇḍita) — A title that identifies a man as learned. In general usage, any Brahman who follows a traditional religious profession.

parampara (paramparā) — Succession or lineage, especially of gurus.

parikrama—The path that circles a sacred tract such as Vrindaban or Braj.

Prabhupad (Prabhupāda) — Title given to Bhativedanta Swami by his followers. Literally, "master of masters."

prasad (prasāda) — Food that has been ritually offered to a deity. Literally, "grace."

puja (pūjā) — ritual worship of a sacred object.

pujari (pūjārī) — Temple priest.

purnima (*pūrnimā*) — The day of the full moon.

raganuga-bhakti (*rāganugā-bhakti*) — Spontaneous devotion to Krishna.

ras (*rasa*) — The full, complex involvement in and appreciation of an emotional state. Literally, "taste," "juice," "flavor."

ras-lila (*rāsa-līlā*) — 1. The circle dance of Krishna with the gopis. 2. The indigenous dance-drama of Braj which depicts the original circle dance and other Krishna lilas.

rath yatra (*ratha-yātrā*) — A festival where deities are taken from the temple and paraded on a cart. This term especially refers to the annual festival at the temple of Jagannath in Puri, and other temples which house a similar form.

sadhana (*sādhanā*) — Disciplined spiritual practice.

samadhi (*samādhi*) — The grave or tomb of a holy man, so named because there he remains eternally in the final, perfect state of mental concentration, also called samadhi.

sampradaya (*sampradāya*) — Religious sect, tradition.

samsara (*saṃsāra*) — The repeated cycle of birth and death.

samskara (*saṃskāra*) — Sacrament; rite of passage.

sanatan dharma (*sanātana-dhārma*) — The eternal, or "natural" religion of mankind. The general term often preferred over "Hinduism" by Indians to label their religious system.

sankirtan (*saṃkīrtana*) — Congregational chanting.

sannyas (*saṃnyāsa*) — The fourth stage of life (ashram), total renunciation of society and material attachments.

sannyasi (*saṃnyāsī*) — One who has become a renunciate by taking sannyas.

shakti (*śakti*) — The active energy of a deity, usually conceived as female.

shalagram (*śālagrāma*) — A round, black stone found only in Nepal which contains the fossilized imprint of a cone shell thought to symbolize Vishnu's discus (chakra). Among devotees of Vishnu, it is regarded as equivalent to an image for purposes of worship.

shika (*śikhā*) — The tuft of hair at the back of the head worn by Indian men and male ISKCON devotees. Same as choti.

shraddha (*śrāddha*) — Hindu post-funerary rituals.

shudra (*śūdra*) — The fourth, and lowest of the traditional varnas. The term also refers to this varna's members, for whom Vedic law prescribes servile occupations.

tanga (*tānga*) — A horse-drawn cart.

thakur (*ṭhākura*) — Scholar, teacher.

tirtha (tīrtha) — A pilgrimage site. Literally, a place for "crossing over," especially to the spiritual world.

tilak (tilaka) — The forehead marking which usually designates membership in a religious sect or tradition.

tulsi (tulasī) — The Indian basil, sacred to Krishna/Vishnu.

upanayana (upanāyana) — The Hindu rite of passage (samsara) where the sacred thread is awarded and, traditionally, the boy's hair is "sacrificed."

vaidhi-bhakti (vaidhī-bhakti) — Ritual activity based on scriptural injunction designed to systematically take the bhakta to a purer devotional state.

vairagi (vairagī) — A Vaishnava ascetic.

Vaishnava (vaiṣṇava) — Worshiper of Vishnu.

vanaprastha (vanaprāstha) — The third stage of life—"retirement" from active family life prior to the sannyas stage.

varna—One of the four main hierarchical subdivisions of traditional Indian society. In descending order, the varnas are: Brahman, Kshatriya, Vaishya, and Shudra.

varnashram (varnāśrama) — The Hindu sociocultural ideal which encompasses the four varna divisions of society and the four stages (ashrams) of an individual's life.

videshi (videśī) — Foreigner.

viraha—The separation of lovers and the longing involved in it. This love in separation is considered the ideal emotional attitude for the devotee to have toward Krishna.

Vishnu (Viṣṇu) — One of the main gods of the Hindu pantheon. Krishna is considered an avatar of Vishnu by most Hindus, but in Braj, Krishna is seen as the supreme god with Vishnu an expansion of Krishna or coextensive with him.

Vrindabanbasi (Vṛndāvanavāsī) — Inhabitant of Vrindaban.

vyasasan (vyāsāsana) — The honored seat (*asan*) or throne of the guru who is considered the representative of Vyas, the reputed author of the Vedas.

yatra (yātrā) — A pilgrimage journey.

Barker, Eileen, ed.
  1982   New Religious Movements: A Perspective for Understanding Society. New York: Edwin Mellen Press.

Bateson, Gregory
  1956   The Message 'This Is Play.' *In* Conference on Group Processes 1955. Bertram Schaffer, ed. Pp. 145–242. New York: Josiah Macy Foundation.
  1975   A Theory of Play and Fantasy. *In* Steps to an Ecology of Mind. Pp.177–93. New York: Ballantine Books.

Beitielle, Andre
  1974   Six Essays in Comparative Sociology. Delhi: Oxford University Press.

Belshaw, C. S.
  1954   Changing Melanesia. Oxford: Oxford University Press.

Berger, Peter L., and Thomas Luckman
  1966   The Social Construction of Reality: A Treatise in the Sociology of Knowledge. Garden City: Doubleday.

Berreman, Gerald D.
  1972   Social Categories and Social Interaction in Urban India. American Anthropologist 74: 567–86.

Bhaktivedanta, A. C.
  1968   Teachings of Lord Chaitanya. New York: ISKCON Press.
  1975   Sri Caitanya-caritāmṛta of Kṛṣṇadāsa Kavirāja Goswāmī, Madhya Līlā. Vol. 7. Los Angeles: Bhaktivedanta Book Trust.

Blumer, Herbert
  1969   Symbolic Interactionism: Perspective and Method. Englewood Cliffs: Prentice-Hall.

Brooks, Charles R.
  1979   The Path to Krishna: Situations in the Development of American Hare Krishna Devotees. Masters Thesis, University of Hawaii at Manoa, Honolulu, Hawaii.

Burr, Angela
  1984   I Am Not My Body: A Study of the International Hare Krishna Sect. Delhi: Vikas.

Burridge, Kenelm, O. L.
  1960 Mambu: A Melanesian Millennium. London: Methuen.

Chakravarti, Janardan
  1975 Bengal Vaishnavism and Sri Chaitanya. Calcutta: Asiatic Society.

Chakravarti, Sudhindra Chandra
  1969 Philosophical Foundations of Bengal Vaiṣṇavism. Calcutta: Academic Publishers.

Cohn, Bernard S.
  1971 India: The Social Anthropology of a Civilization. Englewood Cliffs: Prentice-Hall.

Cottle, Thomas J.
  1977 Private Lives and Public Accounts. Amherst: University of Massachusetts Press.

Daner, Francine J.
  1976 American Children of Krishna. New York: Free Press.

Das, R. K.
  1978 Legends of Jagannath, Puri. Bhadrak: Pragati Udyog.

David, Kenneth, ed.
  1977 The New Wind: Changing Identities in South Asia. The Hague: Mouton Publishers.

Davis, Marvin
  1976 A Philosophy of Hindu Rank from Rural West Bengal. Journal of Asian Studies 36: 5–24.

De, Shusil Kumar
  1961 Early History of the Vaishnava Faith and Movement in Bengal. Calcutta: Firma K. L. Mukhopadhyay.
  1976 History of Sanskrit Poetics. Calcutta: Firma K. L. Mukhopadhyay.

Denzin, Norman K.
  1984 On Understanding Emotions. San Francisco: Jossey Bass.

Dimock, Edward C.
  1966 The Place of the Hidden Moon. Chicago: University of Chicago Press.

Dumont, Louis
  1970 Homo Hierarchicus: The Caste System and Its Implications. Chicago: University of Chicago Press.

Eck, Diana L.
  1982 Banaras: City of Light. New York: Alfred A. Knopf.

Favret-Saada, Jeane
1980   Deadly Words: Witchcraft in the Bocage. London: Cambridge University Press.

Geertz, Clifford
1973   The Interpretation of Cultures. New York: Basic Books.

Gelberg, Steven J.
1983   Hare Krishna, Hare Krishna: Five Distinguished Scholars on the Krishna Movement in the West. New York: Grove Press.

Gerow, Edwin
1977   Indian Poetics. Vol. 5 of A History of Indian Literature. Wiesbaden: Otto Harrassowitz.

Goffman, Erving
1959   The Presentation of Self in Everyday Life. New York: Anchor Books.
1971   Relations in Public: Microstudies of the Public Order. New York: Harper Torchbooks.

Goswami, Satsvarupa dasa
1980a   A Lifetime in Preparation. Vol. 1 of Śrīla Prabhupāda-līlāmṛta. Los Angeles: Bhaktivedanta Book Trust.
1980b   Planting the Seed. Vol. 2 of Śrīla Prabhupāda-līlāmṛta. Los Angeles: Bhaktivedanta Book Trust.
1981   Only He Could Lead Them. Vol. 3 of Śrīla Prabhupāda-līlāmṛta. Los Angeles: Bhaktivedanta Book Trust.
1982   In Every Town and Village. Vol. 4 of Śrīla Prabhupāda-līlāmṛta. Los Angeles: Bhaktivedanta Book Trust.
1983a   Let There Be a Temple. Vol. 5 of Śrīla Prabhupāda-līlāmṛta. Los Angeles: Bhaktivedanta Book Trust.
1983b   Uniting Two Worlds. Vol. 6 of Śrīla Prabhpāda-līlāmṛta. Los Angeles: Bhaktivedanta Book Trust.

Goswami, Shrivatsa
1982   Rādhā: The Play and Perfection of *Rasa*. *In* The Divine Consort: Rādhā and the Goddesses of India. John Stratton Hawley and Donna Marie Wulff, eds. Pp. 72–88. Berkeley: Berkeley Religious Studies Series.

Growse, F. S.
1979   Mathura: A District Memoir. New Delhi: Asian Educational Services.

Hawley, John Stratton
1981   At Play with Krishna: Pilgrimage Dramas from Brindavan. Princeton: Princeton University Press.

Hawthorn, Geoffrey.
  1982   Caste and Politics in India Since 1947. *In* Caste Ideology and Inter-
         action. Dennis B. McGilvray, ed. Pp. 204–20. Cambridge: Cam-
         bridge University Press.

Hein, Norvin
  1972   The Miracle Plays of Mathurā. New Haven: Yale University Press.

Hopkins, Thomas J.
  1966   The Social Teachings of the Bhāgavata Purāṇa. *In* Krishna: Myths,
         Rites, and Attitudes. Milton Singer, ed. Pp. 3–22. Honolulu: East-
         West Center Press.

International Society for Krishna Consciousness
  1983   ISKCON Vrindaban Newsletter. April 11, 1983.

Joshi, Esha Basanti, ed.
  1968   Mathura: Uttar Pradesh District Gazetteers. Lucknow: Government
         of Uttar Pradesh.

Judah, J. Stillson
  1974   Hare Krishna and the Counterculture. New York: Wiley and Sons.

Kane, P. V.
  1971   History of Sanskrit Poetics. Delhi: Motilal Banarsidas.

Kapoor, O.B.L.
  1977   The Philosophy and Religion of Śrī Caitanya. New Delhi: Mun-
         shiram Manoharlal.

Kaul, Narendra Nath
  1980   Writings of Sri Krishna Prem. Bombay: Bharatiya Vidya Bhavan.

Kennedy, M. T.
  1925   The Chaitanya Movement: A Study of the Vaishnavas of Bengal.
         New York: Oxford University Press.

Klaustermaier, Klaus K.
  1984   Mythologies and Philosophies of Salvation in the Theistic Traditions
         of India. Waterloo, Ontario: Wilfrid Laurier University Press.

Kolenda, Pauline
  1981   Caste, Cult and Hierarchy: Essays on the Culture of India. Meerut,
         India: Folklore Institute.

La Barre, Weston
  1938   The Peyote Cult. New Haven: Yale University Press.

Leach, E. R., ed.
  1962   Aspects of Caste in South India, Ceylon and Northwest Pakistan.
         Cambridge: Cambridge University Press.

Lynch, Owen
  1969 The Politics of Untouchability: Social Mobility and Social Change in a City of India. New York: Columbia University Press.

Majumdar, A. K.
  1978 Gauḍīya-Vaiṣnava Studies. Calcutta: JIJNASA.

Malinowski, Bronislaw
  1946 The Problem of Meaning in Primitive Language. *In* The Meaning of Meaning. C. K. Ogden and I. A. Richards, eds. Pp. 296–336. New York: Harcourt, Brace and Company.

McGilvray, Dennis B., ed.
  1982 Caste Ideology and Interaction. Cambridge: Cambridge University Press.

Marriott, McKim
  1966 The Feast of Love. *In* Krishna: Myths, Rites, and Attitudes. Milton Singer, ed. Pp. 200–212. Honolulu: East-West Center Press.
  1968 Caste Ranking and Food Transactions: A Matrix Analysis. *In* Structure and Change in Indian Society. Milton Singer and Bernard Cohn, eds. Pp. 133–72. Chicago: Aldine.

Marriott, McKim, and Ronald B. Inden
  1977 Toward an Ethnosociology of South Asian Caste Systems. *In* The New Wind: Changing Identities in South Asia. Kenneth David, ed. Pp. 227–38. The Hague: Mouton Publishers.

Meillassoux, Claude
  1973 Are There Castes in India? Economy and Society 2: 89–111.

Miller, David H.
  1959 Ghost Dance. New York: Duell, Sloan and Pearce.

Miller, David M., and Dorothy Wertz
  1976 Hindu Monastic Life: The Monks and Monasteries of Bhubaneswar. Montreal: McGill-Queen University Press.

Mooney, James
  1965 The Ghost Dance Religion and the Sioux Outbreak of 1890. Chicago: Phoenix Books.

Morinis, E. Alan
  1984 Pilgrimage in the Hindu Tradition: A Case Study of West Bengal. Delhi: Oxford University Press.

O'Flaherty, Wendy Douglas
  1975 Hindu Myths: A Sourcebook Translated from the Sanskrit. Middlesex, England: Penguin Books.
  1981 The Rig Veda: An Anthology. New York: Penguin Books

Padmalocanadas
n.d.   Cintamani-Dhama (a Guide to Vrindaban). Vrindaban: Krishna-Bal-
        aram-Mandir.

Pelto, Pertti J.
1970   Anthropological Research: The Structure of Inquiry. New York:
        Harper and Row.

Preciado-Solis, Benjamin
1984   The Kṛṣṇa Cycle in the Purāṇas: Themes and Motifs in a Heroic
        Saga. Delhi: Motilal Banarsidas.

Prem, Sri Krishna
1976   Initiation into Yoga: An Introduction to Spiritual Life. New Delhi:
        B.I. Publications.
1976   The Yoga of the Bhagavatgita. Baltimore: Penguin Books.

Raychauduri, Hemchandra
1975   Materials for the Study of the Early History of the Vaishnava Sect.
        New Delhi: Munshiram Manoharlal.

Redfield, Robert
1958   Peasant Society and Culture. Chicago: University of Chicago Press.

Roy, Dilip Kumar
1968   Yogi Sri Krishnaprem. Bombay: Bharatiya Vidya Bhavan.

Rudolph, Lloyd I., and Susanne Hoeber Rudolph.
1967   The Modernity of Tradition: Political Development in India. Chi-
        cago: University of Chicago Press.

Sahlins, Marshall David
1982   Historical Metaphors and Mythical Realities: Structure in the Early
        History of the Sandwich Islands Kingdom. Ann Arbor: University
        of Michigan Press.

Shapiro, Allan A.
1979   The Birth-Celebration of Śri Rādhāraman in Vrindaban. M.A. The-
        sis, Columbia University.

Singer, Milton B., ed.
1966   Krishna: Myths, Rites, and Attitudes. Honolulu: East-West Center
        Press.
1972   When a Great Tradition Modernizes. New York: Praeger.
1984   Man's Glassy Essence: Explorations in Semiotic Anthropology.
        Bloomington: Indiana University Press.

Srinivas, M. N.
1966   Social Change in Modern India. Berkeley: University of California
        Press.

Stirrat, R. L.
1982   Caste Conundrums: Views of Caste in a Sinhalese Catholic Fishing Village. *In* Caste Ideology and Interaction. Dennis B. McGilvray, ed. Pp. 8–33. Cambridge: Cambridge University Press.

Turnbull, Colin
1981   A Pilgrimage in India. Natural History, vol. 90, July 1981: 14–16.

Turner, Victor
1974   Dramas, Fields and Metaphors: Symbolic Action in Human Society. Ithaca: Cornell University Press.

Uberoi, J. Singh
1967   Sikhism and Indian Society. *In* Transactions of the Indian Institute of Advanced Study, vol. 4. Simla, India.

Uttar Pradesh Department of Tourism.
1973   Project Report—Sri Krishna Complex.

van Buitenen, J.A.B.
1966   On the Archaism of the Bhāgavata Purāṇa. *In* Krishna: Myths, Rites, and Attitudes. Milton Singer, ed. Pp. 23–40. Honolulu: East-West Center Press.

Vaudeville, Charlotte
1976   Braj, Lost and Found. Indo-Iranian Journal 18: 195–223.

Vidyarthi, L. P.
1961   The Sacred Complex in Hindu Gaya. Delhi: Concept.
1979   The Sacred Complex of Kashi: A Microcosm of Indian Civilization. Delhi: Concept.

Wallace, A.F.C.
1956   Revitalization Movements. American Anthropologist 58: 264–81.
1966   Religion: An Anthropological Approach. New York: Random House.
1970   The Death and Rebirth of the Seneca. New York: Alfred A. Knopf.

Warner, William Lloyd
1964   A Black Civilization: A Social Study of an Australian Tribe. New York: Harper.

Weber, Max
1958   The Religion of India. New York: Free Press.

White, Charles, S. J.
1977   The Caurasi Pad of Sri Hit Harivams. Asian Studies at Hawaii Series, no. 16. Honolulu: University of Hawaii Press.

Wilson, Bryan
1982   The New Religions: Some Preliminary Considerations. *In* New Re-

ligious Movements: A Perspective for Understanding Society. Eileen Barker, ed. Pp. 16–31. New York: Edwin Mellen Press.

Worsley, Peter
  1968   The Trumpet Shall Sound: A Study of Cargo Cults in Melanesia. New York: Shocken Books.

Yati, Tridandi Bhakti Prajnan
  1978   Renaissance of Gaudiya Vaishnava Movement. Madras: Sree Gaudiya Math.